Deadly Bonds

DEADLY BONDS
Five Years Inside the Ukrainian Mafia

SERGEY MAIDUKOV

ROWMAN & LITTLEFIELD
Lanham • Boulder • New York • London

Published by Rowman & Littlefield
An imprint of The Rowman & Littlefield Publishing Group, Inc.
4501 Forbes Boulevard, Suite 200, Lanham, Maryland 20706
www.rowman.com

86-90 Paul Street, London EC2A 4NE

Copyright © 2025 by Sergey Maidukov

All rights reserved. No part of this book may be reproduced in any form or by any electronic or mechanical means, including information storage and retrieval systems, without written permission from the publisher, except by a reviewer who may quote passages in a review.

British Library Cataloguing in Publication Information available

Library of Congress Cataloging-in-Publication Data
Names: Maidukov, Sergey, 1955- author.
Title: Deadly bonds : five years inside the Ukrainian mafia / Sergey
 Maidukov.
Description: Lanham : Rowman & Littlefiel, [2025] | Includes
 bibliographical references and index.
Identifiers: LCCN 2024027772 (print) | LCCN 2024027773 (ebook) | ISBN
 9781538187036 (cloth ; alk. paper) | ISBN 9781538187043 (ebook)
Subjects: LCSH: Maidukov, Sergey, 1955- | Martirosyan, Samvel (Gangster) |
 Organized crime--Ukraine. | Criminals--Ukraine.
Classification: LCC HV6453.U38 M35 2025 (print) | LCC HV6453.U38 (ebook)
 | DDC 364.10609477/09049--dc23/eng/20240717
LC record available at https://lccn.loc.gov/2024027772
LC ebook record available at https://lccn.loc.gov/2024027773

♾️ The paper used in this publication meets the minimum requirements of American National Standard for Information Sciences—Permanence of Paper for Printed Library Materials, ANSI/NISO Z39.48-1992.

This is for Donetsk, my most beloved city . . . my most hated city.

Contents

Acknowledgments ix
A Note to the Reader xi

Part I: Setup 1
CHAPTER 1: The Open Wound 3
CHAPTER 2: Everything (and Everyone) Is for Sale 15
CHAPTER 3: Chasing the American Dream 29
CHAPTER 4: A Bullet to Remember 41
CHAPTER 5: Money Can't Be Funny 55
CHAPTER 6: Behind the Broken Doors 69

Part II: Confrontation 81
CHAPTER 7: Manners in the Monkey House 83
CHAPTER 8: The Road to Hell 97
CHAPTER 9: Dances with Wolves 109
CHAPTER 10: In the Laps of the Criminal Gods 123
CHAPTER 11: Wicked Business 135
CHAPTER 12: Family Ties 147
CHAPTER 13: A Failed Millionaire 157

Part III: Resolution 167
CHAPTER 14: Violence Virus 169
CHAPTER 15: An Inevitable Partnership 181

Contents

Chapter 16: Waiting for Judgment Day 191
Chapter 17: Crime and Punishment 199
Chapter 18: An Offer I Couldn't Refuse 211
Chapter 19: Between Three Fires 223
Chapter 20: The Last Chance 235

Bibliography 247
Index 249
About the Author 269

Acknowledgments

First, thanks to my brilliant agent and editor, Claire Gerus, without whose experience, energy, and enthusiasm this book would not exist. From reviewing early drafts to suggesting the final title, she was always ready to help.

I also wish to express my sincere gratitude to Becca Rohde Beurer, a managing editor of Rowman & Littlefield's imprint, Lexington Books, who believed in my creativity even before my first book was published in the US.

I am also immensely grateful to those reviewers who read the sample chapters of this book and gave their thumbs up in unison, thus giving this book the green light.

God bless you all!

A Note to the Reader

When necessary, some titles and names have been changed in this book. However, everyone in my family, as well as the many members of the Mafia "family" of the Martirosyan brothers, are called by their actual names.

I must confess that while reading the text, I found myself constantly judging my previous attitudes and actions. I am now painfully aware that the price of confession can be staggering when buried truths rise to the surface.

The writing process itself, though challenging, reminds me why I am committed to sharing this book with an audience. Only by so doing can I find the peace that accompanies painful lessons learned.

> "Turn your wounds into wisdom."
> —Oprah Winfrey

> "The name of God is Truth."
> —Hindu proverb

Part I
Setup

Chapter 1

The Open Wound

As time passes and my life moves forward, I've begun to realize that traces of certain moments remain. Some are like scars that have formed over old wounds. They lie there within us, waiting for the right moment to remind us of their presence. Sometimes the reminder is a gentle whisper. Other times it can feel like a knife slicing open an old wound that never healed. Such an awakening will be jarring, sudden, and unexpected. To my chagrin, that is exactly what happened to me one September morning back in 2019.

It was still dark outside, but there I was, sitting in front of my laptop in the kitchen of my Kyiv apartment, browsing websites for the latest news. My mind and mood were clear. Normally, this was my favorite time of day not necessarily for writing another book, but, rather, because I appreciated my serene environment.

In my hand was a cup of tea, my morning companion as I scrolled and clicked my way through website after website of articles, photos, and videos. I wasn't searching for any specific information, much less looking for news about my hometown, Donetsk, which my family and I had left in 2014 during the Russian occupation of eastern Ukraine. This lay in a distant past now fogged by time. Today I inhabited another time and place, and I was happy.

My writing career had taken off, bringing me money and satisfaction. My wife, Luba, slept peacefully in our bedroom. Our grown son and daughter lived next door, happily married and raising their children. So I didn't expect any tricks from fate when I scrolled through the

Chapter 1

news feeds. I recall humming along with a cheerful Beatles tune on my headphones: "Will you still need me, will you still feed me when I'm sixty-four?" I was just about that age, and I enjoyed feeling the connection.

It was the beginning of autumn—my favorite season of the year. Who could ask for anything more?

Suddenly, a headline popped up on my screen, announcing, "The End of the Most Terrible Mafia King in Ukraine." I wasn't usually interested in crime news and was about to scroll down further when something stopped me. The music continued to play in my ears, but now I found it disturbing. I turned off the player and put the headphones away.

To click or not to click, that was the question. After some hesitation, I clicked on the link, and my life has never been the same.

There was a photograph that portrayed the very Mafia king who'd been announced in the article's title. I recognized him at first sight.

For a moment my thoughts dissolved: "Yes, it's him!" and "No, it couldn't be him!"

I looked at the photograph more carefully. It was a close-up of a man about my age, wearing a white jacket and a baseball cap turned backward. Despite his blurred face and his eyes hidden under dark sunglasses, there was no question as to his identity. It was Samvel Martirosyan—a man who had once saved my life. He was also the man who had nearly ruined it.

My tea got cold while I stared at his photo. I didn't remember Samvel ever wearing a baseball cap, especially with the visor turned back—he'd never worn a cap when I'd known him. But those old eighties, cop-style sunglasses were his constant attribute. And loose sports jackets too. He'd often had to wear a bulletproof vest under his clothes.

He was a man with many enemies and, as far as I knew, no friends. Samvel surrounded himself with associates, accomplices, bodyguards, and servants—anyone but friends. He couldn't even rely on his brother, who had deceived him at every opportunity.

He didn't trust anyone from his circle. Perhaps this was why he had accepted me years ago—an amiable guy looking for work, a man of foreign origins. What kind of threat could I offer to the king of Ukraine's underworld?

As it turned out, he was wrong about me too. He couldn't trust me, because I had learned both to hate and fear him in equal, large doses. I resented every day of the life he absorbed from me, every moment he demanded my servitude. The five plus years I was his indentured servant were a living nightmare. Every day, when I was not discharging my duties to him, I was consumed with plans to escape from his fiefdom . . . and spent the remaining hours figuring out how to keep myself and my family alive.

As I sat reminiscing, the title of the article remained unchanged, insistently reading, "The End of the Most Terrible Mafia in Ukraine."

The end? Indeed? Was it really?

I peered at the screen to scan the article.

> Employees of the Department of Internal Security of the National Police of Ukraine have established that a criminal group was involved in grave crimes in Ukraine and abroad. The gang was headed by a native of the Republic of Georgia, now a resident of Kyiv, Samvel Martirosyan, nicknamed Samvel Donetsky. (Zhukova, 2019)

I leaned back in my chair. Oh, my God! Samvel had become a resident of Kyiv! How long had he been living here? Was he so close that we might have bumped into each other on the street, in the grocery store, or at a café? I couldn't imagine that he'd shake my hand, saying, "Hi, Sergey. Nice to see you again! How's life treating you?"

The abyss separated us. And I felt myself standing on its edge.

I shifted my gaze back to the photo. Judging by it, Samvel Martirosyan hadn't changed much. Since I could recognize him, he might also be able to recognize me. Had I changed much over the past twenty years? He hadn't. He remained exactly as he'd been in my memory.

I remembered his appearance as distinctly as if we had parted yesterday—the cocky set of his bald head, the shape of his hooked nose, and the outlines of his wide mouth. I knew his gestures, postures, facial expressions, and habits very well because constant observation had helped me calculate what mood he was in and what kind of response I could expect from him from one moment to the next. Being in his

Chapter 1

presence was like trying to keep your calm in the presence of a powerful, unpredictable wild animal. He could seem kind and peaceful, but this would be followed by an sudden outburst of rage, and at such moments, Samvel Martirosyan was extremely dangerous. I never felt safe in his presence. Nobody felt safe.

That's why I'd been looking for a way to leave him, and that's why I did it at the first opportunity. It was either that or remain his prisoner for the rest of my life. During the time I worked for Samvel, I had been insulted, minimized, unappreciated, and cheated. Samvel was a danger not only to me but to my young family. He was like a grenade with the pin pulled out. Its explosion was almost certain to kill anyone close enough to be a potential witness. I was, however, forced to remain with Samvel and his gang for over five years. Those were the craziest years of my life. How often I had wished I could remove them from my life story—and my memory!

I don't want to sound insincere by saying that these were the thoughts running through my head that September morning in 2019. I was too confused and anxious to think logically. I actually read the article three times to absorb what was written. It went on:

> Starting from the 90s, Samvel, the most influential mafia king, as he personally called himself, led a criminal group in the Donetsk region, later extended his influence to neighboring areas," said First Deputy Chairman of the National Police Eugene Koval. According to him, the members of the organized criminal group specialized in hard racketeering, kidnapping, arms trafficking, threats, physical violence and contract killings.
>
> In addition, the organizer of the group was wanted by Interpol for committing a premeditated murder in the territory of the Republic of Armenia. In the criminal world, he was famous for his cunning and cruelty. At the slightest opportunity, at any cost, he would seek to occupy a highest level in the criminal hierarchy.
>
> Koval noted that law enforcement officers tried three times to bring Samvel and his perpetrators to justice—for robbery, illegal possession of firearms, and theft on an especially large scale. "However, every time, thanks to corrupt connections in law enforcement agencies,

he managed to avoid punishment or limit himself to the minimum formality," said Koval.

Finally, in 1998, Samvel went to jail for 14 years, but was released ahead of schedule and went back to his old ways. His gang moved about in expensive luxury cars, always armed, and they all used drugs. It was only in 2019 that the leaders of the National Police of Ukraine managed to detain Samvel in order to charge him with a crime. Also seized were several firearms, cars, technical equipment, and drugs. (Zhukova, 2019)

This last line surprised me. The Samvel I had known had neither taken nor sold drugs. I figured that the drugs seized by the police were probably intended for sale. As for weapons, Samvel's men had used them all the time. He himself rarely picked up a gun to avoid being seen breaking the law. He preferred to commit crimes by having someone else do the job. The man was sly as a fox and lethal as a snake. Additionally, I would learn that he was also deeply vindictive and pitiless toward those he considered renegades from his own authority.

I was one of them, and I had good reason to fear Samvel's revenge. He never forgave anyone—for anything.

Would bars and locks keep him inside prison and safe from those who feared him? If so, for how long? The police themselves were forced to admit that it was not easy to keep Samvel locked in a cage.

Rereading the article, I spotted a link to a short video. In it Samvel was standing on the sidewalk of a quiet street, talking to a fat, gray-haired man in a navy-blue suit and a burgundy turtleneck sweater. I recognized this man by his absolutely round head and small, narrow eyes, which made him look like a character in a Mongolian epic. It was Salim, the cruelest member of Samvel's gang. I had always associated him with a boar both physically and intellectually.

Samvel stood next to him in his stupid cap and sheriff's sunglasses. With his white tracksuit jacket, a pair of baggy blue jeans, white socks, and black loafers, he might have been a suburban wannabe racketeer enjoying a warm summer day.

Both of them looked relaxed, expecting no trouble. What were they talking about on that fine Indian summer day, called "granny summer" in

Chapter 1

Ukraine? Were they planning a murder, a kidnapping—or merely debating where to have lunch? With gangsters, you never know . . .

Suddenly, like black knights in their metallic gear, police special forces jumped out onto the scene! Their menacing yells filled the street as they threw Samvel and Salim face down on the concrete sidewalk, kicking their legs apart and tying their hands behind them to await handcuffs. Then both men were forced to stand up and answer questions as curious onlookers began to mill around.

Police removed baseball bats, a machine gun, and a revolver with cartridges from the trunk of a nearby car. As Samvel was dragged off, his cuffed hands behind his back, his face was blank. For him, this was just another day in the life of a Mafia boss.

It took me almost half an hour to watch this two-minute video. Leaning back in my chair, I tried to reassure myself that all was okay. Samvel would end up behind bars again; thus, he'd no longer pose a danger to me. Our paths would never cross again, and now—once and for all—I needed to blank out all memories of my connection with him. The ties that bound us together had been severed a long time ago. For decades Samvel Martirosyan had been out of my life. So to hell with him and to hell with my past mistakes! Everyone makes mistakes, right? And isn't everyone entitled to a happy ending if they repent?

Within a few minutes, I realized that my self-soothing mantras were failing to calm me down. I tried to do some writing, but there was no way I could concentrate on it. The characters for my new novel seemed dull, uninteresting. In contrast, my mental picture of Samvel was as real and tangible as ever—his dark eyes bulging beneath his eyebrows, the veins on his neck swelling to the size of ropes, and his mouth, wide open, as he bellowed at someone. He'd often yelled at people. At such moments, his voice would rise to a shriek, and the high pitch of his voice would hurt your ears, but you could not plug them while still standing before him, hoping his outburst of anger would pass as suddenly as it had begun. And when you thanked him for something, he might say, "One hundred bucks is better than a thousand fine words," and you'd never know if he was joking or demanding money for his services. I thought I knew Samvel inside and out, yet he still remained unpredictable for me.

Twenty-five years ago, I had been very close to Samvel. I remembered everything about him: his passion for the wine he imported from Sicily, the cruelty with which he interrogated his prisoners, the sweeping gestures of disdain that always accompanied his mistreatment of people who worked for him, his childlike attachment to primitive religion, and his inflated desire to become a major drug lord in South America.

Many of the criminal characters I'd created in my popular novels bore Samvel's mental and physical traits. His closest accomplices also played out roles I'd later created in the pages of my books—these, of course, always used various pseudonyms.

Oddly enough, from that point of view, my experience with Samvel had been very productive for my writing! But given the choice, I would have done anything to avoid the experiences I had undergone. For many years, I kept these memories in the darkest closet of my memory, never suspecting that one day, they would break out to confront me.

For days afterward, I sat in front of my glowing computer screen, unable to write a single word. I was deep in thought, distracted, and silent.

One day our son, Sergiy, came to visit us. While Luba was preparing lunch, we decided to sit down to play chess.

"Sergiy, do you remember Samvel?" I asked as we settled in. I wasn't sure whether or not to share my discovery, but I trusted his judgment and needed to get another opinion about my concerns.

"I only saw him once or twice," Sergiy replied. "He was very thin, and his jacket hung on him like it was many sizes too big. But I remember his bandits in their big expensive cars. When they drove up to our house, all the local boys would come running over to look at them. That's all I remember, Dad—along with your almost-constant absence from home. Why do you ask?"

"Forget it," I said. "It's your move."

"Checkmate," Sergey said, moving his queen. "Looks like I beat you again, Dad. You've been kind of distracted lately."

I was not only distracted—I was also feeling a deep sense of remorse. After hours of reflection, I was beginning to realize that the greater span of my life had already been lived. Now time had run out for me, and

Chapter 1

Samvel had returned to haunt my inner life. For the next few weeks, thoughts of him never left me. Day after day, week after week, I surfed the web for information about him. A couple of months later, I discovered that Samvel Martirosyan had been placed in preventive detention in prison in Kyiv and was awaiting trial and sentencing. That calmed me down, but not by much. It was always the same old tune. Samvel was arrested, charges were brought against him, he was sentenced and sent to the prison bunk—but very soon, miraculously, he was free as a bird. What if it happens again? What if our paths should cross?

Every now and then, I scoured the Internet for new information about Samvel, but virtually everything known about him was buried in old newspaper pieces or came from fragmented, piecemeal reports. There were few of them. A biography of the *Most Terrible Mafia in Ukraine* had been poorly covered by the press. Samvel's rise to power and his heyday had taken place during the 1990s, long before social networks appeared.

I couldn't find much about him on the Internet, either, as his impact was felt much later in the countries of the former USSR than it had been in America. The number of Ukrainian web pages has always been extremely limited, and any researcher seeking to trace Samvel's bloody history would find a dozen versions of the same article, rewritten by many authors, such as Kikvidze (2004), Perovitch (2006), Semenetz (2019), and several others. After some thought, I created my own version of the article, which is as follows:

> Every tale of the gangster-Mafia underworld in Donbas would be incomplete without a nod to the organized crime syndicate led by Samvel Martirosyan.
>
> Some reporters portray him with a touch of irony, noting his tendency to boast and his air of self-importance. Nevertheless, the top criminals in Ukraine acknowledged Samvel as a fierce warrior at heart, with his own formidable "army" that held significant influence in the area.
>
> The Martirosyan family, originally from Georgia, relocated to Donbas in the late 1980s as refugees before they eventually became citizens of Ukraine. Initially, brothers Samvel and Tigran attempted to make an honest living by selling pies at a marketplace near the station

square. However, Samvel's ambitious nature led him to engage in various activities, including minor criminal acts.

His ultimate goal was to become a leader, which he started to achieve by forming a small gang primarily composed of Caucasian friends and getting involved in extortion, making it the main focus of his "family."

In 1992 Samvel asserted that he had the ability to assemble a force of one hundred soldiers equipped with rifles, machine guns, and even a grenade launcher within sixty minutes. Alongside the Armenians, Samvel recruited numerous Slavic youths, particularly athletes from the renowned Donetsk football team the Scythians, all under the leadership of a formidable individual known as Silver.

To execute the acts of violence, Samvel enlisted assassins from both Armenia and Georgia. Following the completion of their murderous tasks, these individuals would retreat to their respective homelands, evading capture.

Samvel was not the sole architect of his criminal empire. His brother Tigran played a crucial role in all their illicit activities. While Samvel was known for his physical prowess, Tigran was the mastermind behind their organized crime syndicate. Despite their contrasting physical appearances—Samvel with his long nose and full lips, and Tigran with his slender and handsome features—the brothers complemented each other perfectly. Samvel thrived on making a grand entrance wherever he went, whether it was driving around in a limousine after his release from prison or demanding special treatment at the barbershop with his entourage of guards. He spared no expense when it came to his girlfriend Karina, even purchasing a Toyota Carina for their trips together.

It could be argued that he had ample reasons to boast. Not a single influential businessman in the Donetsk region was left untouched by Samvel's gangsters—all had to pay their dues.

Naturally, this situation didn't sit well with other criminal groups. Samvel had been sentenced to death multiple times, but his vigilance and precautionary measures, such as wearing two bulletproof vests, thwarted any attempts on his life.

Throughout the 1990s he found himself behind bars on three separate occasions, yet it wasn't until his fourth imprisonment that he was finally convicted—until then his wealth had lined the pockets of many

Chapter 1

lawyers, prosecutors, and judges. Rumor has it that his initial release from custody alone cost him a staggering $180,000.

He came to the realization that his life would be in grave danger in Donetsk, prompting him to make the decision to relocate to the coastal city of Berdyansk. In Berdyansk he acquired ownership of a kindergarten from the local authorities and took measures to secure it with a robust fence, intending to establish a residence for himself and his extensive family.

His primary objective was to gain control of the seaport, although he was well aware that any attempt to seize it would result in dire consequences for him.

Samvel was ultimately convicted this last time around. Initially, the trial of Samvel occurred in the Luhansk Regional Court. However, during one of the court hearings, unidentified individuals opened fire on the court, using a machine gun. The primary reason behind this assassination attempt was Samvel's tendency to talk excessively. Prominent police officials and leaders of criminal organizations were concerned that he would provide incriminating testimonies against them.

The entire legal process concluded in Donetsk, where Samvel received a ten-year prison sentence in January 2000. He was found guilty of robbery, extortion, and various other crimes. On November 21, 2005, his sentence was reduced by half, to only six years.

This is roughly what this news article would look like if I were to write it myself—a compilation of facts known to me as well as to journalists. But one of these facts bothered me most of all: Samvel never served this abbreviated term in prison either. Would history repeat itself and release him to the streets again very soon? Would that mean I'd have to walk the streets constantly looking behind me, afraid to look ahead and see someone resembling him coming toward me? Had he ever tried to find me after my escape? Or had he given up on the past long ago, as I did?

As my obsession with Samvel took hold within me, my wife and daughter often pointed out that I looked gloomy and seemed perpetually annoyed. Finally, Luba, fed up with my behavior, asked me directly what was wrong with me. I had to tell her everything.

Luba frowned. "Do you think he's still dangerous?"

"He always was," I replied. "Why would he change now?"

"You must get him out of your head," Luba said firmly. "Bad thoughts attract bad things. Haven't you learned that by now? Forget Samvel, Sergey. Get rid of those memories of him."

Of course she was right. It was sound advice. What was the point of my poisoning my future and that of my family by obsessing about Samvel and his mobsters? Ever since the day I'd driven away from Donetsk, leaving them behind—hopefully forever—I'd been confident that my fate would no longer be entwined with theirs.

Still, Samvel remained in my thoughts like a sharp splinter, piercing my mind, and I hated sharp splinters. What's more, I hated loose ends.

On the other hand, I didn't want to live my life feeling like a victim or an escapee. I knew my mental health was in potential jeopardy. How could I exorcise these demons of the past? And then, one day, as I was mulling my options around, I realized the only way I would be able to move on from the past.

I was a born writer. In the countries of the former USSR, I was also quite a successful writer of crime fiction. The memories I had tried to exorcise had actually helped me to write, mostly because I'd used my old personal experiences for my books.

So why not tell the real true crime story of my imposed servitude to a Ukrainian Mafia king who had commanded my life and threatened me with death when I tried to withdraw my services from him?

The more I thought about it, the stronger and more decisive I began to feel. The writer in me had now taken over. I knew this story to be true. And isn't the truth what gives a book its unique value?

Now that I'd decided to release the burden I had been carrying for the past twenty years, there was no space for fear in me. Instead, the words began to appear in my mind. Accompanying the words were doubts. How will my confession affect my reputation? Will it tarnish my name? How will this affect my work, my career, and my future? And, more importantly, how will this exposure affect my family?

The last thought haunted me. I started work on the book several times and deleted what I had written each time. I hadn't lived and acted

Chapter 1

in a vacuum. I was—and still am—surrounded by people I love and who love me. Would they want my revelations to be made public to readers around the world?

I brought my concerns to every member of my family. None of them tried to dissuade me. I remember best of all the conversation with my daughter, Svitlana—my soulmate, closest friend, and trusted adviser. She listened to my plan carefully and silently. I looked at her and asked, "Do you think I can do this?"

She looked back at me in surprise. "Dad, you're the only one who can. You were there, weren't you? And aren't you a writer?"

"You don't understand," I said. "Can I actually tell people the truth? What will they think of me? What will little Erika and Severine say when they grow up? 'Grandpa, is it true that you were a member of the Mafia?' How can I look them in the eye? And how will I answer their questions?"

"Let me remind you of one thing from my childhood, Dad," Svitlana said. "You have always told me that the truth can be painful, but ultimately, it is liberating. Do you remember?"

"Yes, I remember," I replied. "But—"

Svitlana didn't listen to my "buts." She had a habit of interrupting me because she knew in advance what I was going to say.

"If we move from my childhood to my youth," she said, "there's one more thing you told me, Dad. You always said I should decide for myself what to do with my life. Now I'm repeating it back to you. This is your life, Dad, not mine, not my mother's—no one else's. And this is your book. It's your choice, not ours."

This conversation took place in April 2022, when Ukraine was burning in the fire of war, and we were in the Polish city of Gdansk as refugees. That very day, I sat down to write this book.

Chapter 2

Everything (and Everyone) Is for Sale

Believe it or not, life in the USSR until the early 1980s was somewhat of a paradise. You didn't have to worry about anything, because the future was predetermined and stable. Everyone felt relatively safe.

If the USSR was a prison, it was the largest and most comfortable prison in the world, with its own laws and customs. I spent the first half of my life there.

I wrote my first book at the age of six; it was in a school notebook, where I'd wrote down stories and fairy tales I'd heard on the radio. I told my parents that I made them up myself, and they were very proud of me. (I was filled with a mixture of shame and vanity.) The shame was stronger—I burned the notebook.

Throughout my childhood and youth, I was engaged in creativity. I wrote my books and painted my pictures. I had a whole army of little Plasticine Indians and cowboys under my bed. I played the Beatles tunes on my guitar and composed my own songs. My poems and cartoons were published in the Donetsk newspaper. Later I translated American thrillers, like Peter Benchley's *Jaws* and Harold Robbins's *Carpetbaggers*; typed them; and gave them to my friends to read. This, despite the risk of being locked up for bringing in a foreign product that might entertain and enlighten—like records and jeans. I didn't care. Stalin and Khrushchev had long been lying in their graves, and the general secretary of the Communist Party of the Soviet Union (CPSU), Leonid Brezhnev, was getting older and decrepit, losing his former grip.

Chapter 2

So for me, it really was a heavenly place and a heavenly time. I had a lot of free time to spend on my hobbies. I didn't have to study hard to pass exams and get my diplomas. I also had no shortage of money, friends, or freedom. And I was not surprised that this "socialist paradise" had its own annoying feature, described by H. G. Wells in *The Time Machine*.

Published in 1895, the book introduces a scientist who, amongst other things, pays a visit to the year 802,701 and discovers the descendants of the human race there: the Eloi and the Morlocks. The first group seems to live comfortable lives in perfect harmony, surrounded by flowers and happiness. However, this ends at nightfall, when a race of ugly Morlocks emerges from their underground dwellings. Apparently, the Eloi are living on borrowed time. During the day the Morlocks feed and clothe the Eloi, but when night arrives, they are eaten by the Morlocks.

In a sense, this is how Soviet society was organized. The bright and comfortable environment of the so-called intelligentsia had a very shaky relationship with the inhabitants of the lower classes of society. With each contact I had, I found myself encountering a strange new reality, where strength, rudeness, ignorance, and alcohol ruled. As a teenager I witnessed many drunken fights and even murders. In the evening the streets of Donetsk were filled with youth gangs robbing passersby. Parks, squares, and comfortable neighborhoods at night became sites of physical violence. Schoolyards sometimes resembled battlefields. If you wanted to survive in these conditions, you had to either mimic this behavior or be able to fend for yourself. I did both.

After graduating from the Institute of Soviet Trade as an economist, I was drafted into the army, where the "normalcy" of violence and cruelty exceeded anything that I had ever seen. I knew soldiers who had hanged themselves, unable to endure the bullying and beatings. And I knew a soldier who once picked up a machine gun to shoot his tormentors point-blank. I met him in the garrison prison, where I was spending ten days due to being in a fight. I wasn't Eloi, but I wasn't Morlock either. I was just a young man who wanted to live a decent life.

After demobilization I returned with relief to the paradise of the scientific intelligentsia. In this compact paradise, I found a beautiful wife, cocreated two wonderful children, lived in a three-room apartment, and quickly won a potential career at the Scientific Research Institute of Secondary Nonferrous Metals. Starting as a junior economist, I was given the position of head of the foreign relations department. It was a rapid rise up the social ladder for a thirty-five-year-old beginner. As I climbed the ladder of success, however, its steps wobbled more and more. Only two or three years were separating me from exile from this Soviet Eden.

My ascent took me nowhere.

In the early 1990s, Ukraine was plunged into years of upheaval, including tectonic shifts in social, political, and cultural life in the former USSR. The euphoria of Gorbachev's perestroika, which had begun in 1985, gave way six years later to a severe national crisis. Suddenly, our familiar world was collapsing at the speed of the hyperinflation rolling across Ukraine. In the morning one might leave home with the equivalent of one hundred dollars, and by evening, the value would have dropped by twenty or thirty dollars, depending on your luck.

Prices in general rose by more than 10,000 percent in a year, and even if you had money in your pocket, you felt like a beggar. Monetary designations changed with the ease of cards in a loaded deck—rubles, karbovanets, coupons, and hryvnias, a whole stream of incandescent soap bubbles that disappeared as soon as they emerged. Everything got turned upside down. Life was now a daily struggle to maintain the shaky status quo.

The purchasing power of my salary was shrinking like pebbled leather. In the late eighties, I'd had enough money to buy a car. In the early nineties, it turned into dust. As a department head in a research institute with a thousand employees, I wore one suit, three alternating shirts, a choice of two ties, and one pair of leaky winter boots. I couldn't afford taxi rides or café lunches. I had to save my cigarette money to pay for cheap Chinese dolls for my ten-year-old daughter and Nirvana posters for my thirteen-year-old son. It was a difficult, desperate, and tumultuous time.

And yet it was also a joyful time. Illegal video saloons showed American blockbuster films, interspersed with a cartoon series about Tom and Jerry. Music promos of Michael Jackson and Modern Talking were played on TV. Poorly translated Stephen King novels and dozens of variations of the Kama Sutra abounded in street stalls. Hairstyles and clothes became more and more outrageous. The night shops sold potable alcohol called Royal, which immediately dissolved all your sorrows in a blurred haze. And the next morning, the rat race would begin all over again.

For me and my workmates, the days passed in a feverish search for earnings. Those of us who still had jobs were never paid wages on time, keeping us off balance and tense. We never knew if we would have enough money to live another day. My family was no exception: when I looked into my wife's eyes, I saw silent reproach. My teenage son kept asking when I would buy him an electric guitar while my daughter dreamed of a Barbie doll, plus accessories. The word "soon" accompanied all my responses to their wishes, and for a long time, I believed this to be true.

Occasionally, a job opportunity might appear, and then the question would arise: "Should I leave my present job and take a chance on the unknown? Or should I stay where I am, on shaky but familiar ground?" I couldn't muster the courage to leave my well-trodden track to take a new, untested route. But soon, as it turned out, I would have no choice.

In the spring of 1993, the director of our institute gathered the heads of departments for a meeting and announced that the funding for scientific research had been cut off. From now on everyone would have to look for sources of income on their own, or, in the director's words, "become self-sufficient." We were all being let go. Stunned, we all packed up our things and glumly went home to share this turn of events with our families.

When I returned home that evening, my family was gathered together for dinner, watching me expectantly. I took a deep breath and delivered the news no one wanted to hear: that I was now unemployed, and consequently, our lives would be changing drastically.

For Sergiy and Svitlana, this meant that the purchase of an electric guitar and a Barbie doll was now off the table—indefinitely.

For Luba, it was the news she had feared the most—a major loss of income for our family. She shot me a look, and I read the doubt in her gaze. Could I support my family under these new conditions? I tried out a confident smile and the line, "It's all for the best, you know. We're starting a new life."

She hesitated, then said, "I hope you can pull it off."

"Sure," I said, nodding. And I thought, "So do I!"

A hopeful approach is half the battle when things go sour, but it's easier said than done. I had to start from scratch, with no one backing me up. In what direction should I move? Where should I begin? I would compare my condition with suddenly turning into a helium balloon that's fluttering in the wind. Who knew where I'd end up or when the string would break?

Two of my workmates had similarly been affected by this turn of events. We all felt utterly out of our depths, haunted by the uncertainty facing us. However, our combined experience in the field of nonferrous metals suggested a possible way out for us. After conferring, we turned our attention to a heap of scrap metal in a nearby factory that contained objects made of copper, brass, aluminum, and lead.

We approached the director of the factory and paid him off with a box of cheap cognac in return for six months of free access to his scrap metal. We set up our ad hoc business to extract copper wire from old electric motors with a single piece of equipment: a blowtorch. When the fire burned out the insides of the engines, it allowed the copper braids to be pulled out with a crowbar. At that time it was the most valuable product in the nonferrous metal market. We found a potential buyer willing to pay us a dollar for each pound of refined copper scrap. The three of us felt like gold diggers who had found El Dorado.

By the end of the month, smoke fumes followed me everywhere. My hands were so black it was impossible to wash them with any existing detergents. But our small group persevered, and we finally collected half a ton of copper wire. That was enough for each of us to receive a decent amount from the sale.

To the group's shock, however, one member decided that a decent amount was not enough for him. He grabbed all of the copper and then disappeared without a trace. I was left penniless, stinking of smoke, and with dirty, scratched hands. Luba called me a gullible fool, and I could hardly defend myself.

Another equally gullible fool was my former employee Yura. We had become friends while firing up electric motors. The damned things were

Chapter 2

heavy, requiring both of us to move them. Doing hard work can bring unlikely people together as they establish a new common ground.

I must confess I'm not a born leader. I don't like being in charge, preferring instead to be a support person. But I was always reluctant to go it alone, so I tried to bring someone along for support. Unfortunately, this meant sharing not only the responsibilities but the profits. In the past I hadn't minded: it was a small price to pay for a colleague and a companion.

In time, Yura became my ward. He was a red-haired, freckled guy—good-natured and lazy, like a well-fed, amiable young lion. He willingly accepted my leadership and was ready to carry out my orders, even though I wasn't always sure what to do next.

Although we lacked the resources to start our own company, I got lucky when a city official offered us a small room in the state building. I promised to pay him as soon as Yura and I made a profit. In those naive times, there were no rules and no controls. Everyone acted on their own. The only motivation was the prospect of money appearing somewhere down the line.

Newspapers were filled with ads for the sale of all sorts of unexpected things, from used cars to red mercury and mammoth tusks. The main task was to find buyers for all this stuff. We searched by phone. Day after day, Yura and I called different numbers, offering to act as intermediaries for the sellers. Alas, all our efforts were in vain. More often than not, the ads were either outdated or false. It was called "selling air." I can't even imagine how many tons of this "air" we sold in a month. And of course, our revenue was consistent with the product: air.

To our relief, however, a commodity exchange was opened in the building where we had been offered an office. We immediately became brokers, which didn't change much for us. We still called thousands of numbers to find out whether Japanese computers, Cuban cigars, and Vietnamese balms actually existed. As a rule, they did not. At best we managed to earn money for cigarettes and beer.

Meanwhile, life at home was deteriorating. Pasta and bread were our primary staples, and occasionally, I would bring home a case of chocolate or cans of tomato juice, but those were very rare occasions.

Everything (and Everyone) Is for Sale

One day Luba asked me why I was spending money on transportation every day when I arrived home empty-handed every night. Wouldn't it be better if I stayed home with the kids so *she* could look for work?

"Well, today we had an interesting prospective client . . ." I began.

"You get new prospects every day," she said. "Unfortunately, you can't feed your children with prospects, Sergey."

She was right. But I was right too. The new client did turn out to be promising. At first it was a mustachioed man with the fixed eyes of a dead fish. On his second visit, he was accompanied by a plump woman with a very tight perm. Apparently, they had large quantities of wood for sale. In fact, they had a whole sixteen-car freight train loaded with Siberian timber! For cash!

Yura and I were to receive 10 percent of the total amount of the sale. It was huge money. Fantastic!

Then three miracles occurred one after the other. First, the logs at the railway station turned out to be real, not mythical. Second, Yura and I managed to find buyers for the wood. Third, the buyers actually paid us the agreed amount!

The four of us sat in a shabby apartment near the railway station, sorting through, then counting, a mountain of banknotes. Oddly, the surname of the man with the mustache was Zhurba, which means "sorrow." His girlfriend was named Nadezhda, or "hope." There was something whimsical about working with Hope and Sorrow—and their names didn't seem appropriate for their personalities. They were tough, selfish, and calculating. When we finished counting the money, we sat down at the table, opened a bottle of vodka, and drank to our success.

After drinking one glass of vodka, Zhurba told us that he worked as a warden in a Siberian penal colony. The authorities had instructed him to sell the felled wood, which had been illegally cut down by the prisoners. Nadezhda, who worked as an accountant at a freight railway station, had helped to carry out this dark deal. One might say that Sorrow and Hope found each other, and then they found us.

Was this a portent of things to come?

Does a fish swim?

Chapter 2

I must confess I was not alarmed that I was getting involved in an illegal scheme. To judge me, you would've had to live in Ukraine in those crazy days. It's difficult for a resident of a modern, civilized country to imagine the almost medieval chaos into which my countrymen had fallen. The laws didn't work. The police merged with criminals so closely that you couldn't tell one from the other. Students became prostitutes; prostitutes became talk show hosts. Markets grew like mushrooms, and racketeers in tracksuits roamed through them, harvesting and establishing new orders.

Bandits in leather jackets and businessmen in crimson jackets were the heroes of the day. Their bodies were adorned by gold chains, and they drove luxury cars, were drowning in funds, and despised the law. These fortunate few aroused the admiration and envy of the younger generation. Everyone was intoxicated with the air of freedom, a concentrated mixture of permissiveness and unscrupulousness.

When there is no air to breathe, one can die. But too much oxygen can be just as deadly.

Now sitting in front of me was a mountain of money tied in bundles with rubber bands. Twenty of these packs were mine. Twenty more were owed to Yura. The rest belonged to Zhurba and Nadezhda. We drank cheap vodka, ate monstrous railway station pies, and looked sideways at money and watches.

"Okay, buddies," I said. "We drank on the deal. It's time to part."

I picked up the briefcase, which I had prudently taken with me.

"There will be another wood train next week," Zhurba said, watching my hands. He was very drunk and constantly licked his mustache, which made him look like a Cossack.

"Great," I said and put the first pack inside the case.

"Um . . . put the money back on the table, Sergey," said Zhurba, his eyes dull with the drink.

"Isn't this ours?" I asked, puzzled.

"Not yet," he replied. "We will pay you after the next round. This money needs to be paid for the next batch. Do you understand?"

"It's an advance payment," Nadezhda said. "Do you know what advance payment is?"

She was the soberest of us all, and her eyes shone with a sense of superiority.

"We did not agree to that," Yura and I exclaimed in unison.

"You'll have to," Zhurba said.

We argued some more. Throughout this conversation, I kept putting wads of money in the briefcase, which I had taken to work at my Research Institute. But those days were in the distant past, and I clearly didn't understand anything about modern business.

Three unknown men were waiting for us in the adjoining room. We hadn't heard them come in, but now they awaited us, sitting on the couch in a row, with shaven heads, tattooed arms, and steel and gold crowns in their mouths. Zhurba had not only brought logs from Siberia; he had also brought some prisoners for reinforcement.

One of them took the briefcase from me while the other two showed us their knives. We left without saying goodbye. Neither Zhurba nor Nadezhda came out to see us off. For them, it was routine. I was stunned and crushed.

Yura, however, looked smug. "I grabbed two packs while you were talking," he said. "So we win after all."

My wife didn't agree. Yes, I had brought home some money, but it seemed a mockery after our grandiose expectations. Her dreams had deteriorated before her very eyes, and she didn't want to hear any tales of criminals and their intimidating knives. She needed her money. My son and daughter looked at me as if I were mentally ill. Perhaps they were right.

The very next morning, I went to see Eugene, an old friend who ran a big company and traveled in a Mercedes with a personal driver. During the years since we'd last been in touch, Eugene had grown stout. Now he sat in a large leather armchair at a massive desk as confidently as if he had spent his whole life there.

His long-legged secretary hovered beside him, which made me embarrassed about what I had to do next. Gathering my courage, I asked Eugene if he could lend me some money.

He gave me a look that said my stock had suddenly plunged in his estimation. "I don't lend money, Sergio," he said. "But we can sign an

Chapter 2

agency agreement. You look for a buyer for my product, and if you sell it, you'll get your percentage."

Eugene was three years younger than me. When we first met, he was still a schoolboy, and I was a student at the institute. I had treated him as an equal and supported him through troubling times; I had thought we were friends.

Now he was sitting before me in his magnificent chair and offering me the opportunity to be his errand boy. I took the lousy form that his secretary handed to me, crumpled it up, and threw it on the floor. On top of that, I uttered a few unflattering words about Eugene. He took a quick look at his secretary, leaned back in his chair, and said, "That's your decision, Sergio, and no one else's."

Yes, it was my decision. And it was another humiliation.

All my life, I had been taught that the Communist Party would take care of everything for me. Soviet citizens were taught that any independent initiative was punishable. That was one reason why market relations took us all by surprise. We only knew the socialist economy. Capitalism was a wild new territory. I felt like a house cat set free—what should I do with this freedom? In fact, I was finding the concept both fascinating and daunting.

The following months passed in turmoil. I worked as an insurance agent, then sold cars. I also traded Turkish sneakers in the marketplace. I was even employed in various firms where they paid not with money but with empty promises.

In the end I got an interview at a company with such a tricky name that it flew out of my memory. But I remember the owner very well. His last name was Grousko.

"What can you do?" he asked me during my interview.

In the course of my previous deal, which had involved a railcar full of steel rods, I had met the production manager of a metallurgical plant. We had stayed in touch, and my mind immediately flew to him as a potential entrée for this job.

"I can arrange a supply of rolled metal," I said.

"Abroad?" asked Grousko quickly.

"Abroad too," I said without hesitation.

"I'll pay you two hundred dollars a month," he said. "And if you can bring me an export supply of metal, you'll receive 3 percent of the profit."

"Five," I said.

"You take me by the throat," Grousko said, biting his fingers. "Okay, Maidukov. Agreed. But we will count from net profit, I warn you."

"Net profit is okay," I said.

Grousko did not look like a swindler. I was impressed with the professionalism demonstrated by his company. It was reassuring to see the polite, well-dressed young men and women working in his firm. Here it was customary to congratulate employees on their birthdays and arrange five o'clock tea parties. Everyone was polite and helpful to each other.

I was delighted when Grousko gave me a separate office, complete with a new set of furniture. I got a chair, not as grandiose as Eugene's had been, but it was still leather, and it even spun around. This was my first real business job, and I actually received my first advance in a long time. It wasn't much, but it was a possible link to future stability. Even life at home began to improve!

The operation to send steel rods to Turkey took two months. The manufacturing and shipping process was demanding, but Grousko unquestioningly supplied me with the money to bribe the employees of the plant, the railway workers, and, of course, customs.

At the beginning of winter, two freight cars disappeared, and for a week and a half, I wandered around the stations, searching for them. The sums we paid to the customs officers were simply monstrous, but the real vultures were the port workers! Knowing that the Sea of Azov would soon freeze and that shipping would stop, they slowed down the loading of the wire rods onto the ship, extorting double bribes. I froze my toe and got a stomach ulcer, but I coped with the task. On New Year's Eve, Turkey reported that the cargo had successfully arrived at its destination.

Looking back, I realize how miraculous it was that I alone had executed this operation. All the company had done was prepare the necessary documents and provide me with transport. By my calculations, the net profit exceeded $100,000. I told Luba to choose a car, and she immediately signed up for a course to get her driver's license.

Chapter 2

All winter I asked Grousko when the Turkish partners would transfer money for the delivered goods. He asked me to be patient, and I tried to be, but my wife was becoming more and more urgent with her questions. Where was her car? How soon would I be paid?

In March I once again went to Grousko's office to ask my usual question: "Where's the money I'm due, boss?"

He looked surprised. "What money are you talking about, Maidukov?"

I patiently reminded him of our deal with the wire rods.

Grousko shook his head impatiently. "You are a staff member of the firm, Maidukov," he said. "Our contract does not provide for remuneration for outside work. You do your job and get paid for it."

He meant a contract of employment. We had not signed any other contract. Realizing what an idiot I was, I demanded, "I want my money. I earned it!"

Looking down at the documents lying before him, he declared, "You're fired, Maidukov, for violating labor discipline. Leave my office now!"

Seething, I stepped toward him, and as if on cue, two guards appeared. One took me by the shoulder, but I threw off his hand.

"Listen to me, Grousko," I said. "Listen carefully. You owe me five grand. You don't always have your gorillas with you, and one day, I'll take you by surprise. Alone. Without guards and witnesses. And then you'll regret it, I promise you that!"

The guards turned to look at Grousko, who gave me a pensive look. "I'll think about it," he said. "You'll get my answer in half an hour. Give me your phone number."

I gave him my parents' number because my route home might take an hour or more, and I couldn't wait that long. I was sure he would pay me—if not the whole amount, then at least half.

I arrived at my parents' home, sat, and waited. The phone rang forty-five minutes later, and I eagerly picked up the receiver.

A male voice said, "It would be worth cutting off your tongue so you never use it again. Along with your head. But there are better methods. Your kids go to School Number 37, right? Who do you think will get there first, you or us?"

I couldn't speak. Who was calling me? Was it the goons? It didn't sound like them; this voice had more authority. How did they know about my children? When did their classes end? What time was it now? Was this a real threat, or were these people simply trying to intimidate me?

Suddenly, the money was repugnant to me. I just wanted to hug my kids and make sure they were all right.

"Don't you touch them!"

My voice was hoarse, my heart beating hard inside my chest.

The invisible speaker laughed. "You're a fool, Maidukov. You can't threaten us. Your boss works for very serious people, so forget what happened here today. If you bother Grousko again, I won't even bother to call you. Do you understand?"

"I understand," I said, my voice now a whisper.

Actually, I didn't understand *anything* at the time. Was there one honest businessman in this country? I still had a long way to go to learn from my own mistakes.

Chapter 3

Chasing the American Dream

That night I lay in bed, awake, for a very long time. I wondered if I would ever be able to adjust to the new, harsh circumstances. Knowing myself, I thought it was probably impossible. I certainly had an instinct for acquiring potential money, but I lacked the assertiveness, if not the rudeness, for making business deals with unscrupulous partners. The threat to my children had completely broken my spirit. I felt worthless as a man and as the head of a family.

In the middle of the night, I awoke to find Luba, sleepy eyed and disturbed, shaking my shoulder. "You have been moaning in your sleep," she said anxiously.

I told her everything. Her expression changed so much that it was noticeable even in the dark.

"How could you risk the lives of our children in such a reckless fashion?" she hissed.

"Don't we need the money?" I replied defensively.

Luba didn't say anything. She turned away, lay on her side, and fell silent. Her stiffened back told me more than a thousand reproaches ever could. "If you weren't such a stubborn loser," her back seemed to be saying, "we would have a sweet and cloudless life. We could have been infinitely happy, gone swimming in summer, shopping in winter, traveling in our own car . . . we could have an apartment twice as big as this tiny one, eat fantastic food, and wear fashionable clothes. But now, you're spoiling everything!"

Chapter 3

I should have accepted Luba's silent reproaches, but I was genuinely offended. And being so was the easiest way I found to avoid conflict resolution. So I also turned my back on Luba. Our bed had become a battlefield following a quiet respite. Marital wars are, after all, often filled with silences.

In the morning, instead of taking into account all my mistakes and going back to fight with a surge of renewed energy, I gave up. Swimming against the current required too much strength and perseverance from me. Now I would take the path of least resistance. I would swim downstream.

During the next week or two, I left my home early and spent my days tippling with some drinking companions, shutting off thoughts of work, family, and other obligations. My buddies and I boasted of possible prospects while sitting on our asses and feeling sorry for ourselves. Sometimes I didn't come home until very late, and sometimes I didn't come home at all.

I knew that I was destroying myself. I wasn't giving myself time to sober up completely. I hardly ate and became addicted to smoking two packs of cigarettes daily. When I happened to be at home, my family didn't even look in my direction. It was like I didn't exist. My sense of shame was unbearable, forcing me to get drunk again and again. Only then could I forget my miserable life. Looking back now, I see what a miracle it was that I wasn't felled by a heart attack or crushed by a car appearing in the dark of night, when I was out carousing. Somehow I survived. One morning I looked in the mirror and saw a stranger there. He was so disgusting that I wanted to punch him in his bloated, raw face, swollen from drunkenness and sleeplessness.

"You're dead!" I hissed, speaking to him . . . speaking to myself.

I took a razor and shaved carefully, making my face as clean and smooth as my conscience should have been. Then I drank two cups of the strongest tea in the world. I forced myself to boil two eggs and had breakfast. Then I went back to sleep, where I fell into a black abyss.

In the afternoon I put on my formal suit and went downtown, where I sat down on a bench near a phone booth. I grabbed a newspaper and began to look for job advertisements. Pigeons arrived at my feet, waiting for handouts. I had nothing to give them. I had just enough change in my pocket for several bus trips and some phone calls. Every coin should have been used as rationally as possible.

In the evening, I returned home, now sober and hungry. Sergey walked past me as if I were invisible. Svitlana peeked out of her room to look at me for a moment or two, then disappeared. I winced at the pain that shot through me. But it was pain I deserved.

"I'm going to work tomorrow," I announced to everyone as I entered the kitchen.

Luba was silent, busy sorting through pay stubs spread out on the table. Her expression was impenetrable.

I cleared my throat and said, "Can I get something to eat, my dear?"

Without saying a word, she gathered the receipts into a pile and tucked them into a drawer. Then she set a platter of mashed potatoes on the table, then a bowl of fried fish. I've never eaten anything better in my life.

I told Luba about how much I liked her dinner. She didn't answer but busily washed dishes, standing with her back to me. Her shoulders, her posture, the tilt of her head wordlessly told me that only the worst bastard could leave his family to their fate in such poor circumstances. It was true—I had behaved like a bastard. But I didn't want to be a bastard anymore.

I approached Luba from behind and put my hands on her shoulders. "I'm sorry," I said softly. "I'm so sorry."

She remained silent, but her shoulders had lost their tension. It was a sign that she had relaxed, softened. We had begun a new phase.

The next job I found was hardly lucrative, but I considered it a stepping stone to begin with. The Globalinvest company that hired me was American and seemed solid enough. I was surprised, however, to find not a single American in the office. The interview was conducted by a pleasant young woman named Angelika. Later I learned that she was the company's chief accountant. The entire time she interviewed me, she didn't look up once, instead staring at her list of questions.

In the middle of our conversation, a tall man entered the room and sat next to her. I sensed there was a certain closeness between them, a hidden, intimate relationship. I also knew that this man was the boss. He looked arrogant and self-confident. For a while he listened to my responses wordlessly, blowing cigarette smoke up in the air. When I said that I had made several successful deals, he interrupted me sharply, saying, "If you were so successful, then why are you here?"

My answer was as frank as possible. He nodded and told Angelika to continue questioning me. As I answered her, I glanced at him from time to time. He was smoking king-sized Camels incessantly, and a cloud of gray smoke now curled around him; his round face, the color of a badly baked pancake. He had pale blue eyes and large yellow teeth. I estimated him as roughly ten years younger than me, though he looked much more solid and impressive. I felt him staring at me, studying my appearance and behavior. I tried to be as confident as possible.

He listened carefully to my dialogue with Angelika and sometimes interrupted us to make certain points. I learned that his last name was Momot, which suited his big stature and heavy build. He was not an American but an ordinary Ukrainian, a native of Donetsk. If there was anything foreign about his company, it was its name: Globalinvest Corps.

"Okay, you're in," he suddenly announced, arising and leaving the room.

Angelika jumped up to open the window wide, eager to release the smoke from the room and bring in fresh air.

"You're lucky," she said. "Sergey Viktorovich [Momot] liked you. But don't relax. He's very . . . er . . . demanding."

I thought that she'd meant to say *picky*, which turned out to be accurate.

I joined the company as a sales manager, not knowing what product I'd be promoting. For me, it was just another job where you do what you're told to do, go home, and forget about work until tomorrow. The staff was young, the average age around twenty-five, and looking at my much younger colleagues who surrounded me, I felt old in my late thirties, now closing into forty. My workmates treated me politely but did not take me seriously. I think they regarded my position at Globalinvest as temporary. I, too, suspected that this was the case. But a job was a job, and I was glad I had one—for now.

The company occupied a part of the second floor in a run-down hotel building in the heart of town that overlooked the main square with its obligatory monument to Lenin. Our office was a stretch of the corridor and had a long red carpet, well worn, heralding every doorway. There were a dozen doors that opened off it on either side, and the walls were covered with shabby wallpaper. The beds were taken out of the hotel rooms, but greasy sofas, heavy plush curtains, and landscapes in gilded frames remained inside. The whole picture called up images of a nineteenth-century brothel.

"We're moving out of here in about a month or two," Momot informed me when we talked in his smoky office. "You can't make much money sitting in a miserable office with peeling wallpaper. Do you know anything about building?"

I had recently completed repairs on my parents' cottage and told Momot about it. He nodded and handed me a list of building materials: "Check the prices. I wanna know if my president is cheating me out of my money."

The president of the company was a burly young man who consistently showed up in tight trousers. When he heard that I was checking out hardware stores, he ordered me to stop immediately, but I refused, citing Momot's instructions. Then he tried to snatch the paper I'd been writing on, but I resisted because, by then, I had figured out that the prices on the list were overpriced by at least double, if not more. He told me, "I'm the boss here," then threatened me, saying I would be fired.

"Who's fired?" asked Momot, standing in the doorway. His overweight figure did not prevent him from walking as silently as a cat.

The young man in tight trousers pointed at me, but he'd made a mistake. It was he who found himself unemployed. Momot picked up a sheet of paper with my notes, ran his eyes over the numbers, and signaled me to follow him. Half an hour later, I left his room, filled with swirling clouds of cigarette smoke, as the new head of Globalinvest Corps with a salary of $150 per month during my probation period.

I learned from employees that I was already the company's third president, but it didn't stop me from accepting the offer. It was my only lifeboat amid an ocean of turmoil and confusion.

Chapter 3

Every day, firms went bankrupt, banks burst, and queues lined up in front of labor exchanges. A police patrol car could stop you anywhere and rob you, in broad daylight, under the pretext of checking your documents. Local backyards bore the corpses of frozen beggars and knifed drunkards. Thousands of lonely old people were killed by those in a rush to take possession of their apartments. Today it sounds like a nightmare. It was. However, working for Globalinvest was increasing my chances of survival.

Momot favored me from the very start, perhaps because we were namesakes. He was seven years younger than me, and I liked the way he called me not by my first name but by my patronymic—Georgevich—as if respecting my seniority in age. I couldn't allow myself the same liberty. For me, he was Sergey Victorovich, the Slavic equivalent of the Anglo-Saxon "mister."

Momot smoked two packs of Camels a day and drank so much instant coffee that his eyes beneath his dark blond bangs were constantly pink. One day Angelika confided to me that Momot had once been an alcoholic. Nicotine and caffeine were acting as substitutes—a shield against his addiction.

Following his example, I also got hooked on coffee, drinking cup after cup throughout the day. The frequent instant coffee did little to invigorate me, but it caused me to smoke more often than usual. In Ukraine in the nineties, it was not customary to take care of one's health. The most important requisite was to simply stay alive at all costs.

My typical working day began with an obligatory visit to Momot's office, where the two of us would sit for several hours, talking over our plans and discussing possibilities. As a rule, while talking to me, he didn't stop playing with colored balls, lining them in a row on the bulging glass screen of his monitor. It was another bad habit I picked up from him. Millions of small multicolored balls floated before my eyes at night, causing insomnia. In those days, when I was ruining my health with such intensity, I felt detached from my body, like it could have belonged to someone else.

When we were alone, Momot could be sincere and natural, but when it came to appearing in public, he could turn off politeness and camaraderie like a light switch. Instead, he would puff himself up like a pompous peacock. He would go all out to "look like an American." During negotiations, he would, as if by chance, pull out from his pocket the Chase Manhattan Bank's credit card and twirl the small golden rectangle in his fingers, proudly showing it to his conversant. In the store, also "accidentally," he would take out a hundred-dollar bill instead of Ukrainian hryvnias, which, of course, impressed his audience because it caught everybody's attention.

Although he pretended to be a rich American, Momot didn't speak English at all, except for a few customary greetings, such as "Hello," "Good-bye," and "How are you?" His only American phrase was "Let's go step by step," and he repeated this whenever possible. He also knew how to exclaim, "Oh, yes!" That was his linguistic limit.

On the other hand, I could speak some English after years of listening to rock music and reading cheap paperbacks. Now my knowledge was coming in handy. Momot entrusted me to negotiate by phone with US companies in the motor vehicle parts industry. He would offer them access to the Ukrainian market through our "network of car dealerships" (which existed only in his imagination). At that time, we owned only a couple of unfinished concrete hangars on the outskirts of Donetsk. I had purchased them cheaply from the city administration, along with land. We only had to pay for the land plots since the authorities knew nothing about the existence of these abandoned constructions. Turning them into car dealerships would have cost tens, if not hundreds, of thousands of dollars.

When I wanted to know how big Momot's capital was, he gave me a long, suspicious look.

"Why are you asking, Georgevich? My money is my money. Stay out of things that don't concern you."

I'd noticed more than once that he had a highly suspicious nature, bordering on paranoia. Part of him never trusted anybody; thus, he would distance himself even from those who were loyal to him. He surrounded himself with a cohort of bodyguards, but he didn't trust them either. His heads of security changed with kaleidoscopic speed. The rest of the employees didn't stay with the company very long either.

Chapter 3

In time Momot revealed himself as a pretty nasty character and seemed to enjoy punishing subordinates for the most minor of faults. His tolerance only extended to Angelika and me. She probably had a romantic relationship with Momot, while his attitude toward me was more pragmatic than genuinely cordial. He also liked to brainstorm with me in sessions sometimes lasting deep into the night, trying to pull fresh ideas out of me, such as distributing software to state institutions, bartering manufactured goods for agricultural products, installing ATMs in supermarkets, and so on. True, when it came to funding, Momot usually paused and then canceled projects.

I discovered that his money, no matter how much he had, did not work for him. He could spend it on the construction and maintenance of our office, including staff salaries, but he stubbornly refused to invest in the business. It was a great mystery to me. The company's revenues barely exceeded its operating expenses. I had the impression that money had fallen from heaven upon him, but he didn't know what to do with it. His majestic black Mitsubishi Pajero—a limited-edition model—cost him almost $30,000, while Globalinvest's working capital was close to zero. Like most local businessmen, Momot would throw dust in the eyes of the people—and the dust was golden.

Luba, after seeing Momot's expensive car, began to urge me to demand an increase in my salary. She believed that he should pay me at least double. After all, I had been putting long hours and effort into Globalinvest Corps. She kept pointing out that I acted as if it were my own company, and I thought she was right. Actually, I was beginning to regard Globalinvest as my creation. There were too many weekends in the office, too much nerve, too much strain, too much coffee, and too much smoking. My intensity around the office not only required long hours of thought and conversation, it was also beginning to affect my health.

"I'm going to talk to Momot this week," I said.

"I suggest you talk to him tomorrow," Luba replied.

We exchanged glances. I shrugged and nodded.

The next morning, when I went to Momot's office, he was placing the color balls in a row on the screen in front of him. One cigarette was perched lazily in an ashtray. Another stuck out of his mouth. I took a deep breath and blurted out, "I need you to double my salary," hoping to get an extra fifty at best.

Keeping his reddish eyes on the screen, Momot snapped, "Okay. But four thousand dollars a month is the limit that I can offer at the moment. Don't ask for more, Georgevich. Be patient. Let's move step by step forward, and then we'll see."

With double pay, I could definitely be patient! Momot's generosity endeared him to me even more. From morning to night, we were inseparable. Like him, I began dressing in jeans instead of business suits. Blue Levi's pants, denim jackets, and cowboy boots emphasized our "American heritage." This image set us apart from other Donetsk businessmen. When the two of us went to government offices, the officials looked at us like we were aliens. Many more of them believed that we'd flown straight from the States to them and looked up at us, waiting for miracles. The whole country was under the spell of the magical motto "Made in USA." Although Soviet propaganda continually presented the image of America as an imperialist hell with militaristic instincts, for us, it was a wonderland inhabited by reincarnations of Marilyn Monroe in a white dress and the Marlboro cowboys—men of strength and freedom. We looked at the United States as a country full of promise and prosperity, freeways and skyscrapers, film stars and millionaires, Coca-Cola and Cadillacs. Americans might consider the Stars and Stripes the national symbol, but we were more inspired by Ben Franklin's iconic portrait on the face of a hundred-dollar bill.

The phrase "American investment company" produced a hypnotic effect on our partners and customers. I never saw the company's statutory documents, as Momot kept them in a safe, but he claimed he was married to a US citizen who had cofounded the company with him. My plan, devised to further enhance the privileged position of Globalinvest Corps, was to set up an offshore company in the Bahamas and create another founder. With the help of a computer and the best color printer we could find, we "issued" a thousand $1,000 shares that were "contributed" to the charter capital of Globalinvest (in other words, put in Momot's safe). Thanks to this maneuver, we acquired many benefits, including almost complete tax exemption. Along with those handmade shares of stock, we had gained the status of a $1 million investment company, which meant we could enter any administrative door we chose. It was a minor offense when compared to the terrible crimes rampant then—murder, racket, kidnapping, raiding, bribery, and corruption. The government was in a coma. The rotting odor emanating from the corpse of the USSR was drawing the attention of countless predators and parasites.

The city of Donetsk, where we lived, was now considered the criminal capital of Ukraine. (Our future president was from the Donetsk region and had two convictions for robbery and rape.) It was commonplace to read in the news that yet another businessman had been killed for refusing to pay protection money to racketeers. When you regularly see big, tough guys on the street, you know who they are: soldiers of a criminal army. Instead of hiding, they quietly stand beside their black cars—mostly BMWs and Volvos—with heavily tinted windows, weapons always at the ready. When Momot and I walked past them in our denim suits, they followed us with wolfish eyes.

Only Momot's numerous guards forced them to stay away from us. There were eight or ten in all, mostly martial masters with huge calluses on their knuckles. They didn't obey me; only Momot could give them orders. However, before leaving for New York, he put the security service at my disposal.

The month was June. By this time, Globalinvest Corporation had moved to a new office. We occupied the second floor of a large building on a quiet side street. Because of the summer heat, the windows were always open, letting in poplar fluff, but the front door was locked and guarded by a security camera. As a rule, the guards were in their room, equipped with trainers, a punching bag, and an armoire for pump shotguns.

I remember Momot said, pointing out their door to me, "These lads are strong enough to fight with street gangs, but they can hardly be called heroes. It's not them who are my main defense."

"Then who?" I asked, intrigued.

"You will know in due time," he responded. "Until then, I want you to memorize the phone number I'm going to give you." He dictated the figures. "Now you know who to call in case of emergency, Georgevich. No names. Just call and say you need help. They'll take care of everything."

Momot flew away on Friday, and on Monday, I realized what he meant when he told me about the emergency. That afternoon, as I was sitting in my office, I heard loud voices and a lot of commotion outside. I looked out the door and saw a bunch of strangers walking in my direction along a long, forty-foot corridor. The two company security guards were sitting on the floor, their noses and mouths bleeding, and several others were standing, motionless, pressing their backs against the freshly painted walls and making no attempt to stop the intruders.

I must confess my heart sank into my heels, but it would be all right as long as my brain remained coldly calm.

"Who are you?" I asked the intruder who'd walked ahead.

"You'll find out soon," he promised, pushing me back into the office with his outstretched hand. "Better sit down, or you're gonna fall down."

The guys behind him laughed. None of them had weapons in their hands, but I did not doubt that they were armed. They were tall and wide, with a tough look on their faces. This was the first time I'd seen real mobsters up close. They radiated aggression like high-voltage energy, which seemed to flow and pulse in waves throughout the room.

Remembering Momot's instructions, I glanced at the phone.

Their leader caught my eye and shook his head slowly.

"Don't even think about it," he said. "The cops won't come."

I looked up at him. All his features showed strength and self-confidence. The tip of his nose and upper lip were cut with the thin white scar that a razor would have left.

"What do you want?" I asked.

"Money," he answered without hesitation. "With your miserable guards, you need additional protection, right? So you're gonna pay us 15 percent of all your income. The Greek said so. It's him who sent us out here to give you a message. Heard about him?"

"Yes," I said.

That was true. Akhat Bragin, nicknamed Alik the Greek, was then the biggest Mafia figure in Donetsk and the owner of the city's football

Chapter 3

club. His name alone inspired fear in anyone. No one then imagined that the Greek had only four months to live.

On September 15, 1995, after a bomb attack at the football stadium, he would be dead, and Rinat, his beloved nephew, would have taken his place. For the time being, Rinat remained in the shadow of his uncle, who seemed powerful and indestructible.

"The Greek, he asked me to tell you something more of what he wants you to do for him," the intruder continued. "You gotta let us keep an eye on these numbers you put into your bookkeeping—a debit and a credit and other stuff. We wanna be sure you're not just winding us up. Do you follow my train of thought?"

"I've got to talk to my boss," I said. "I'm not in charge here."

The intruder winced. "Then why the hell am I wasting my time talking to you? Go get your boss now."

I reached for the phone, summoned the contact number from my memory, and dialed it. I had no idea who would answer or what he would say.

"Hello?" a neutral male voice said.

"It's Sergey Maidukov speaking," I said promptly. "I have a problem. There are unknown people here, and they—"

"Give it to me!" The intruder grabbed the phone out of my hand. "Hey, who's here? Do ya hear me?"

The man on the other end of the line had heard him perfectly well, and began to say something in a somewhat metallic tone. I noticed that while the intruder was listening, his face grew longer and longer and more and more strained. He was listening so hard that his brow was wrinkled in concentration.

"Sorry," he finally said. "I didn't know. We're leaving, so there won't be no more problems."

He handed the phone to me, turned away, and quickly left the room, his gang at his heels. In less than a minute, the corridor was empty. The shaken employees peeked out of their doors. The guards stayed at the locations where they had been taken by surprise.

"All of you, please go back to your work," I said in a loud voice. "The incident is over."

CHAPTER 4

A Bullet to Remember

DURING THE TWO WEEKS OF MOMOT'S ABSENCE, I HAD A GOOD REST and was able to devote sufficient time to my family. I didn't have less work to do, but I was spared long and often pointless conversations with my boss. As a result, I had enough time to review all our cases before noon, and then I just supervised the subordinates and solved minor organizational issues.

As for the business, our income barely covered the company's expenses. Sometimes we resold batches of perfumes or auto parts, but it never went beyond that. I was puzzled by this situation, seeing a lot of useless people on Globalinvest's staff.

There was a former director of a construction company who'd been hired by Momot to set up a network of car dealerships that were, so far, not being built. There was a highly paid lawyer who spent days and weeks doing nothing. There was a naval navigator who'd been hired in case we decided to go into shipping. The company also had a translator whose duty it was to conduct meaningless correspondence with the giants of the US auto industry.

On payday Angelika and I just shook our heads as we signed the payroll. This money could be enough to organize a serious business, but it was being tossed into the wind. Momot seemed to be playing the *role* of a businessman—not being one. He also tended to inflate costs instead of trimming them. I knew that this was usually the behavior of people who steal other people's money and do not earn their own.

Chapter 4

When I shared my insight with Angelika, she looked away uneasily and said, "It's none of our business, okay? Sergey Viktorovich knows what he is doing. He doesn't like it when someone sticks his nose into his finances."

I thought to myself, "Okay, then, it's none of my business. Everyone manages his money as he likes. Forget it."

And I turned to other things. In my carelessness, I was like a butterfly, not thinking about who owns the flowers over which it flutters. How long does the carefree life of a butterfly last?

Momot showed up at the office unannounced, as if he wanted to take me by surprise. His eyes were redder than usual, and he looked thinner. The secretary brought us coffee.

"Now, tell me everything, Georgievich," Momot said.

Even when he had been visiting the States, he had made daily transatlantic calls to me, so he was aware of the racketeer invasion. But he wanted to hear my story down to the smallest detail. Over the course of the conversation, he made comments and posed questions. It was evident that he enjoyed the power of his mysterious patrons . . . which were becoming part of his own personal power. After listening to me, he smiled with satisfaction, his lips curled back, revealing his yellowed teeth, stained from coffee and nicotine.

"Georgevich, now you see how influential my friends are," he said. "Thanks to them, we are protected and safe. But they are waiting for a response from us. Our job is to make money, but nothing is free in this world. Every favor has a cost."

This was something new. I looked at him carefully. He was smoking, squinting as he spoke, and waiting for my answer.

"Sergey Victorovich," I said, "do I understand correctly that we are paying people to protect us from harm?"

Momot lit a new cigarette, took a puff of smoke, and replied, "No, no, you have a completely wrong idea about what's going on here, Georgevich. Our protectors are not racketeers. But they do have a reason why they're helping me, understand?" (I didn't understand but nodded anyway, being a careful listener.) "They expect us to increase our profits," Momot went on. "Don't ask me who these people are. I'll tell you when the time comes. First, you have to show them what you're worth . . . uh, what *we're* worth. Got it?"

I nodded again, watching him closely.

"Remember when you told me how you exported steel wire rods to Turkey? I mean, you probably could pull off another deal like you did then."

I shook my head. "I doubt it, Sergey Victorovich. That guy, Grousko, has invested a whole heap of money in the deal. Such a scheme is impossible without an infusion of capital. You know, factory shipments are moving on a prepayment basis. You pay the money, then you get your rolled steel. That's the only way it works. Grousko spends $200,000 to earn $100,000 profit."

"Well, I ain't going to risk my money," said Momot quickly.

"Okay, then—" I shrugged.

But he was not about to let me close the topic on such a vague note. For several days he repeatedly told me that we had to increase our profits without investing a significant amount of money. He wanted me to go to the metallurgical factory and secure a supply of rolled metal for export—the sooner the better.

I continued to point out that without money, I had nothing to offer the sellers. At that time, exporting wire rods and steel fittings to Turkey was a very profitable business, and the demand for rolled metal was high. Why would a factory give us its product for free if they could sell their metal to other buyers?

I explained this to Momot with varying degrees of politeness, but he refused to listen. He insisted. He hurried. He overreacted. His main argument was that the patrons of Globalinvest were very influential people with whom it was better not to fool around. "Okay," I said, "if they're such big ones, then maybe they'll convince the director of some plant to sell us rolled metal in installments?"

Momot's round face was almost pleading as he said, "I have to prove that I can make money on my own. Otherwise, what's the point of keeping me?"

It was unexpected frankness on his part. My hunch was confirmed. Momot's relationship with his mysterious patrons was far more complex

Chapter 4

than I had realized. Certainly, he depended on them more than they on him. Moreover, he was afraid of them. While I hesitated, he looked at me, trying to put an ingratiating expression on his face. It was unbearable to see him so fawning, so flattering.

"Let's try," I said.

Momot slowly released the air that he had been holding back in his lungs. I felt relieved.

We often make decisions based on feelings rather than on logic. Then we wonder why we are not where we thought we would be. I can't tell you where our sympathy and empathy come from, but I know for sure that they often lead us to the wrong destination.

The next morning, I headed for the Alchevsk Metallurgical Plant to meet with a familiar production manager, Michael Petrovitch. Momot was going to come with me, but I firmly asked him not to. I explained that this was a journey I preferred to make on my own because the manager would not want to speak in the presence of anyone he hadn't known before.

In fact, I was afraid that Momot would ruin the professional atmosphere I intended to develop by saying or doing something inappropriate, like making his usual comments about how rich and successful he was or waving his golden credit card around. Michael Petrovitch was a fifty-year-old man whose life had been spent in the USSR, where one did not brag about one's wealth. This man required a more subtle approach.

For the trip I took off my "denim armor" and put on my old business suit, complete with a wide-striped tie. I did not want to appear as a "white crow among the black ones"—a common Ukrainian expression. I wanted the plant managers to see me as "their guy."

In my pockets I had four envelopes filled with cash, ranging from $2,000 to $5,000. The size of the bribe depended on the behavior of the production manager. Momot gave me the money without any questions, but the expression on his face mirrored doubt and suspicion. I assured him he had nothing to worry about.

"Georgevich, it is *you* who should worry," he said. "Fourteen thousand bucks is a lot of money, even for me."

A Bullet to Remember

Two of his new bodyguards accompanied me to Alchevsk. Presumably, this was evidence of the confidence and trust reposed in me. I suspected that the guys were assigned to me for the exact opposite reason. In what was then Ukraine, $14,000 *was* considered big money. With this amount, you could buy a three-room apartment or start your own business. However, my escort was amazingly carefree. On the way the guards were fooling around and laughing, like schoolboys who had gotten away from their strict teacher. I was tense and focused as I contemplated a difficult job ahead of me. The main effort was to find the right approach to Michael Petrovitch. (Giving a bribe is a real art.) The taker does not know if it's a trap, and the giver has no guarantee that his request will be filled. I had embarked on a risky adventure. Unfortunately, this remains a troublesome habit for me.

Michael Petrovitch was absent from the office, so I went looking for him. He was probably in the mill—a virtual city with countless yards, factories, and stores, where everything was pounding and smoking and roaring.

The loading area was cluttered with huge coils of wire rods. Michael Petrovitch was arguing with some businessmen in colorful jackets. Listening to their nervous discussion, I realized that the businessmen were demanding that the wire rod they had purchased be immediately sent to its destination. Michael Petrovitch explained to them, clearly frustrated, that this was impossible.

"How many times do I have to repeat the same thing to you?" he shouted. "There is only one access railroad, and now it is jammed with cars. Can't you see the freight train is on the rails? I can't just push it off the rail line!"

As far as I understood, the train consisted of thirty-two boxcars loaded with steel rebar. The purchasers of the lot still hadn't paid for it and didn't answer calls. Michael Petrovitch had found himself in a hopeless position. The railway line was blocked. The production capacity of the plant was paralyzed. The businessmen wanted to take their wire rod immediately. Facing high fines, they were nervous and even began to threaten Michael Petrovitch with physical violence.

Chapter 4

The workmen and loaders watched grimly, sitting on steel rings, their cigarettes in their dirty hands. Downtime meant a gap in their earnings, and they didn't like it. They could rebel at any moment, as often happened with many factories in those troubled times. In other words, Michael Petrovitch was in a desperate situation when I appeared before him and said, "I'll take the rebar. All thirty-two cars."

All eyes turned to me as I stood there, smiling politely. Michael looked at me, read determination in my face, and then, with an impatient gesture, invited me to follow him. Five minutes later, we were received by the director of the plant. The chief engineer also joined the meeting. Back and forth, the bickering went on for more than an hour.

The three of them flatly refused to give me rebar without at least a 30 percent advance payment. They had given up after I contacted a Turkish purchaser of hot-rolled steel, who agreed to buy the entire batch of rebar and sent me a copy of the contract by fax. The price he agreed to pay was much higher than the factory's selling price.

My company was left with about $90,000 after paying for transportation costs and loading and unloading operations. I signed an agreement with the plant, we shook hands, and the train loaded with rebar set off in the direction of Berdyansk Port.

It was a victory. I returned to the company as a hero. The employees looked at me with adoration. Momot rewarded me with a carton of long-sized Camel cigarettes and asked how much money was spent on bribes. Instead of answering, I laid the four envelopes on the table in front of him.

His face fell. "Are they all empty?" he asked.

"They're full," I replied proudly. "All of them."

I was now the nominal head of Globalinvest. I believed that my duty was not only to earn money for the company but also to save it.

Momot opened each envelope in turn, counted the money, and put it in the safe. His face was solemn as he shook my hand and said, "Georgievich, I always knew I made the right choice when I appointed you president of the company. This is not only my opinion. My friends are going to meet you in the coming days. They're officers of the Security

Service of Ukraine, so there's no limit to their possibilities. Consider this as your lucky chance."

I was intrigued and worried. The Security Service of Ukraine (SBU) was the immediate successor to the KGB, the USSR Committee for State Security. This organization's purpose was to instill fear in anyone who dared to act, speak, or even think in ways that could be construed as anti-Soviet. In my youth, when I'd listened to Voice of America radio programs, read James Bond novels, or bought scratched Beatles records on the black market, I automatically fell into the category of traitor. Every Soviet institution had its own special department staffed by KGB officers. Anyone you knew could be a secret agent who gathered information on you or your surroundings. You had to watch your every step, your every word, and you had to be very selective if you wanted to tell a political joke to your buddies. Probably, the Americans had experienced something close to that in the late 1940s and early 1950s, during the "witch hunt" period. For those of us born in the USSR, the SBU seemed like a ghostly reincarnation of the KGB. An aura of secrecy surrounded the organization.

The two men of mystery arrived at our office in the evening, when all the employees had left their workplaces and Momot's bodyguards were waiting for him in the car, so we were all alone in the building. The SBU officers introduced themselves as Andrew Andrewich and Ivan Ivanovich; they were operating under pseudonyms, which was not difficult to guess.

They looked like ordinary middle-aged men. Both were of medium height; both, in their standard dark suits, with their equally unimpressive figures and their expressionless faces. Their appearances were somewhat similar because they spent so much of their working lives together. And they radiated the superiority that their status provided. Although they were emphatically friendly, I did not feel safe in their presence. There were reasons for that.

If the SBU was a Ukrainian analogue of the FBI, then it was in its worst possible form. No one knew what the official duties of the Security Service members were, but in their free time, they acted as defenders of businessmen, taking them under the so-called *krysha* (roof), which was illegal protection from gangsters and corrupt police. It was the main source of income for the majority of representatives of power structures. Based on this, I decided that Andrew Andrewich and Ivan Ivanovich were the *krysha* for the Globalinvest.

Remembering this, I was tense and cautious while we talked a little about general topics like weather, politics, and so forth. But soon our guests dropped their formal business manner and engaged in the kind of small talk characteristic of close friends. I learned that Andrew Andrewich would be a major and Ivan Ivanovich, a colonel. They seemed interested in my life and wanted to know about my plans for the future, though I suspected that they already knew everything about me. They questioned me about my latest deal and said that they appreciated the initiative I took.

"You should continue in this direction, Sergey," said Ivan Ivanovich.

"We're going to continue," said Momot quickly.

As for me, I kept silent. So far, I hadn't received any reward for my efforts, and this didn't seem encouraging. I was expecting something more substantial than praise. It was I who had earned $90,000 for our company, which, by the way, was not taxed, thanks to my foresight. Still, Andrew Andrewich and Ivan Ivanovich didn't say anything about my bonus. They just finished their tea and left.

Momot breathed a sigh of relief and relaxed into his chair. I had never seen him so unsure of himself. His relationship with Andrew Andrewich and Ivan Ivanovich was anything but equal. He perceived them as his masters and played a subordinate role in this alliance. It was highly likely that the SBU officers may well have been the shadow company's investors, who expected profits from their contributions. But Momot showed no desire to reveal the secret to me. He pretended he hadn't been feeling small and frightened, and I pretended I didn't notice. This encouraged him. He squared up his shoulders and began to view the evening with more optimism.

"Georgievich, we won," he said. "It was evident that my friends were extremely happy with us. This means that we have reached a new level and, in no small part, thanks to you."

"Not so small," I thought. Momot saw the hint of disappointment in my eyes and smiled reassuringly. He reached into his pocket and pulled out a Chase Manhattan Visa card.

It was his habitual gesture, which I had constantly observed since the beginning of our acquaintance. What the heck was he trying to do, anyway? Show off in front of me again? Impress me with his wealth?

"Take it, Georgevich," Momot said, handing me the card. "Keep it in a safe place and don't lose it, because it's your future. Now you have your personal bank card. I registered it in your name while I was in New York. Yesterday, I deposited $15,000 into your bank account."

His words took my breath away. I knew virtually nothing about ATMs. I couldn't even imagine what they might look like. Not far from the truth were those who saw the people of the former USSR as a naive, aboriginal race. We had traveled into the future and now found ourselves face to face with terra incognita.

This was the first time I had held a bank card in my hands. Momot watched me with a reassuring Santa Claus smile. I ran my finger over the raised numbers on the plastic and asked how I could get the money. Momot shook his head.

"You don't need to right now, Georgevich," he said. "Wait till I take you to the States. Americans pay with cards in stores, at gas stations, at the movies—anywhere. You'll learn when we get there. Until then, I can assure you your bonuses will be good, and you will accumulate enough not only to buy a car but also for two or three years of life in America. Are you satisfied?"

I was not only satisfied but happy—so happy that all my doubts disappeared at once, and in the evening, I returned home with a huge cake and a bottle of champagne. It was a big family event. Svitlana received an electric piano as a gift, and Sergey got the money to buy a new pair of jeans. On the table was a vase containing a dozen fragrant scarlet roses.

Luba said she felt as if she were on cloud nine. We all felt that way. Finally, my efforts and abilities were being appreciated, and I'd been rewarded appropriately.

The next day, I set to work with redoubled energy.

CHAPTER 4

In early spring I made another export shipment of rolled metal, which turned out to be less successful but still profitable. There were some complications that prevented my return to Alchevsk. As a start-up businessman, I'd had no idea how fierce the competition in the steel industry could be. Now, I would learn—the hard way.

I tried to call Michael Petrovitch several times, but he had stopped answering my calls. I managed to get his home number and called there. His wife answered. She said that Michael had died, then burst into tears and hung up.

Afterward, I remember Momot and I sitting in his Pajero, parked on the Donetsk Theater Square, discussing the fallout from Michael Petrovitch's death. Momot thought we could probably do without him because I knew other factory managers. However, the news of the production manager's sudden death upset me. Michael Petrovitch had not appeared old or sick. Looking through the wet windshield of the car, I thought about him, not about the export of rolled metal.

It was drizzling cold rain outside. The opera house building was yellow stucco, with white columns—the oldest and finest theater in the city. The buildings across the street were old gray brick. Even at the late afternoon hour, many of the windows shone with light from within. Along the street were some showcases: a jewelry store, the Theater Caffe, a tobacco shop, and a place selling ice cream and fried chicken legs (then known as Bush's legs). The tobacco shop looked posher than the jewelry store. People walked back and forth along the street, some with umbrellas, some not. No one was buying anything.

Momot sensed my mood and fell silent. The two of us were looking absently up the city street across the road when the Pajero was surrounded by a dozen tough guys in leather jackets. The back door opened, and a man wearing a black leather coat climbed in and sat down behind us. Momot started and grew pale as he glanced at the rearview mirror. I remember that the man's shiny black coat rustled, giving off the scent of brand-new leather. Speaking quietly and distinctly, he identified himself.

It was Jakob the Samson, the most dangerous mafioso in Donetsk, who headed a large criminal group. His name was as intimidating as Alik the Greek's.

"I don't like it when someone sticks his snout into my bowl," he said. "So you boys stay away from Alchevsk."

"I've never been there," Momot said quickly.

Both of us were equally nervous. As Samson was directly behind my back, I couldn't see him, and it heightened my unease. I couldn't tell if he was armed.

"I know who was there and why," he said.

His torpedoes stood outside, hands in their pockets. They looked around to make sure no one approached Momot's car. For some reason, Momot's bodyguards were out of sight. The rain intensified and drummed on the car roof. It was gloomy outside, and the streetlamps were beginning to come on, one for every two lamps, as the city was saving electricity. At night Donetsk was as black as a coal mine. I would have given a lot to find myself at home, sitting in an armchair under a brightly burning floor lamp.

"It's only business," I heard myself say.

"It's not yours anymore," Samson cut me off abruptly. "Here, grab this."

He touched my shoulder. The back of my head went cold. I turned around and looked down at him. Some small brass cylinders glittered in his fingers. It was a bullet, or, more precisely, the cartridge of the AK-47 Kalashnikov assault rifle—I had seen such little things in the army.

"Take this, man," Samson said again, this time more forcefully. "This is a little souvenir of our meeting. I hope you're around long enough to remember it."

Before I could say anything, Samson had climbed out of the car and went back to a black Mercedes, surrounded by his mobsters. The bullet resting on my palm still radiated the warmth of his hand as we watched the gangster cars drive away from the square. Momot's bodyguards ran toward us. They were lucky they hadn't arrived earlier. I stared at the bullet in my hand.

"Don't worry, Georgevich," Momot said. "You're not alone. Our friends will take all the necessary measures to make sure it doesn't happen again."

Chapter 4

His tone was deep and reassuring—but not reassuring enough to dispel my doubts and fears. At night I would wake up from the noise of approaching vehicles and stand on the balcony for a long time, peering down in the darkness. During the day I would constantly look around, making sure I was safe.

A week or two passed. Momot gave me a personal driver with a pistol, but how could he help me? I flatly refused to go to Alchevsk again, and Momot didn't insist. Even he, surrounded by his numerous guards, did not feel completely safe.

It was pretty inhumane, but I experienced real relief when I learned that Jakob the Samson had been killed. This happened on April 12, 1995. Samson had just left the Theatre Caffe opposite the opera house. He and his gunmen had been shot to death from a car parked opposite the café exit. His younger brother, Arthur, took him to the hospital and threatened to kill all the doctors if they didn't save a bleeding Samson. It was in vain. Samson died without regaining consciousness.

The next morning, Andrew Andrewich appeared at the office specifically to congratulate me on the news of Samson's death. "Now you can work in peace, Sergey," he said. "I believe Jakob the Samson is no longer a menace to you and your business. You can make money without any risk. No obstacles."

My thoughts were not about money or obstacles.

"Do you know who killed him?" I asked.

"Some bandit," Andrew Andrewich replied recklessly. "You know, bandits always kill each other, nothing new. Which is precisely why they are useful."

I can still see his grin as he spoke those words.

Was he a bad guy or a good guy? And what kind of man was I becoming since I'd become part of this murky business?

After many long and painful reflections, I told myself that Samson's death was not my fault but that he'd become a victim of circumstance. Though I may have been self-justifying, to some extent, it was the way I saw it (and see it still). Circumstances determine our actions, while our actions, in turn, create circumstances. As a philosopher once said (who else could have said it?), each one of us is the creator of our own destiny. Or, I would add, the destroyer.

Instead of drawing the right conclusion from my ominous premonitions, I chose to stop thinking the situation. I even threw Samson's bullet away and told myself never to think about it again. Well, there's no bigger fool than a careless fool, right? And a bullheaded careless fool has even more to learn in this game called life.

Chapter 5

Money Can't Be Funny

AT THIS POINT OUR TURKISH PARTNERS WERE READY TO BUY ROLLED metal on a permanent basis, but after three weeks of negotiations, I had to regretfully decline the offer. The Alchevsk Metallurgical Plant suddenly went bankrupt and was closed. Such was the practice of the state-owned company directors who wanted to buy out plants, factories, and mines from the government. They had consistently bankrupted their enterprises in order to acquire them at bargain prices. Then bandits would descend upon those clever directors and take away their prized possession at an even lower price. This was also common practice.

You cannot act dishonestly and expect to be treated fairly. If you live in swamps, be prepared to deal with snakes and crocodiles. It's so easy for me to write about it today. But it was so difficult for me to comprehend this at the time. I remained at Globalinvest. I remained in the crosshairs of responsibility as I was running a very dubious business.

My search showed that all the metallurgical plants in Donbas were now in the hands of new owners who exported their products independently. Monopolists were determined to keep outsiders out of their business, so I had to find new ways to get the products I needed.

The Visa card Momot had given me warmed my heart in the days of these trials; it offered me strong motivation to remain in the middle of a confusing road. Since I had received it, I considered it the apple of my eye. The little plastic card was my key to the future. Luba once turned it over in her hands and said she would prefer cash, but I enlightened her about the benefits of having an account at Chase Manhattan.

Chapter 5

Our new confidence about having enough money had made our family relations more loving and comfortable. We ate delicious food and wore snazzy clothes. Our children's rooms were equipped with electronic toys for every taste, from a game console to a computer and a synthesizer. We felt we were living a life of luxury. If you knew how much one could buy for four hundred bucks a month in Donetsk at that time, you'd be surprised. But you'd still stay away from this place, wouldn't you? And that would be perfectly reasonable.

Donetsk was the unofficial capital of Donbas, and it embodied all the worst qualities that accumulated there. Since the Stalin era, when Donetsk bore the name of a Soviet dictator, it had become a large mining city. That meant it was less of an outpost than it was somewhere on the outskirts of the USSR. We were an industrial center, the second biggest in Ukraine, situated between the Azov Sea and Moscow. Industrialization had begun here in the late 1920s, when masses of ruined peasants, impoverished proletarians, and detainees had arrived here from all parts of the country. The area was a composite of poor and evil people—our own version of America's Wild West.

There was nothing significant in Donetsk, nothing advanced. It was a rather provincial city, poor and tough, dotted with black pyramids of waste heaps. And the locals had aggressive temperaments because they were under duress, so they were always ready to snap.

For all of my childhood and youth, I'd had to walk around with clenched fists, waiting for the sudden attack. Mass fights constantly took place on the streets and in the parks between the inhabitants of different parts of the city, from small kids and teenagers to adult men, who were mostly demobilized soldiers and drunk miners.

The very name Donetsk still evokes unpleasant associations in me. It was a goddamned city where horrible things were constantly happening. Many of my classmates and childhood friends had come to a sad end. Some, when drunk, fell out of windows, were hit by cars, or drowned in the river. Others committed crimes and ended up in prison. Two of my college buddies killed a third, cut off his head, and were caught trying to burn it at the stake. The guitarist from our youth band was jailed for ten years for rape. The drummer became an inveterate drug addict and hanged himself. It was an endless series of crimes and accidents. It was Donetsk, a mining town, and perhaps not in vain did some believe that it had an underground corridor to hell—a place you want to get out of so that your children could grow up in a normal environment.

Because I had some money placed in an American bank account, I began to make plans to move to a more civilized place. Alas, it was a remote prospect. Despite my fervent need to get the hell out of there, my immediate future was connected with Globalinvest Corps. I saw my well-being as inseparable from the prosperity of the company. I was constantly looking for new sources of income, which seemed an easy task, given the number of visitors who flocked to our office in hopes of getting investments, like teams of winged cockroaches that fly at night to the lamplight.

One of our visitors marked the beginning of a new era in my existence, although, at the time, I was unaware of it. He was a good-looking guy in his midthirties. There was something about how he presented himself that reminded me of a big cat; his walk perfectly matched his name: Tigran. He was Armenian, as his surname—Martirosyan—showed. Black-haired and neatly bearded, he spoke with a heavy accent and wore a snow-white blazer over an open-necked black shirt. The handset of his radiotelephone was a rarity in those days, implying the existence of a special antenna on a high tower.

Before starting a conversation, Tigran reached down and picked up a leather men's purse, placing it on the Momot's desk. His silk trousers were pressed to perfection; his elegant loafers made me cringe as I looked down at my tattered cowboy boots. He looked at us with his sad hazel eyes and invited us to invest in his sewing shop.

Curious, Momot asked him how much he wanted. Tigran said he would like to have $50,000 and promised to return $80,000 in two months. I saw Momot's brows lift in surprise. The offer was very generous and very tempting.

"*Too* generous and *too* tempting," I thought.

I shook my head slightly, giving Momot a "Don't do it" sign. But my boss seemed to have forgotten his usual policies of caution and suspicion. Instead, he swallowed the bait and began to ask questions.

Chapter 5

Tigran told us that he had bought Japanese sewing machines and was going to make uniforms to fill a firm order for the students of all the schools in the country. Now he was looking for money to purchase fabrics and accessories and to pay the salaries of twenty seamstresses. He had now spent his last allotment of cash on equipment for the sewing workshop. It had cost him about $50,000, and now he was desperate for the same amount—or perhaps even more. His dark Armenian eyes looked at us pleadingly and sadly.

I had to admit I felt ambivalent toward Tigran. On the one hand, it was hard not to fall under the spell of a man whose face and manner expressed the most perfect cordiality. On the other hand, he failed to inspire confidence in me. Maybe it was my intuition. In any case, I was wary. That could not be said about Momot. His nostrils were already quivering with the scent of money, so he allowed himself to be drawn into the affair with Tigran.

I thought I knew the reason for this decision. My boss decided not to tell Andrew Andrewich and Ivan Ivanovich about the deal because he had no intention of sharing either the risk or the rewards with them. He regarded it as his "personal business." And of course, he never even asked me for my opinion. Considering himself very cunning, Momot said that he was ready to lend Tigran not $50,000 but only $40,000, with the return of the same $80,000. Tigran sighed and agreed.

"That's not all," Momot said, squinting through the cigarette smoke. "You'll have to put up your sewing machines as collateral for the loan. My president will check them personally. I'm warning you, Tigran, don't even *try* to trick him! Maidukov has a smart head on his shoulders."

Tigran gave me an up-and-down look, assessing what he saw. His gaze seemed to penetrate my skull like an X-ray beam. I waited, stone-faced, for his assessment.

To my relief, what he saw seemed to please him.

"Deal!" he said.

When we went outside, I saw Tigran's red Jeep. I couldn't stop myself from asking him why he hadn't decided to sell it to get the money he needed. He replied that it was a cherished gift.

"I believe I'm rather sentimental about presents," he said.

He hardly struck me as a sentimental person, but I nodded and said nothing.

The road was leading us to the satellite city of Donetsk: Makiivka. Tigran was driving his red car with tinted windows at a risky speed. Along the way he asked how much Momot was paying me, and I told him. He shot me another evaluating glance and barely suppressed a sneer.

"Hell, that's not a heap of money for a man in your position," he said.

I let it go.

Makiivka was an ugly industrial city with gray buildings and gray people under a gray sky. The factory chimneys gave off smoke that mingled with the clouds. Against this background billboards with palm trees and white-toothed beauties looked like bright patches on worn rags. A surprising thought welled up in me: Donetsk wasn't really such a bad city to live in.

Tigran's sewing workshop was located on the ground floor of a two-story, yellow-plastered building with wooden window frames and a jumble of television antennas on the roof. Tigran unlocked the door, and we entered the workshop. It appeared abandoned, with clutter and dust and poor lighting. Some of the cutting tables were actually old doors resting on wooden boxes. Sewing machines and sergers were partially disassembled and clearly *not* made in Japan.

"Ninety percent of them are just junk," I said.

"No, no, they're good machines," Tigran said. "They only need to be refurbished a bit."

"They're only good for scrap!" I countered.

He laughed. His laugh was a weird mix of cackling and hissing.

I didn't understand what he found amusing. In fact, I was ready to leave the workshop as soon as possible. I told Tigran that I'd take a taxi back to Donetsk, but he put his hand on my shoulder and asked me not to tell Momot about what I had seen here.

I was shaking my head—no, no, no. Tigran promised to reward me for my silence, starting with $1,000 and ending with three times that. He said that it wouldn't be a crime, because he would pay his debt to Momot anyway. He urgently needed money, and he was going to get it one way or another. I listened to him for a long time, still shaking my head, and then I said: "Sorry, Tigran, but you're asking for the impossible. Momot is my boss, and I can't fool him. I'll tell him the truth and let him decide. Call him tomorrow, and you'll get an answer. I'm sure Momot's answer will be no."

I had misjudged both men. Momot's answer was a shocking yes. My report on the deplorable state of the sewing shop had been swept aside, and all my efforts to convince Momot to send Tigran packing were rejected. The next day, Tigran visited our office and left it with four thick wads of bills. When he'd left, I said to Momot that it was a mistake, but he then told me that he never makes mistakes.

"I don't care about sewing machines," he said. "Have you seen Tigran's car, his phone, his clothes? He's just flashing his gold baubles around. He's worth a lot more than the $40,000 I gave him. I'm betting that I'll get my investment back. If not, my boys will make Tigran pay."

Disgusted, I decided that it was not my problem. I had warned Momot not to lend Tigran money, so I was in the clear.

For a while my worst fears seemed unfounded. A week later, exactly on time, Tigran showed up at our office with $5,000, which he handed over to Momot with emotional expressions of gratitude. According to him, the sewing shop was now working full speed ahead, busily fulfilling orders. It sounded so convincing that I almost believed him.

But the following week, Tigran arrived with only $1,000, citing increased production costs. After that he limited himself to a skimpy weekly phone call, persuading us to wait patiently until he could return the rest of the money he owed.

"Don't worry," he kept repeating, "everything will be fine soon. Just be patient, please."

As the weeks rolled by, Momot's face took on a grayish tint, his eyes glowing like two tiny red lanterns. I have never seen a person consume so much caffeine and nicotine; he was clearly addicted to both substances, and it was taking a physical toll.

Momot literally ruined himself. Soon the only subject he would discuss was how he had parted with his money so thoughtlessly. Gone was his confidence that he would receive double the amount owed to him. All he wanted was to get his $40,000 investment back again.

As the weeks went by, Tigran never showed up again. After the hundredth phone call, he stopped answering his phone. Finally, Momot's patience snapped. He declared that tomorrow, he would send his guards to Tigran.

"They'll teach him to respect me," he growled, pacing the room. "I'll order them to beat the hell out of him. Either Tigran finds the money, or he'll see himself in a hospital bed, if not in a coffin. This Armenian is going to get what he deserves. He will remember me forever! He doesn't know who he's fucking with!"

I should have shared Momot's outrage, but instead, I began feeling sorry for Tigran. He had impressed me as being a bright, cheerful person. Yes, he was a fraud, but I didn't want him to get hurt. My diplomatic Libra nature rose to the challenge, and I decided to convince Momot to resolve the conflict peacefully. Perhaps Tigran would change his mind if our own SBU officers talked to him.

"Are you crazy?" he shouted. "They don't need to know about our problems!"

"About *your* problem," I thought, but I said nothing. Momot was in a state now. There was no point in trying to convince him to go easy on Tigran. Momot knew he had deceived his patrons and was afraid to confess the unhappy outcome to them. This only confirmed my guess that Globalinvest's money did not belong to him. At the same time, he was too greedy to recoup the company's losses out of his own pocket.

The bottom line was Momot had made a mistake, and I was determined to correct it. I hoped I could persuade Tigran to pay off Momot and left the office early to take a taxi to Makiivka. Along the way I tried to ignore a growing sense of foreboding. Something bad was about to happen—I sensed it in my bones.

The receipt that Tigran had given us included the legal address of his business, but, as I suspected, it was nothing more than a fake. Now I had no choice but to go to the sewing shop to confront him. It was almost a hopeless undertaking. How great was the probability of finding Tigran there? One chance in a hundred? A thousand?

The sewing shop was empty, its windows broken. Glass shards littered the sidewalk. I looked inside, and the room was a mess of broken

Chapter 5

pieces of metal, bits of plastic, and strands of electrical wire. It looked as if someone had come in with a giant bat and crushed everything in a rage. I thought that Momot probably was not the only one who'd lent money to Tigran.

A car honked behind me. By now my nerves were frayed and on edge, so I spun around to confront the driver. Before me sat a familiar red Jeep Cherokee. Tigran was peeking out of the front window. He watched me, his gaze stern and reproving. It seemed to me that he was about to stomp on the accelerator and speed away, but he surprised me by beckoning me over with a wave of his hand—less of an invitation and more of a command.

This was a different Tigran than I had known earlier. Gone was the friendly, engaging, and easygoing version of the man. Now he looked menacing and severe. Somehow we had switched roles: it was I who was his guest, feeling as if I'd entered an alien ground where Tigran was suddenly the master of the situation.

I felt a strong pang of regret for my ill-conceived decision to come to Makiivka. My taxi had long since departed, which left me alone in an unfamiliar place, face-to-face with a man who sat in his car with the engine running and who was looking at me without any emotion in his face as I walked toward him. He owed us $34,000, not to mention interest. In the 1990s in Donbas, you could easily be killed for ten bucks. (You could also be killed there for no reason at all.) Such were the times and such were the circumstances in which we were placed.

I approached Tigran, and we greeted each other. Contrary to my expectations, the expression on his face was far from hostile, and he didn't show signs of irritation, though his tone was cold, if not stern. He asked me why I came. I told him that I was looking for him.

"Why don't you just call me?" he asked.

I almost laughed. "We've called you again and again. You're not answering your phone."

And then his excuses began. Tigran told me he had serious problems to solve and pointed to his destroyed workshop. According to him, someone had thrown a grenade inside the room, and he suspected it had been an attempt on his life. While he was explaining this, he looked up at me several times, and I thought I saw ominous flashing in his eyes, as if he was letting me know that I, too, could be assassinated. I felt intensely uncomfortable, but I didn't show it—otherwise it would have made me seem like I was scared. Instead, I tried to look cool and calm.

"Were they your competitors?" I asked. "I guess they were going to take those miraculous Japanese machines away from you, yes?"

For a moment or two, Tigran looked at me suspiciously, but suddenly, he laughed. Gone was his mask of cold reserve. Now his laugh was one of relief—light and happy—rather than the laugh of a man preparing to attack or defend. I realized that my joke had penetrated his fear of retribution, and he no longer saw me as an enemy.

"You're kidding," he said cackling and shaking his head. "Who needs that junk?" Then in a split second, he grew serious again. "They wanted to kill me because of my older brother," he said, looking around. "I'm his right-hand man, you know, so they so tried to get rid of me."

I had no idea Tigran had a brother and asked him his brother's name. That was the first time I heard the name Samvel. It didn't mean anything to me back then. Instead, I shelved the information and reminded Tigran of his debt. Glaring at me, he said, "Samvel's name is known to everyone here in Makiivka."

I shuddered and reminded him that I was from Donetsk. He said that very soon, the name of Samvel would thunder throughout the country, and when he said this, I knew he meant it.

He described his brother, who was in prison, and hinted that it would be better for me not to get further involved in this situation.

Our conversation went on for quite some time, and the sun was already low, sinking behind the rooftops. There was a chill in the air. Tigran and I were alone near the Jeep Cherokee, but in the distance, I noticed a black car with tinted windows. That damn black car had snuck up behind us while we were talking. I thought it was time for me to say goodbye and go home. Instead, I made another attempt. I told Tigran that if I were him, I wouldn't mess with Momot.

"He has a dozen tough guys ready to cripple anyone they're sent to visit," I said. "And that's not all, Tigran. Even bigger men from the SBU

Chapter 5

are standing behind him. Now do you understand what kind of shit you've gotten yourself into?"

Tigran smiled and shook his head dismissively.

"Nobody likes losers," he said. "Serious people won't stand up for a dumbass throwing his money around. No one took that forty grand from your boss by force. He's just a greedy asshole, and people like him will lose everything. Everyone pays for their mistakes out of their own pocket, Sergio. So go and warn Momot not to fuck with me, because my brother will nail his ass to the wall!"

I shook my head and said that putting pressure on Momot would only make him even angrier. I reminded Tigran that Globalinvest had strong security and support from the SBU. Did he need problems? He thought for a bit and agreed that it made sense to cool down my boss a little.

"All right, then tell him he'll get his money later," he said. "As you already know, my brother is in prison. The charge is false, but the punishment may be real, so I've gotta get Samvel out of there. And yeah, that's why I needed the money. As soon as my brother's free, we'll pay off Momot."

I felt a huge weight being lifted—until his next words.

"There's just one condition: if your boss is smart enough to wait until all the legal stuff is over. Go tell Momot to stay put until I call, got it?"

"You don't know this guy," I told Tigran. "Far-off promises will only make him angrier. He's already mad at himself for being played by you."

"Well, if he doesn't smarten up . . . it will be a lot worse for him," Tigran said. "I like you, Sergio, so let me give you one good piece of advice: whatever you do, stay away from your boss—as far away as you can."

With that new threat in the air, he looked at his watch and offered me a ride home.

I replied, "It's okay. I'll get a cab."

He looked at me closely, then nodded. "I understand. *Loyalty.* You're a loyal man. This is a good thing, but you chose the wrong side, Sergio. Don't trust Momot. He'll let you down."

"My boss is my boss," I said.

Tigran winced and said, "Let's hope you won't regret it later on."

Then we shook hands and parted.

On my way home, I kept looking back over my shoulder, watching the same black car with tinted windows that had appeared at Tigran's demolished workspace. It kept a discreet distance from the taxi all the way back to Donetsk. Only near my house did the car slow down, then turn around and speed away.

I remember standing in the street long after the ruby lights of the car's tailgate had disappeared. Anxious thoughts were tugging at me. Why had Tigran put a tail on me? Did he want my address? Damn it, I seem to have crossed a line into a heap of trouble. Why had I poked my nose into my boss's business? Now I was being set up for more problems between two hotheads and a guy doing jail time.

Tigran's behavior toward me had conveyed a level of sympathy—when he wasn't scowling—but it's hard to trust someone who has a habit of embezzling other people's money. And what about his jailed brother, Samvel? This guy might be dangerous.

The next morning, I told Momot about my conversation with Tigran. I shouldn't have been surprised when he got pissed off and yelled at me, accusing me of betrayal. He didn't even listen to the whole story. Then he went on a rampage, smashing his computer mouse against the wall, stamping his feet, shaking his fists in the air. It was truly something to behold. I sat there in silence, waiting for the next scene to unfold.

Momot called in all his guards and ordered them to go to Makiivka, pronto! "There isn't a minute to waste!" he yelled, then demanded that they capture Tigran and bring him to the office in the car's trunk. The guards, armed with pump-action guns and gas pistols, surged out the door.

"You shouldn't have done it, Sergey Victorovich," I told Momot. "You ought to think twice. It's not too late to stop them."

Momot didn't even look in my direction. He told me to get out of his office and sat down to play color lines. His eyes were bloodshot.

As it turned out, the guards quickly found Tigran. Two of them were taken to the hospital with severe head injuries and fractures to their limbs and rib cages. Four quit without severance pay. Only two guards were standing in front of Momot when he called me in to him. I think one of them was called Lehman, though I'm not sure. They were very young guys, who had seen too many Bruce Lee films but had never before encountered real gangsters. Their faces were so bruised and swollen, I didn't recognize them at first. Lowering their heads and shifting from foot to foot, they told Momot how their "strike force" had been surrounded by some hefty guys who ran all over them.

"If you're attacked, you ought to fight back!" Momot shouted, waving his fist. "You had a weapon!"

"They also had weapons," one of the guards answered. "And they didn't need a license to use their guns."

"And they promised to come to you, Sergey Victorovich," the second one said.

Momot muttered some curses and sent the guards away. He began to pace the office, shaking his head like a restless stallion. I waited in silence until he spoke again. Finally, he asked me, "What should I do now?" I advised him to call his patrons.

"I wish I could," he mourned and then admitted that the money he had wasted actually belonged to SBU officers.

I said they would find out anyway, so it would be wiser to tell them the truth. Momot sighed resignedly. Putting aside his hesitation, he picked up the phone.

A face-to-face meeting with Andrew Andrewich and Ivan Ivanovich took place in the evening of the same day, when there was no one left in the office who could hear or see us. They entered Momot's office without knocking or bothering to say hello or shake hands. They just appeared and sat down in the front of us.

At this point Momot no longer looked troubled . . . he looked frightened and desperate for forgiveness. The SBU officers listened to his confused recounting of his humiliating takedown and then condemned him for having committed "an unforgivable offense." They ordered Momot to return $40,00 to the "common pot" and fined him an additional $20,000.

"That's all I have!" he exclaimed in despair.

The SBU officers said they knew, so they'd fined him $60,000, otherwise the punishment would have been even more severe. They also said that in the event of a new mistake, Momot would be removed from the management of the company. With this, Andrew Andrewich and Ivan Ivanovich looked at me. I shook my head. It was too much. I wasn't going to take the place of the man to whom I owed my job.

They shrugged their shoulders and headed for the exit. Stopping near the door, Ivan Ivanovich turned around and, looking straight at me, said, "When we want someone to work for us, they usually work for us. See you."

When the SBU officers left, Momot sat in his seat for a long time, staring blankly. He looked like a man who had lost everything at the gaming table. When we shook hands in farewell, his palm was cold and soft, like a dead fish.

That was the last time I saw him.

Chapter 6

Behind the Broken Doors

Over the next few days, it fell upon me to run operations. Momot had vanished as if he had never existed. He didn't appear in the office or at home, he didn't answer the phone, and he didn't return all the calls I made to him.

Momot's absence left me with an uneasy feeling of responsibility for the situation. Where's my boss? Was he kidnapped by gangsters? Should I report his disappearance to the police, or is he in hiding?

I couldn't get through to Andrew Andrewich or Ivan Ivanovich. Tigran didn't pick up the phone either. I was all alone, left to figure things out on my own, and I didn't even know what was going on behind the scenes. Was I in danger? Waiting for the unknown threat to materialize was even worse than being able to face it.

Day after day, I sat in my office at the big L-shaped desk with the glass screen monitor, wondering how to deal with all the problems I faced. The company was left not only without its leader but also without a source of income. The construction of the car dealership had been halted due to a lack of funding. The two trucks we used to transport daily goods were standing idle and useless without fuel. I had no funds allocated to pay for customs clearance of imported merchandise. The office staff now had to make do without printer cartridges and free coffee. The safe was empty. My head was empty, too, and I was unable to come up with a plan to keep the Globalinvest activities current. How could I come up with a plan when my thoughts were being tossed about by waves of burden and confusion?

Chapter 6

How long did it take? I don't think it was more than a week, because, in fact, the events unfolded very quickly. One day, when the ghost of bankruptcy was breathing down my neck, I dialed Andrew Andrewich's number again. To my relief, he answered. My relief was short-lived, however. He told me that Momot had taken all his money and flown to the States.

"Do get ready, Sergey," he said, while I struggled to absorb this latest news.

"Ready for what?" I asked.

Andrew Andrewich paused for a short chuckle and said, "Ready for the worst. Your company is finished. And don't call us again. Forget we ever existed. This is not advice; this is a warning. You don't know us and never did. If we need you, we'll find you."

The line died, the dial tone buzzing in my ear. I was sitting there, numbly holding the telephone receiver, when Angelika entered my office. Conservative as always in her black business suit, she sat down in a chair across from my desk. As Momot's lover and his chief accountant, she was in a privileged position within the company. In fact, Angelika's position was equivalent to mine.

Shortly before these events had occurred, her brother had died in Chechnya. He'd been a very promising young artillery lieutenant in his late twenties. He was torn to shreds by a land mine and was buried in a zinc coffin, its lid soldered down. I attended the funeral and witnessed Angelika's inconsolable grief. Somehow, it brought us closer. We were almost friends—as far as our professional duties allowed.

In recent days Angelika had been visiting me often to talk about Momot. After the death of her brother, she began to smoke two or three cigarettes a day. After Momot's disappearance she was never seen without a packet of Salems and a lighter. While she was lighting her cigarette, I lit my own and told her about Momot's escape to the USA.

"I think it's highly unlikely that he'll call us from there," I added, watching her for a reaction.

Her head jerked up, and she swallowed visibly. Her eyes suddenly went from remote to haunted, and I waited until she recovered a little, then told her everything.

Angelika stubbed out her cigarette in the ashtray and asked what would happen to us. We both knew that Momot had shifted all the responsibility onto us by his escape. All contracts, invoices, and reports bore our signatures. As long as the SBU had supported us, we could feel safe. Now this protective dome had been removed, and we were left defenseless. Our financial tricks and quasi-legal frauds now threatened to backfire on us. Boomerang is the main and highly accurate weapon of Karma.

It seems doubtful to me that I was capable of thinking about boomerangs and karma on that ill-fated afternoon, when Angelika and I sat across the table from each other, separated by a large walnut table. All our thoughts were concentrated on the critical situation in which we'd found ourselves.

"We're done," Angelika finally said, shaking her head. "Oh, my God, we're done, we're finished."

Her earrings dangled back and forth, like those of a fortune teller. I didn't like her prophecy.

"You'd better go home, Angelika," I said. "Right now. This minute. Take all the accounting records with you. They need to be hidden somewhere."

Her eyes widened, and she jumped up from her chair, ready to run from the office. But it was too late.

The security guard downstairs called to report that a group of armed men in masks and black uniforms had driven up to our building, kicked the door, and rushed in. In a matter of seconds, I could hear him speaking, then the connection was lost. Thuds, shouts, and sounds of a struggle came up from below.

"Looks like the special forces of police broke in," I told Angelika. "Follow me! Quickly!"

She became white as paper, ready to faint, but that did not prevent her from obeying me promptly.

Momot's office and mine were separated by a shared bathroom with shower, sink, and toilet. The two opposite doors leading inside were hidden behind laminated wall paneling to keep out prying eyes. The

Chapter 6

company staff hardly knew about the existence of this secret room. It was our only chance to escape retribution and remain unnoticed.

I pushed Angelika into the bathroom and shut the door. She and I stood perfectly still and waited in the dark room. We could hear cops stomping and yelling throughout the office downstairs.

"If they find us—" Angelika began, but I put a finger to her lips to silence her.

I didn't dare turn on the light. The bathroom was completely dark. We were afraid to move, trying not to make a sound. Breathing low and slow, we became part of the darkness. I had heard my heart beating, the blood pounding in my ears. It was like a child's game of hide-and-seek, only with terrible consequences.

A couple of times, Angelika tried to speak, but I held my hand up in front of her mouth, making it clear that I did not want to hear anything from her. Our shelter was our trap. It was the wrong place and time to talk.

At first the outside noise produced by cops was distant and muffled, but with each passing moment, it became louder and more distinct until it sounded as if it were right outside our secret doors. I almost saw a stream of police commandos outside, crashing and crushing everything in its path. Their heavy boots were pounding along the corridors, running from room to room.

Despite all the deafening cacophony, I could clearly hear Angelika's ragged breathing and knew she was close to fainting. I guided her to the toilet seat, with its lid closed, so she could lean against the wall.

My eyes gradually got used to the darkness. I could see via the faint rays of daylight streaming through the cracks beneath the doors. I awaited the moment when I'd come out of our hiding place and show myself. However, my intuition said, "Stay where you are."

My memory has not retained the thoughts that flashed through my head, but I can easily assume that I was close to panic. The possibility of being arrested and eventually punished had never felt so possible as it did that afternoon. All I knew was that I didn't want to go to jail and be killed, maimed, or raped with a mop handle. So I stood in the dark and waited for fate to step in. I felt like a small child who hides from adults, hoping that his offense will be forgotten once he appeared to his elders.

I imagine that Angelika's thoughts were similar to mine. I don't know how long we hid in the secret bathroom. Everyone knows that the passing of time can appear skewed in the darkness. Minutes could stretch to infinity or shrink into moments. An hour of tedious waiting is not equal to an hour spent in work or play. So I lost track of time.

We remained motionless, growing numb in our shelter as we listened to what was going on outside. My ears were picking up screams, sobs, cursing, doors slamming, and staccato commands. There were sounds of scurrying inside Momot's office, followed by a grating noise directly behind the door, as if someone were moving furniture.

I looked into the crack and saw men in balaclavas and black uniforms pulling out desk drawers, tossing folders out of the file boxes, and yanking books from the shelves. Turning back, I saw the same scene in my own office. I couldn't say what organization these men represented, but I assumed they were from the Department for Combating Economic Crimes.

Leaving us without SBU cover, Andrew Andrewich and Ivan Ivanovich had actually thrown us to the dogs of law.

My nostrils caught the smell of burning tobacco. The men in black had finished searching the office and were now on their smoke break. Two of them were sitting on my desk, talking. Their voices sounded lazy and relaxed. They talked about me and Angelika, calling us a pair of effing assholes, and they regretted not finding us at the office. But they were sure we would soon be caught and punished. They already knew about Momot's escape and called him "a bloody cunt but the smart cunt—the smartest in the company." It was true. Momot proved to be more prudent than me. Now I wondered, How much trouble I was in for being his official and unofficial partner?

While the men smoked and talked, sitting easily on the top of my L-shaped walnut desk worth $1,000 (delivery bill, $300), our office telephones rang constantly, but no one intended to answer them. Now and then, excerpts of interrogations reached me from outside, and my heart sank every time the cops asked the staff where their president might have

Chapter 6

gone. Thankfully, my subordinates had no idea, or if they did, they were not about to admit it. Yet it was awful to be sitting there, in a dark, stuffy room, dripping in sweat and waiting for someone to let slip something about my secret hideout.

Finally, the interrogations and searches were completed. I heard our employees being taken out of the office. A deep, commanding voice called out something like the following: "Folks, give me your attention, please. I want to warn you to take only your personal items. All property of the company has been confiscated. The front door will be sealed. It's closing time, gentlemen. Get the hell out of here!"

After a long ten minutes, silence reigned in the office. I wiped sweat from my forehead. That unventilated bathroom was like a sauna. Angelika asked in a whisper if we could go out. I replied that it would be wiser to wait a little longer, so we spent some more time in the hideout's oven. When we walked out of there into my office, I was wet from head to toe.

Angelika was breathing heavily and fanning herself with a folder taken from my desk. Our eyes squinted from the sunlight. I felt as if I'd awakened from a living nightmare. I still couldn't absorb the fact that this was all too real.

After making sure we were alone, we made a round of the office. It was trashed as if a pack of wild animals had frolicked there. The floors were littered with wires, cords, ripped stationery, and sheets of paper covered with boot prints. Computers, files with contracts, and Momot's safe were gone. I couldn't find the cardboard box with the Bahamian shares and other valuable documents, and the shelves of the bookkeeping room were empty.

Angelika sank into a chair and put her head in her hands. I started telling her to be brave, to be calm, not to worry, and to believe that everything would be fine.

"Oh, come on, Sergey," she said tiredly. "Can't you see that sounds like bullshit? Just shut up and let me think. I need to figure out how the fuck I'm going to get out of this shit."

Under the circumstances, I didn't find it surprising that she sounded so impulsive and was not carefully choosing her words. I shrugged and went back to my office to call home. As I walked, slivers of glass and plastic crunched under my feet. With every step I took, one thought swiftly followed another: Globalinvest Corps no longer existed. I had become president of a nonexistent company. Moreover, I had become—by association—a wanted man. And I was being pursued.

Upon entering my former office, I gathered my thoughts, trying to think of how best to tell my family my shocking news. I picked up the receiver, took a deep breath, and let it out before I dialed my home number. The phone rang. I cleared my throat.

Then Luba picked up. She was trying to speak calmly, but her voice was high and shrill. I heard elements of both panic and rage as she demanded, "Why haven't you answered all my calls, Sergey? You have no idea what I've been through these past two hours! Some sons of bitches conducted a search of our flat! Imagine how I felt when I found them breaking into our home! Thank God our kids were in school! They smashed dishes in the kitchen, kicked over chairs, and broke the closet door off its hinges. They're gone now, but they left a mess. Everything is trashed, and there's nothing that hasn't been turned upside down! Why, Sergey, why? What is going on?"

I took a deep breath and told her about the raid on the office, explaining that I'd have to go into hiding for a few days. Not surprisingly, she gave me a tongue-lashing and became even more agitated. The more I tried to soothe her, the more upset she became. Finally, I told her that our phone might be tapped, and I wouldn't be calling home for a while.

At this point Luba's patience went out the window, and she blurted out a few harsh suggestions and hung up.

I felt very lonely and useless. It was a relief for me when Angelika came in. She was my only ally. And she seemed to feel the same way about me while the two of us stood in the middle of my wrecked office. Angelika didn't have anything with her, just a small purse slung across her shoulder. I noticed her hand was clenched around the purse strap so tightly that her knuckles were white. Her face was pale, and her eyes were wide and dark. I asked her if she had any idea what to do. Angelika nodded.

"We must stick together," she said. "Alone, we will fall. So don't leave me, Sergey. Otherwise . . ." She shuddered, probably at the thought

Chapter 6

of going to jail. I said nothing. She took a short, almost imperceptible step in my direction; I remained silent and immobile. I didn't know how to react to Angelika's proposal.

Should we stick together or split up? She was a young, attractive woman—much too attractive for my wife to accept her as my fellow sufferer. Both of us were married with families, and now we were facing another tricky situation.

Perhaps I should have reminded Angelika of this. I didn't. In the end I was not going to cheat on my wife. Neither Angelika nor I had ever flirted with each other. What was at stake was a possible life as fugitives. Would it be alone? Or together?

I remember we went out the building together, descending the stairs stealthily, like a couple of offenders leaving a crime scene. And so it was, to a certain extent. The office of Globalinvest Corps had been the scene of numerous economic crimes. Now, instinctively, we both wanted to be as far away from this place as possible. I opened the door to the street and, in doing so, tore apart the police seal: a white piece of sticky paper with the data and a signature on it. One more crime, one less crime—it hardly seemed to matter.

Standing on the porch, Angelika and I looked around. No one was waiting for us with handcuffs at the exit. The parking lot was free of police cars. The occasional passerby walked down the street, unaware that they were seeing two lawbreakers in front of them.

Angelika pointed her finger toward her blue Peugeot and said, "Let's get out of here!" I disagreed. I felt it was better not to use her car because its license number might have been on the wanted list.

"Well, then, what are we going to do?" she asked.

I suddenly realized how dangerous it was to stand like this, on a sunny street, in full view of everyone. At any moment we could be arrested and thrown into jail. I experienced a fit of despair. I had not the slightest experience of hiding from the police. Where should I go? What should I do? I had no clear plan for either the distant or the very near future.

It seemed that Angelika had caught my condition. She lowered her head and said that she should take me to her aunt's place, where we could stay temporarily until things got sorted out.

Immediately, my thoughts sprang to my wife, who would probably clobber me for even considering staying with Angelika, no matter how innocently.

"It sounds ambiguous, I know," Angelika said as if reading my mind. "I just want to help you, Sergey. We can't go to our homes right now, so why don't we go to my aunt's together? I'm guessing you have nowhere else to go, am I right?"

My circle of acquaintances was fairly large, but all my friends were married, and their wives would not have been happy to have me for an extended visit. Any hotel could be a trap. The houses of my parents and relatives were not a safe haven, because that would be the first place the cops would look for me.

Angelika's invitation sounded acceptable except for the prospect of staying alone with her in the same apartment. Noticing my hesitation, she sarcastically mentioned that she wasn't going to take away my virginity. It worked: I felt embarrassed and agreed to go with her. Angelika grinned, having won me over. She led me through the streets to her aunt's house. It was a pleasant, quiet, and uncrowded part of Donetsk. Everything looked the same as I remembered it from childhood—trampled lawns, sparse small shops, and tall trees with whitewashed trunks. The borders were also whitewashed—this was the only decoration of the city's landscape that the municipal authorities could afford.

Finally, we came to a twelve-story building that towered over the surrounding Khrushchevkas—cheap, rapidly built houses of the Khrushchev era.

"We're here," Angelika said. She handed me the keys, gave me the apartment number, and told me that she'd be back in an hour or more. Then she left before I could ask any questions.

I smoked a cigarette and entered the house. The elevator's huge barred steel door reminded me of a jail cell. Suddenly, I wanted to get out of there, but I forced myself to calm down and ride it up to the fifth floor.

Chapter 6

The apartment Angelika had lured me to was a small, one-room unit. A white and gray cat came out to meet me. That explained why Angelika's aunt had left her the keys. The cat stared at me unblinkingly as I moved around the apartment. I found some coffee bags in the kitchen, put the kettle on the gas stove, and took a few cookies from a pack. I needed to get something into my stomach. It was still only three in the afternoon, and I realized I hadn't eaten in twenty-four hours.

While I was drinking coffee, I asked myself how this bizarre situation could have happened. Was it my naïveté? How could I have believed in an omnipotent Momot when he turned out to be an ordinary scoundrel? My gullibility was my damnation. I could only thank God that Momot had partially paid me with a bank card. According to my calculations, at least $15,000 had accumulated in my account. However, I had no idea how to get to this money. Chase Manhattan Bank was located thousands of miles away from the modest flat where I now hid from the police.

I felt the bile of despair rise in my throat. I had experienced a similar feeling once in my childhood, when I succumbed to the persuasion of some local boys and climbed onto the top of a hundred-foot factory chimney. Climbing up the steel rungs was much easier than going down. In fact, I *couldn't* get down on my own! Until the firefighters arrived, I was lying helplessly, with my stomach on the curved wall of the pipe, clinging to the bricks with both hands, waiting every second for the wind to throw me to the ground. The culmination of this event was a black bird that suddenly flew out of the pipe right into my face. Only a miracle allowed me to hold on.

Would another miracle happen this time? Once again, I had climbed too high and felt all alone, not knowing if I could ever regain the ground beneath my feet.

Now time crept slowly. The resident cat didn't care about my problems. Its purr motor revving, it stretched out across my lap. An hour and a half later, the cat raised its head, listened, tensed, and then jumped down to the floor and ran to the door. There was silence, and then I heard the key turn in the lock. The front door opened.

"Angelika?" I called, getting up from the sofa.

It wasn't Angelika. Three unfamiliar men entered the room—and they were all looking at me.

"Sergey Georgevich?" asked the one in the middle. "Maidukov?"

"Who are you?" I asked, fearing the worst.

These were pointless questions. One glance was enough for me to recognize the men as plainclothes cops. They twisted my hands behind my back and quickly led me to the exit of the apartment building.

My friend Angelika had certainly made good use of the time she'd had at her disposal. Realizing that she had turned me in, I clenched my teeth and again cursed my incurable innocence. I could only hope that I was strong enough to endure the trials that lay ahead of me.

Part II
Confrontation

Chapter 7

Manners in the Monkey House

When you read about the police in this book, keep in mind that in the former USSR, there *were* no police in the 1990s. They existed somewhere in the West. We had the *militsiya*, first Soviet, then Russian, then Ukrainian... I'd only ever heard the word "cops" in American movies. We used to think of our *militsioners* as *musora* (trash). To a certain extent, the "police" did protect citizens from criminals. At the same time, the Soviet and post-Soviet *militsiya* was itself a criminal organization. Moreover, it was considered "legal," or at least semilegal, which meant citizens could not resist men in *militsiya* uniforms. They had the law and the courts on their side. Nothing and no one could oppose it.

The "trash" could beat you on the street or rob you under the pretext of "making a search." When you saw *militsioners* on the street, you were wise to hurry past without looking back.

Now that I was under arrest, I prepared for the worst, although I tried not to show it. I kept my shoulders high and didn't slouch, but inside, I felt sick at heart. Mentally, I bade farewell to my freedom. When I was led into the Department for Combating Economic Crimes and I heard the door slam behind me, I felt like a mouse in a mousetrap.

The police department looked like any other government office. There were fluorescent lights, green walls, notice boards, and lines of peeling white doors with signs on them. Along the walls were chairs for visitors and detainees. When I passed by, the occupiers lifted their heads to look at me. They were probably trying to determine if my situation was as bad as theirs.

Chapter 7

I don't remember the name of the investigator who handled my case. But I do remember him nodding at a chair in front of his desk, saying, "Now sit down, and let's talk about your future—if you have one."

He was a youthful man with a pleasant, open face and snow-white hair, carefully combed with a side part. Although he wore civilian clothes, I knew that he was a major, as he'd introduced himself to me as such. In his right hand, he held a pen, poising it over the blank record form. His first questions were the usual police questions—my age, my birthplace, my social position, and so forth, leading up to my current job and my work responsibilities. He wrote down the answers and then put his pen down on the desk and nonchalantly told me that Angelika had expressed the desire to testify against me, accusing me of forcing her to sign all the questionable documents.

Another betrayal from someone I had trusted. The news felt like a punch to the gut. Angelika had framed me. Enjoying my reaction, the investigator continued: "Your position is unenviable, Citizen Maidukov. Now there's only one main suspect: you. Being a head of a company does mean you are automatically held responsible for the actions of the company. Consequently, prepare yourself to be accused of being a criminal. This means your life will not go on as before, and your old patterns of living will be altered—irrevocably. The vital question will not be whether you will drive a white or black Mercedes but, rather, how long you'll stay alive once you find yourself behind bars."

I saw that the investigator enjoyed scaring me, so I made an effort to keep my face impassive. I told him that I never owned a Mercedes or any other car. His expression hardened; I could tell that he didn't believe me. For some time he questioned me about the real estate and personal property that I owned. My honest responses did not satisfy him. Finally, he leaned across the table and said testily, "Now listen to me carefully, Citizen Maidukov. The judge will make a decision based on the evidence that I'll present to him. Do you see the connection between these two events?"

I nodded. Then the investigator asked me how much money I had earned as president of the company. I told him, and he shook his head in disbelief.

"Do not try to mislead the investigation with your lies," he said. "You're the man who ran a company with $1 million in authorized capital. Do you think I'll believe that you haven't helped yourself from the cashbox?"

It seemed to me that the investigator winked at me, although it could have been a nervous twitch of the eye. I didn't react. I stood my ground, repeating that the position of president of Globalinvest had never enriched me. The investigator listened to me with a sarcastic smile on his face. It was obvious that he didn't believe a single word I'd told him. He kept insisting that I must have a lot of money hidden away—money Momot never knew about, and that theory was something that interested him much more than my actual malfeasances.

As if by accident, he mentioned the cramped conditions in which his family of five lived. They should have moved into a larger apartment a long time ago, but they hadn't enough savings to allow them to do so. Saying this, the investigator looked at me as if I had personally caused him all this distress. I held my ground.

He leaned back in his chair, laced his fingers across his stomach, and said, "What I'm telling you now is off the record, Maidukov. I'm not greedy, and I shall be satisfied, say, with $30,000. That's a pretty good deal. Isn't it better than spending years in jail and being a criminal for the rest of your life? Why don't you get smart and cooperate?"

I relayed that I didn't have that kind of money, repeating my refrain of "I've only got $1,000 in cash."

Now tired of this game, he sat up straight and assumed an official air. He no longer winked at me, and his face no longer looked even remotely pleasant. For several moments he fiddled with the pen in his hands, as if about to throw it angrily on the desk, but he restrained himself. When he spoke, his tone was cold.

"Don't you realize it's stupid to lie to me?" he demanded. "Your future hangs in the balance. By refusing to cooperate with me, you risk landing in prison—very soon and for a very long time. Don't you see? I'm the one who gives you a chance to escape punishment and commence a new life. Are you getting the point, Maidukov? I may be the only man left on earth who can save you. So now, go home, and think carefully about this mess you've made for yourself."

I got up and walked toward the door, silently swearing that nothing could get me to return to this place. The investigator's voice stopped me.

"Hey! Be here tomorrow at ten sharp, and I mean sharp. Don't try to run and hide because it will not help. We'll find you wherever you go. You also have to understand the state you and your family are in. I suppose we understand each other. So you can go. Till tomorrow."

Before I left, I looked into his eyes. They were stern and cold, and his jaws had shut tight. He knew I had nowhere to go, and I knew it too. I got scared, really scared.

Immediately after leaving the Department for Combating Economic Crimes, I rushed to the nearest telephone booth and dialed Andrew Andrewich's number. There had been a glimmer of hope in my mind that perhaps he had nothing against me personally and would help me in a time of trouble, but as usual, he didn't answer my calls. I had no one to rely on anymore, no one to tell me how to act in these new and alarming circumstances. It was entirely on me—but what the hell could I do?

The bus I took home was packed like a sardine can; the working day over, people were hurrying back home. All the seats were taken, so I ended up standing and holding on to a bar. Traffic was only allowed to go twenty miles an hour. It was exhausting, but there was nowhere to go and nothing to do except to stay and wait. The air was thick with the smell of body odor. Apart from this there was a mournful vibe inside, as if the passengers were being driven to a funeral.

I couldn't take the pressure anymore. Pushing my way through the mass of bodies, I finally got off the bus. Unfortunately, it wasn't my stop—and it was raining. I ended up walking about two miles in the rain to get home. I didn't mind. Walking gave me the opportunity to put my thoughts and feelings in order. Now everything depended on my courage, composure, and commitment.

As I walked toward my block, wet from head to toe, my eyes fell on a stray dog running back and forth down the median strip that divided the busy street. Continuous streams of cars that sped up to forty miles an hour with flashing lights didn't allow the dog to cross the road in either direction. The poor animal looked the way I felt: despairing and pleading for help. Without thinking, I stepped into the road and raised my hands, calling for the cars to stop. The drivers slowed down one after another as they saw a human figure in front of them. Ignoring their curses and honking, I stood still and waited for the dog to get out of the trap and return to the pavement. It didn't even look in my direction, rushing away at full speed toward some unknowable destination. I moved on, wiping the rainwater off my face. Will there be someone to guide me through my *own* obstacle course?

I came home wet, hungry, and dog tired. The first thing that struck me when I crossed the threshold was the coat closet door broken off its hinges, now leaning against the wall.

"Hello everybody, I'm home!" I called out.

"Then why don't you just take a damn screwdriver and fix that damn door?" Luba called back to me from the kitchen. "And then, Sergey, come here real soon, and tell me what the hell is going on. I hate to see the empty side of our bed and those fucking cops stomping around our house in search of *you*!"

Quietly, I reminded Luba that it was better for our children not to hear such strong expressions from their parents.

She responded passionately, "It's better for our children not to see the cops rummaging through their mother's underwear."

Sergiy and Svitlana left their room to hear my answer. Their looks were more eloquent than any words. I muttered something unintelligible.

"That sounds unconvincing, Dad," said Sergiy firmly.

"We're not having a trial here," I said. "Better get on with your homework."

"We've completed our homework," my son said. "How about you?"

He left and Svitlana followed him, leaving me face-to-face with Luba.

It took me about half an hour to calm her down and answer her questions. After that I told her about my interrogation at the Department of Economic Crimes and the investigator's ultimatum. She looked at me straight in the eye and said, "As long as you have your bank card, you should have no problem withdrawing money from your account. I would

Chapter 7

rather have you penniless, Sergey, than see you in prison. This would be a bad example for our children."

I told Luba that I could not leave her without money. She told me not to talk nonsense. Sometimes you don't have to speak sweet words to show your love. This was such a case.

Now, thanks to Luba's suggestion, I began to feel better. I even called the Chase Manhattan Bank in New York, where it was morning. Momot hadn't lied; the card was real and money was stored on my bank account. The full amount? A staggering sixty-seven dollars. Not fifty, not a hundred—just sixty-seven dollars. For some reason, I found this discovery particularly offensive. Momot had never intended to repay me from the very start. As he shook my hand and expressed his gratitude, he knew he was going to reward me with a nothing burger.

"Will there be anything else, sir?" the operator asked.

"No, that's it," I said.

There was a sharp clunk in my ear as the operator hung up. Luba wisely said nothing; from the dark expression on my face, she knew I had failed. Now she helpfully suggested I use my credit card as a bookmark, then sailed out of the room. Before going to sleep, I heard her and Svitlana talking about me and my future.

"Well, your dad is a lucky man," Luba's voice said. "He always manages to get out of the scrapes he invariably gets into."

"And what if he doesn't get out?" Svitlana asked worriedly. "What if they lock him up or send him away?"

"I don't like thinking about that, so I don't," Luba said.

"But . . . what *if*?"

There was a long pause before my wife spoke again. "Then we'll have to learn to live without him," she said calmly.

"Don't you think you're being cruel, Mom?"

"Reality is cruel, sweetie. If your father is convicted of economic crimes, he will be under arrest, and all our property will be confiscated. Our apartment, our possessions—everything. Consider that, sweetie!"

I didn't sleep well that night, waking up every half hour to realize that I was lying on my bed next to my wife. That moment of awareness was, for me, the greatest happiness in my life—and I wanted the night to last forever. But the sky outside the window was slowly changing its color from black to gray. We could hear the birds chirping outside from our bedroom. What a blessing!

At some point I looked again at the sky outside and saw that it was light blue. The new day had arrived, and I could no longer stay in bed, pretending to be asleep. It was time to stand up and face life straight on. We are here to live as long as we are alive, and each of us has a path we will follow. Such is the personal journey known as life.

I arrived at the Department for Combating Economic Crimes an hour before the scheduled time and spent sixty minutes outside, walking around the building. I knew that these could well be my final moments of personal freedom. How quickly they flew!

At five minutes to ten, I entered the building. Just before I stepped inside, I sighed and breathed in a huge gulp of air as if pretending to dive underwater. This habit has remained with me to this day, when I am forced to make critical decisions or take risky action.

The investigator greeted me with a beaming smile as if we were old friends. His smile quickly faded when I repeated that I had no money except the thousand bucks I had in my pocket.

"Who's talking about money?" he said. "Did I mention money? We're talking about the law—the law you broke. You're a criminal, Maidukov." These words were spoken with a great deal of gusto. "And you ought to be isolated from society."

Until then, I had led a comparatively sheltered life, and the thought of spending some time in a jail cell—not to mention years!—was enough to induce a surge of despair in me. I fought to keep my expression from betraying my shock at the thought of internment.

"Do you have an arrest warrant?" I asked briskly.

"No," the investigator replied, shaking his head slowly. "Not yet. But I have the right to detain you for seventy-two hours without charge. The holding cell is waiting for you, Maidukov. Whenever you want to get out of there, just ask the warden to call me. But don't waste your time. A lot can happen in three days and three nights. Especially at *night*."

He grinned slightly.

"Are you threatening me?" I asked.

Chapter 7

He shook his head again.

"No, I'm just warning you, Citizen Maidukov. Prisoners don't like smart-asses and treat them badly. By the way, I'm going to make sure you get proper cellmates and have a good time tonight. Maybe you'll be more accommodating the next time we meet. Until then, enjoy yourself."

At that point he called the guard and ordered me to be taken to the holding cell.

This was new—and frightening as hell. Like everyone born in the USSR, I had a fairly clear idea of the inhumane conditions in our penitentiary system. Although Stalin's repressions had ended long ago, the former Soviet republics still had plenty of prisons, strict regime colonies, and forced-labor sites. Terrible rumors had been leaking from there, including stories about the so-called press huts, or pressing cells, where prisoners selected by the administration would torture, beat, and rape other inmates to make them more compliant or to obtain information from them. Officially, these practices did not exist, but the underground reported this as widespread practice.

I was ready to go through all the circles of hell when the guard pushed me into an open holding cell and locked the barred door behind me. At least I wasn't in a press hut yet. I was relieved to know that I had some time before nightfall. Any small consolation seemed better to me than none. I looked around my new temporary digs.

The cell was brightly lit, rather spacious, and relatively clean, though it smelled of bleach, probably from cellmates rubbing the floor to get rid of the smell of the urine and vomit. There was only one long wooden bench along the back wall, which had a drunken bum lying on it. He was blissfully snoring, lying on his back with his toothless mouth open. In the corner on the floor sat a disheveled girl in an evening dress embroidered with rhinestones, her back against the wall, her arms wrapped around her bent knees. She looked up at me and rubbed her eyes, blinking.

"Hi," she said. "Welcome to the monkey house."

It was a suitable name for our open cell with its iron bars and cement floor, and I was beginning to feel like a caged zoo animal. When people outside passed by, they could see the three of us inside, behind the bars.

Some of them looked at us curiously, others acted as if we made them sick, and many didn't even turn their heads.

"Why are you here?" the girl asked me.

I looked over my shoulder. She was standing one step away from me, her eyes glassy. She looked slightly stoned.

"Because," I said and turned away, looking through the grates.

"Do you have some cigarettes?" she asked.

"I was searched," I muttered. "My pockets are empty."

"Did you have money with you?"

I didn't answer, but I remembered the thousand bucks that had been taken from me during the search. "Don't expect to get your cash back," the girl said. "Cops are vultures. They even took my lipstick away from me. Why do they need lipstick, can you tell me? To paint their piggy snouts?"

I didn't speak with her but kept my gaze staring between the iron bars at the people in the lobby. They were free! I was locked in a cage, forced to endure the company of a girl of dubious morals and a drunken tramp.

After trying to strike up a conversation several times, the girl in the evening dress gave up. She stepped out and sat down on the floor again, leaving me alone. For a long time, I stood still, watching the people that came and went. Suddenly, I saw a squat young man walking across the lobby to the stairway. He was bearded and wore a black shirt with a white tie. I recognized him right away, even though he was turned away from me.

"Tigran!" I called out to him. He ignored me. "Tigran!" I shouted again, trying to get him to stop before he reached the stairway.

He looked in my direction and stopped walking. For a moment he stood there, one hand stroking his beard thoughtfully; his other hand held a small leather briefcase with brass clasps. Then he stepped forward and approached the cell.

"Sergio, buddy?" he exclaimed. "What the hell are you doing here?"

I explained my situation to him, trying to make it as short as possible and not to sound as whiny or depressed. We talked in low voices to avoid

Chapter 7

being overheard. When I gave him the name of my investigator, Tigran nodded his head, indicating familiarity with him.

"You're lucky, Sergio," he said.

"You're serious?" I asked.

He threw back his head and hissed with laughter.

"You're lucky that *I'm* here," he said. "It's a big day for pig feeding." He patted his briefcase meaningfully. "It is our good fortune that I found you here, Sergio."

"As for me, it would be far better if we had met somewhere else," I said.

Tigran chuckled and then frowned. "Have you ever had to go to jail?" he asked. "Do you have any idea what's going on here?"

I told him that I'd heard a thing or two of what happened in our prisons. Tigran's face became stern.

"Remember, Sergio," he said in a cautionary tone, "you must be calm. Talk confidently, stand up straight, don't keep your eyes down. Rule number one in a jail is never show your insecurity. It will be taken as a sign of weakness. Don't let anyone scare you."

"I'll try," I said.

"No," he said. "Not try, but do it!"

I nodded. "Okay, I'll do my best, Tigran. But I don't know how long I can last."

"In about twenty-four hours, I think I can promise you you'll be free," he said. "Until then hold on tight, Sergio. Once you're in front of those prison fellas, start with two of your trump cards. Do you know what they are?"

When I shook my head, he laughed in his odd hissing voice.

"Use our names—mine and Samvel's," he said. "That should be enough."

"And if not?" I asked.

"Then you'll have taken away your last trump card," Tigran replied. "You yourself. Your character. Your resistance."

He winked at me and left.

"Your friend seems like a nice chap," said the girl in the evening dress, who was still sitting by the wall on her heels, hugging her knees.

I shrugged. Was Tigran really a nice guy? Good men don't cheat their partners. On the other hand, I remembered the day Tigran warned me to stay away from Momot. And he had insinuated that he'd get me out of here. I didn't even have to ask him about that. So what kind of man was he? He was, I decided, not one of the nasty people. Nor was he really a nice chap. He fell into another category: bighearted and friendly—but dangerous.

The girl's voice interrupted my thoughts. "That guy reminded me of an actor in the gangster movies—I forget his name."

She may have been right, but I didn't want to blab about it at the prison cell, and I was relieved when the girl's parents came and took her away. In the afternoon a policeman pulled the drunken bum out of the cell, and I was left alone. I was not given any food or water, nor was I allowed to use the toilet room. It was a kind of torture, but I knew the worst was ahead of me.

At the beginning of the evening, a policeman came into the cell. He had a baton in his hand and a look on his face as if he'd just stepped in dog poop and was grossed out by it.

"Get up and go! Now!" he commanded. "Put your hands behind your back. Don't turn around or anything, just walk straight down the corridor."

The time had come. The biggest test of my life awaited me only a few steps away. I didn't know if I could take it, but I told myself there wasn't anyone who could scare me to death and stop me from being a man. My childhood and youth weren't hard, but I'd had some experience with confronting teenage gangs. I also served with the Soviet Army, which, in many ways, was equivalent to a two-year prison term. And I was not used to giving up just because something was difficult. As Tigran had said, my main ace in the hole was me!

We made our way down to the basement and stopped in front of a massive green-painted iron door. I was ordered to stand facing the wall. Keys rattled in the lock, the heavy bolts were drawn back, and the door swung heavily on its hinges. A wave of thick stink rolled out from inside and slammed my nostrils. The light inside the cell was dim and rusty.

"Get in there," the policeman ordered.

Chapter 7

I crossed the threshold and found myself inside a cramped, cube-shaped room without a window, with four concrete walls covered in obscene graffiti. At the farther end of the room was a three-foot-high wooden platform—the privileged area for relaxing, sitting, and sleeping. The platform was occupied by two men in sleeveless black T-shirts and side-stripe track pants. Their faces were blurry because my tears were running from the unbearable stench. A lone bulb hanging from the high ceiling seemed to be shrouded in mist. It was so quiet I could hear water dripping from the tap into the tin sink.

The door behind me slammed shut with a metallic clang. The stink around me was so sharp I could taste it. I coughed, putting my hand to my mouth.

"You puke here, you eat it up," one of the men said.

I suppressed the urge to vomit and raised my head. "I'm not hungry," I said.

Neither of the two even smiled. Both of them just stared at me from their decking.

I had to decide immediately what to do next. I couldn't continue to stand near the door, motionless, while they were sitting there, watching me. I also couldn't sit down on the floor, because it would humiliate me in the eyes of the cellmates. So I took five steps forward and squeezed into the free space between the wall and one of the prisoners, somehow not touching him, though the gap was narrow.

"Hi there," I said. "Name's Sergey. Tigran used to call me Sergio."

I moved farther onto the platform, then leaned against the wall and stretched my legs out in front of me, carefully avoiding touching my cellmates. They turned their faces toward me and stared at me with astonishment in their eyes. They were shocked by my impudence.

"Who the fuck is Tigran?" the younger one asked.

"Samvel's brother," I said.

"Samvel what?"

"You ought to know."

They exchanged glances. The older one slightly nodded his head. The younger one turned to me again. "Do you know Samvel? Can you prove it?"

"Why?" I said. I felt instinctively that this was the best answer possible.

They looked at each other again. Moments later the elder made a gesture to his mate, who went to the door and knocked with his fist. He was gone for about twenty minutes—the longest twenty minutes of my life. When he returned, he whispered something to his mate, and they started whispering to each other while keeping an eye on me. I was pretending to be asleep, but I was very thirsty; I wanted to drink and urinate at the same time, but I didn't dare change my position.

After a while I actually fell asleep. When I awoke, I was alone: the two jailbirds had flown. I peed in a bucket in the corner of the cell and drank from the tap. The stink of the cell no longer bothered me, but my thoughts assailed me relentlessly. I couldn't sleep, so I lay on the hard wooden deck and tried to imagine what it would be like to spend not one night in prison but 365 . . . 3,650 maybe? For me, the prospect was worse than death.

When the guard came for me, I thought it was four hours later. In fact, it was only noon. I was overwhelmed and felt dirty from head to toe. To my great relief, the guard took me not to the holding cell but to the duty room, where I got back my passport and small personal belongings. The policeman who was there told me that I could leave, then turned away. I asked him where my money was.

"What money?" he asked, his eyes as innocent as a baby's. "Look, you better get out before we change our minds."

Tigran was waiting for me outside, near his big red Jeep.

"I thought you wouldn't come," I said to him when we climbed into his car.

"How could I leave my friend in trouble?" Tigran said. "If you're a man, then you must keep your word. Your case is closed, Sergio. I settled the matter."

"How much did it cost you?" I asked.

He smiled smugly.

"Hardly anything, Sergio. As you can see, my brother and I have influence that we use when things come up."

"I don't know how to thank you, Tigran," I muttered.

Chapter 7

"It's simple," he said. "Come work for me, Sergio. I just started a new company. No sewing machines, no bullshit, only serious business. I need a general manager because I'm often busy with other things." He put his hand in a pocket of the trousers and took out an impressive wad of Ukrainian money. "Here's an advance," he said, handing it to me.

"Don't, Tigran, don't," I protested. "I haven't agreed yet."

"A little extra cash never hurts," he insisted, putting the money into my hand. "We're friends, right? Friends must help each other in whatever damned way they can."

He had called me a friend. He had pulled me out of prison. He had given me money. And most importantly, he could be, when needed, an incredibly charming man who had charisma and knew how to use it.

"When should I start, Tigran?" I asked.

Chapter 8

The Road to Hell

It was a sunny afternoon the next day, when Tigran halted his red Jeep Cherokee in front of the large beige-tiled building that rose above everything nearby. I had no idea what kind of business could be done in such an isolated and remote spot.

"We're here," Tigran said. "How do you like the place, Serge?"

"It's big," I answered evasively.

"Oh, yes," Tigran nodded. "Well, we deserve to have all the biggest and best things in life, don't we?"

As we slid out of the car, he took off his white jacket, revealing a black shirt with a white tie—typical mafioso style. His greased hair shone in the sun. The strong scent of his cologne lingered behind him.

The entrance to the building was decorated with a mosaic of two cosmonauts, a man and a woman, wearing spherical helmets and very tight suits that showed off their grotesque muscles and genitals, possibly an effort to compensate for the lack of erotica in Soviet culture. The black polished sign on the wall by the door said that we had arrived at a research institute along with an indecipherable abbreviation that was written in gold capital letters.

Tigran gestured to proceed inside, and our steps sounded abnormally loudly in the lobby's morgue-like silence. The entrance to the building itself was blocked by a turnstile. Beside it was a glass enclosure that contained a female porter busily working on her knitting. She glanced at us and hurriedly lowered her eyes, as if she'd seen two ghosts. The turnstile opened silently, and we walked through.

Chapter 8

"Does the entire building belong to you?" I asked as we climbed the stairway to the second floor.

"We're renting half of it," Tigran answered. "At present."

"It doesn't look very crowded," I said.

"We don't need extra eyes on us," Tigran said.

The corridor along which we walked was deserted except for a lone male silhouette at the far end. At his feet sat a large pit bull, and suddenly, I wanted to be back outside under the open sky. Too late! We were now standing in front of a large double door with a "Reception" sign on it. Muffled voices drifted through it.

"Slow down, Sergio," Tigran said. "I want to warn you about one thing."

"What?" I asked.

The pit bull gave a low, short bark. The guard leaned toward it and spoke a few words in a soothing voice, but I saw that the leash he held was pulled tight.

"When you talk to my brother, *don't look away*," Tigran said. "He doesn't like it."

"Which brother?" I asked dumbly.

A chuckle came from Tigran's chest. "My older brother, Samvel," he replied. "We're always together, Sam and I, 'cos we're as close as can be. We're sort of like twins with a telepathic link." Tigran touched his forehead with his index finger. "You see one of us, you'll see the other, got it?"

I saw no reason to rejoice in this fact. "Tigran, wasn't it you who told me that your brother is behind bars?"

"Yeah, he was," Tigran said. "But the court acquitted him on all charges. So Momot's money wasn't wasted, you can be sure."

"I didn't know I'd have to deal with Samvel," I said, shaking my head slowly.

Tigran chuckled. "Well, now you know, so come on in and meet him. And don't forget, Sergio. Keep looking at Sam straight through his eyeballs, intently and unblinkingly, you dig?"

With these words, Tigran put his fingers into a Y shape and held them up to his own eyes. As I nodded, he opened the door, and we stepped into a large, bright room full of people.

They were all young men, five or six of them—very tall, athletic, and holding rifles and machine guns in their hands. Then I noticed an unarmed man of around forty standing among the others. His hawk's face was in stark contrast to the others' Slavic features. He looked small compared to the young giants who stood around him, although he carried himself as if he were a head taller than any of them. There could be no doubt that it was the infamous older brother of Tigran, Samvel Martirosyan, the criminal boss and leader of the gang.

Tigran embraced him, and they exchanged a brotherly kiss on each other's cheeks. During this ceremony Samvel's eyes were fixed on me. Bearing in mind Tigran's instructions, I did my best not to look away or even blink. This allowed me to examine Samvel in detail.

His hair was cut extremely short, like a prisoner's or someone hiding the bald patches on his head. The pale, grayish color of his skin suggested he rarely saw the sun. The stubble on Samvel's face and the dark circles around his eyes made him appear older than his real age: at that time, thirty-six.

"Hey, why the fuck are you staring at me like that?" he asked me. "Tigran, who's this? Who the hell did you bring here with you? He looks to me like a total rat fink."

The young giants stared up at me with acute concern. I didn't look at them directly, but I saw that two of them raised the barrels of their weapons higher.

Tigran chuckled, sounding like the hissing of a spray can.

"This is the same businessman I told you about, Sam," he said. "Sergey Maidukov. An economic genius and so on. He will lead our company."

Samvel calmed down as quickly as he'd blown up.

"Aha," he said. "I see. Sergey Maidukov. Fine. Then why do you gawk at me like a damned fool, Maidukov? Have you been told that I can't stand it?"

I glanced at Tigran reproachfully. He made another hissing sound.

"Don't nag at him, Sam," he said. "The guy just didn't know. I'm sure he'll never do it again. Say hello to my brother, Sergio."

"Hello," I said.

Chapter 8

Samvel spread his hands to the sides. A huge gold ring with a black onyx stone glittered on the fourth finger of his left hand. Two big guys approached to put a massive bulletproof vest on him. While they were doing this, I had time to look around.

The room we were standing in was in the standard office arrangement for any low-level Soviet official, with a grandiose desk, potted ficus plants, and dial phones that apparently hadn't been used for a long time. There was no portrait of Lenin on the wall, but the bookcase was still filled with thick volumes of his writings. The living-giant bandits among us looked grotesquely out of place among these everyday objects.

I wanted to rush out, slam the door behind me, and forget about their existence, but I continued to stand still. You can't just quit a room full of armed men who have you in their sights.

The big guys put a sport coat on Samvel over the bulletproof vest, and he began to look like a turtle peeking his small head out of the shell. I didn't laugh. Didn't even smile.

Samvel looked down at himself and then looked at me.

"I have an important meeting today, Maidukov," he said with a strong Caucasian accent. "Very important, yes. Our family business depends on it."

"Good luck, then," I said.

They all stared at me, and I felt the room temperature jump up a few degrees. The pause was long. Obviously, Samvel didn't know how to react to my words. Were they too familiar? Was there a mockery in them? He stood and looked at me. I kept my face impenetrable.

"I'll need some good luck today," he said finally.

"We all need some luck," I said.

It was an unwary thing to say, but my tongue was ahead of my brain, as I was nervous.

Samvel goggled at me. There was another pause.

"It's time to go, Sam," said the tall guy in the green tracksuit, who shifted from foot to foot as if he were uncomfortable with the entire scene.

Like his fellow athletes, he had a typical Slavic appearance. As I found out later, Samvel surrounded himself with ex-players from the

Scythians football club. It was American football, so all the guys were well matched—powerful, tall, healthy.

"Shut up, Cowboy," Samvel said, raising the pitch of his voice. "If I want you to talk, I'll tell you to talk."

The big guy blinked and bit his tongue. Samvel fixed his dark eyes on the bridge of my nose. "I like you, Maidukov," he said. "You're a brave fella, yes, it's obvious. Admit you're a narc, and I won't hurt you. We might even be kinda like friends, I guess."

His guards waited, holding their breath. This was like having a bad dream where you cannot wake up and are filled with the certainty that something terrible is about to happen to you.

I heard myself saying, "I'm not a narc."

"Sam—" Tigran started.

"Shh!" Samvel stopped him with a warning wave of his hand, his dark eyes fixed on me. "If you're not a narc, Maidukov, then what are you?"

"I am Tigran's friend, Samvel," I said. "He offered me a job and—"

I wanted to swallow, but my throat was dry.

"Oh, come on, come on," Samvel said. "Who sent you? Criminal Police? Security Service? Prosecutor's office? Which is it?"

One of the giants stepped forward and pointed his machine gun at me. His face showed no more emotion than a plaster mask. I opened my mouth but didn't make a sound. I had nothing to add to what was said.

Finally, Tigran came to my aid. "You're crazy, Sam!" he yelled at his older brother. "You probably see a cop in me, you're so stupid! You probably think that your own brother is betraying you! It's me who brought this fella. Not trusting him means not trusting me."

"You just mind your business, Tigran!" shouted Samvel back. "Don't tell me mine!"

Both of them switched to speaking Armenian. While they bickered, my fear passed. I began to feel angry. It happens. Sometimes irritation is stronger than the instinct of self-preservation.

"I'm not a narc," I said in a loud voice. "I'm just a guy who heard you need a manager for your company. I agreed, but now I'm changing my mind. It will be better if I leave."

Chapter 8

I was ready to regret my temper when I saw that Samvel and Tigran were looking at me with a kind of amazement, as if somebody else had taken my place.

"Who told you that you can leave, Maidukov?" Samvel asked after long moments of silence. "Our conversation isn't over, man. I'll see you later, and we'll talk some more. And now I must go. Some sons a bitches won't hand over to me what I want just like that, so I gotta whack them a little."

He made a gesture of a smack and laughed. The giants picked up his laughter and followed him out of the room. We were left alone, Tigran and I.

"Well done, Sergio," he said. "Looks like Samvel liked you. To tell the truth, I doubted whether it would happen."

"Then why did you bring me here?" I asked, my temper beginning to rise again.

"He who does not risk does not win," he answered as he shrugged his shoulders.

"Your joke could have cost me my life," I said, reminding him of his advice to constantly look Samvel in the eyes.

Tigran laughed. "But it was so damn funny, wasn't it?"

"No," I said. "Not to me."

Upon returning home, I told Luba what had happened and how I felt about it. My story about Samvel and his armed gangsters didn't shock or overwhelm her. It was a time when we were desperate for money, and working for the Martirosyan brothers seemed to be the quickest and easiest way to get some.

"Do you think they'll hire you?" she asked.

"I'm pretty sure that they will," I said. "But I'm not sure I'm ready for that kind of job."

Luba reminded me that, without Tigran, I could end up in jail again and that, as recently as yesterday, we had lost our last thousand dollars. Then she asked how much I would be paid. I told her that I had no idea yet. Luba frowned.

"This is the most important question, and the most important questions should always be asked first," she said. "I think they could easily afford to pay you a thousand a month."

"I don't know," I said. "I really don't know. And I think I want them to forget about me and my existence."

My wish didn't come true. The doorbell rang later that night, and there stood two big guys, who told me that Samvel was waiting for me *right now*. They called him Papa, which meant "father" and sounded like "pope." As far as I could see, both of them were unarmed, but they still looked dangerous, which was part of their job. Inviting them into my home was like letting predators in. I left them outside the door and got dressed.

My children and my wife were watching me with worried expressions in their eyes. I told them to relax and smiled reassuringly. Before I left Luba came up to me and kissed me, not on the cheek but on the mouth, and it was like a farewell kiss. Somehow, deep inside us, we knew that once I left this room, nothing would be the same. And so it was: this would be the night that completely changed my life.

I got into the car and was immediately assailed by the smell of air freshener and loud music. I glanced back up to the glowing window of our bedroom. It started to float away as the car moved off.

"How far are we going?" I asked.

"You'll see," the driver said.

This was our entire dialogue. I didn't ask any more questions. As for the guys, they didn't talk to me or to each other. Chris Rea's hoarse voice was coming over the radio, instead: "Son, what are you doing here? / Son, this is the road to hell."

"What am I doing here?" I asked myself. "Why am I in this damn car, awake at this hour? Why the hell did I ever let strangers take me to the devil knows where?"

I knew the answers to my questions, but I didn't want to admit it, because doing so would hurt too much. So I just sat and looked out the window and listened to Chris Rea finish his song ("The Road to Hell," 1989) with "This ain't no upwardly mobile freeway / Oh no, this is the road, this is the road, this is the road to hell."

Chapter 8

Since the Gorbachev perestroika, the streetlamps had not yet been lit, and the city had been plunged into darkness. The oncoming headlights were blinding. After a twenty-minute rally through the city streets, the car drove past the cemetery, with its shabby walls, and began to wind through narrow little streets with small houses, many of which were primitive wooden shacks. As we proceeded, we now and then passed darkened cars at intersections, and our driver exchanged flashing headlight signals with them. It was not difficult to guess that we had entered a carefully guarded area.

I saw Samvel's house from afar. It was two stories high, and its windows shone in the dead of night. When I climbed out of the car in the inner yard, a dog emerged from the darkness. As I expected, it was a pit bull. Another one was lying in the hallway. My guide stepped over it. I followed his lead, and we walked into the brightly lit room, where I was told to sit and wait alone.

With all the windows and curtains shut, the room was stuffy. At the center was a table with the remnants of supper. The table was shrouded with a starched white cloth stained with coffee and tomato sauce. I looked around the room for empty wine or whiskey bottles. There were none, nor were there overflowing ashtrays. This seemed strange to me because I always imagined mafiosi as men with cigars in their mouths and glasses of strong liquor in their hands. It was hard for me to picture them arranging their dark affairs over a cup of coffee.

Judging by the photographs on the walls, I realized this was someone else's home, not Samvel's. They showed a happy Slavic family, including the obligatory wedding, army, and first-day-of-school pictures. The room itself was old-fashioned and cozy and seemed isolated from the rest of the house.

Samvel was already here. I recognized him by his high, raspy voice sometimes breaking into falsetto. I later learned that when he was nervous, his voice broke like that of a teenager on the cusp of adulthood. As far as I could tell, Samvel was on the phone with some person whom he'd called a "fat-assed fag," and the conversation irritated him. The room I was in no longer felt cozy.

One or two minutes later, dressed in a white terry bathrobe, Samvel entered and sat down at the table across from me. Without saying hello, he closed his cell phone and put it back in his pocket. A tall bodyguard stood behind him. Samvel snapped at him and told him to wait outside. The guy disappeared as if the wind had blown him away. Samvel turned to me and asked, his voice still piercing, "Why did it take you so fucking long to get here, Maidukov? You were supposed to be here half an hour ago."

"The roads are bad," I said. "Your lads drove me as fast as they could."

"My lads," he repeated. "My lads, hmm. What, you don't have a car?"

Unlike, say, in America and Western Europe, until the early 1990s, car ownership in my country was very limited. Passenger cars in the USSR were in rather short supply, and most of them were models like a Moskvich or a Lada, which had been manufactured in the Soviet Union. By purchasing them, you automatically turned into a taxi driver and carrier for all your relatives who did not have their own cars.

In addition, you had to be a mechanic, as Ladas and Moskviches were constantly breaking down and there were not enough service stations for vehicles in the country. By the time the situation had changed for the better, I had developed an enduring distaste for driving and everything connected with it. I never dreamed of having a car. My mind saw it as a burden, not a privilege.

Of course, I refrained from explaining all this to Samvel. I just replied that I didn't have a car. And that was the moment when I first called him Sam. It just slipped out. I looked at him, trying to determine his reaction to such a familiarity. There was a short pause. Then Samvel continued the conversation as if nothing had happened, and I thought that it would probably be all right to call him simply Sam.

Aping a typical Westerner, he stated that "a man without wheels is like an eagle without wings" and began nagging me about why the hell I had not bought myself a car. My demurs didn't impress him.

"Don't give me all that crap, Maidukov," he said. "Mebbe there's something else there, huh? Mebbe you had your license revoked for drunk driving?"

Chapter 8

He stared at me, waiting for an answer. His eyelids were red from lack of sleep, but there was a power in his eyes that I had never seen in anyone else's eyes in my entire life. His gaze was magnetic.

When I said that I had never had a car or a driver's license, Samvel leaned back in his chair. A five-inch gold cross gleamed on his furry chest under the open collar of his bathrobe.

"I hate alkies," he finally said. "I can't stand booze or smoke."

Later I would learn that Samvel's father had been a heavy drinker who, when drinking, would beat his children and wife savagely. This went on for many years. When Samvel turned sixteen, he threatened his father with a kitchen knife and promised to kill him at night if he abused them one more time. Apparently, by then, he had already developed his trademark look, and his threat worked. There was another reason for this. Samvel *always* carried out his threats. I was aware of this from the very first hours of our acquaintance.

When he asked me how much I drank, his eyes turned into slits, as if he were trying to see straight into my brain. I assured him that I drank no more than anybody else. On that first day, sitting in front of Samvel, I still retained the illusion of independence, so I took the liberty of adding that it is a personal matter for everyone to decide whether he drinks or not. He didn't actually say, "Bullshit," but he gave me that look that said, "Bullshit."

Then he asked if I smoked. I answered in the affirmative. "You better quit, Maidukov," he said. "I'm telling you, you better quit."

I chose to keep quiet. In fact, I was going to quit smoking (every smoker dreams of giving it up one day), but I didn't want to do it under someone else's pressure. We sat quietly for some time. Samvel looked at me, drumming his fingers on the table. I saw that he was deciding for himself how to deal with my silence.

"Tea!" he shouted all of a sudden.

I shuddered.

Almost immediately, an attractive, if slightly overweight, brunette with a pageboy haircut walked into the room, carrying a tray with a teapot, sugar, and one cup. Her blue satin robe was tied tightly around her waist. Putting the tray on the table, she didn't even look at me, except out of the corner of her eye.

Who was she—Samvel's wife or lover? How did she know the tea for him had to be ready? Why didn't he even thank her?

Still not looking in my direction, she sat next to Samvel, tore one grape from a bunch on the plate, and put it thoughtfully into her mouth. She had huge dark eyes with full eyebrows and a snub nose that gave her the appearance of a young girl, though she was far from one. She definitely looked like a woman closer to thirty than twenty. When she yawned, covering her mouth with her hand, I noticed she was wearing a wedding ring.

We sat together for a while without saying a word. Samvel drank tea in large gulps and looked into space. When the cup was empty, he put it on the table and told the brunette to go on to bed because he needed to have a man-to-man talk with me. Addressing her, he called her Oksana. She said that she would not sleep until he came. Without looking at her, he waved his hand as if to chase away a fly buzzing over his head.

Oksana stood up abruptly and walked toward the door. I couldn't see her face, but I sensed that it registered both resentment and disappointment. When she'd left the room, closing the door quite loudly behind her, Samvel looked at me. I kept a neutral expression. I wanted to get out of this stuffy room as quickly as possible. I felt burdened by Samvel's presence. I decided to tell Tigran directly that I didn't intend to work for his brother. I was going to do it tomorrow.

Both Samvel and I simultaneously remembered Tigran.

"My brother told me you were a smartass, Maidukov," he said. "And you're smart, indeed, but no matter how big your head is, we're smarter than you and always will be. Get it through your skull." He tapped himself on the head with a finger. "Fellas that aren't clever enough end up working for the fellas that are."

His statement hurt my pride. I shrugged and muttered that some people work for themselves. My remark was met with hostility.

"Bullshit," Samvel snapped. "You can't go backward, Maidukov. Promises don't work in reverse. Tigran is your boss from now on, and I'm your boss's boss, so just take it, and be glad for the opportunity."

Chapter 8

I said I'd think about it. Samvel grimaced as if from a toothache.

"I'm not asking you!" he exclaimed, irritated. "I'm *telling* you! You're gonna work for us. Do you understand me clearly, Maidukov?"

"But—" I started.

"Don't jerk me around with this but-but-but shit!" Samvel yelled in falsetto. "Answer directly the question I asked you: *Do you understand me?*"

His face quivered with rage, and his eyes looked about to pop out of his head. Meanwhile, the veins on his neck were bulging through his pale skin like blue ropes.

Eventually, I was to learn that sometimes Samvel would feign anger in order to shake up his opponent. I have to admit the ploy was effective!

I lowered my head down and nodded: "Yes, Sam. I understand."

"That answer's correct," he said in his normal voice, then yawned and turned away.

The trap had closed, and I was locked inside.

Chapter 9

Dances with Wolves

Working at the Martirosyan brothers' company was the strangest job I'd ever had in my life. Initially, leading the company meant doing nothing all day long.

In the morning a car would come for me. It was a pretty old-fashioned white Mercedes with German license plates and a silent driver behind the wheel. I don't know where he came from or where he went after. All I can remember is a tattoo in the shape of a spider on his right arm. Not a name or a face. Just the tattoo on his forearm—a weird black mark. And his boring voice. He would constantly ask me for money for refueling and repairs, even though we traveled no more than twenty miles a day from Donetsk to Makiivka and back.

On the way we would drop off Tigran, who then lived in a Romani quarter located between the two cities. The area was built up with two-story and one-story houses behind the high walls and fences. Most taxi drivers flatly refused to go there, even in daylight. When I asked Tigran why he chose such a strange place to live, he explained to me that Romani kids were always on the alert to discover strangers and to give timely notice of their approach. The quarter was also guarded by dogs barking warningly at each car in unison.

In Tigran's yard lived a huge Caucasian shepherd dog, a real monster in a furry coat. It never barked at you; it only watched you and growled from its pen enclosure. Tigran used to let it out of there at night. He told me that once, this dog had bitten a random burglar to death, and I believed him. However, Tigran lied as easily and naturally as he breathed.

CHAPTER 9

It was his gift. He could have fooled even the apostle Peter, guarding the gates of heaven.

My visits to Tigran were a kind of ritual that brought with them both mandatory and meaningless routines. Each time, he'd promise we would do something important the next morning, but again and again, I found him sleeping in his bedroom on the second floor. I can't remember a day when he got out of bed before ten in the morning. Most of the time, he stayed in bed when I went up to him. His regular girlfriend (there were so many of them that their names cannot be reconstructed) usually made coffee for us.

Still yawning, Tigran chatted with me about this and that and then sent me to the office, where he himself appeared only in the late afternoon. I didn't understand how it was possible to waste so much daytime, and I constantly asked him to set specific tasks for me. It never happened.

This went on for a long time until, finally, Tigran announced that the next day, we'd start for real. The next morning, exactly on time, I was at his gate, but it was closed. Tigran's girlfriend (Natasha? Tanya? Sonya?) didn't answer the intercom despite the urgent buzzing. His phone, as always, was switched off. Determined to wake up Tigran and get down to business, I used the nearest tree and climbed over the wall.

The shepherd dog was in the yard, not in a cage. I almost ran right into it as I walked toward the porch. It was my luck that I didn't have time to be frightened, otherwise I'd have been torn to shreds. I walked past the dog, up the steps, and into the house. As soon as I closed the door, the giant beast threw himself at it with all his hundred-pound weight.

Tigran was very amused by my story and laughed for a long time, making puffing little pump-like sounds. It seemed that he liked to see me in dangerous situations. His sense of humor was as ingenuous as that of a savage.

He met me not in the bed but in the living room, washed, combed, dressed, and energetic. He said that great things are ahead of us in the not distant future. Samvel had decided to settle fully in the Scientific Research Institute, where we rented an office. The director gave us an entire wing of the building with a basement and big courtyard in the back. I asked how much it would cost to rent, and Tigran told me not to fill my head with more worries than necessary. He and I had to organize the construction of the most pompous and modern business office in the district.

Tigran told me that the builders were already waiting for us at the worksite. We had to purchase building materials, plastic windows, lamps, laminate flooring, paint, and hundreds of other things to equip the office.

"My brother allocated eighty thousand bucks to finish work as promptly as possible," Tigran said proudly.

I was to learn the real reason for his enthusiasm a little later.

The purchasing process followed a familiar pattern. Tigran took goods from the owners, promising to pay later. But he made only the first payment in cash and then forgot about the owners' existence. If they called or came to see him, he threatened to pit his older brother against them, and they prudently disappeared.

Our brand-new office was equipped with magnificent oak doors, which Tigran received for free. For air conditioners and roll shutters, he also paid mostly with promises, not cash. I didn't know then that this tactic allowed him to pocket the money received from Samvel. But I certainly understood the dirty nature of the game I was involved in. After all, I accompanied Tigran in the process of these "purchases" and looked into the eyes of the people he'd deceived. I was making no attempts to warn them. I was only trying to dissuade Tigran from continuing this dangerous practice. Usually, he would smile contemptuously, saying, "Stop being afraid, Sergio. Things are going fine. These traders, they are a bunch of gullible fools. These are valuable lessons for them. They need to be taught."

His words were touching a painful wound in my mind that had never healed despite all my efforts to forget those episodes when I myself had been deceived. Each such memory was like a rusty nail in my brain. It was corroded. It was painful. But I was not going to be a fool anymore. I preferred to be among the winners than among the losers. Tigran was a winner—always had been. I never saw him "used," and this testified to the effectiveness of his tactics.

Chapter 9

Suppressing my doubts, I consoled myself with the thought that I had not committed any crimes personally and, of course, had not engaged in racketeering or violent activities. I only signed papers, remembering my sad experience at Globalinvest. I would do it with my left hand, creating signatures that were completely different from mine. Tigran did the rest of the work, and he did it flawlessly.

As I said before, he was a born winner, and, what's more, he was a charismatic leader who could motivate others. His main distinguishing features were deceit and generosity. Though I didn't know in what bizarre way these qualities were combined in him, the mix was amazing. Many people were fascinated by him, including me. In his best moments, he tended to make grand gestures, bestowing his gifts and money on those around him.

The next day, he could just as easily rob or deceive you. You knew he was lying, but you still believed him because he'd persuaded you by looking into your eyes and holding his hand on your shoulder.

Tigran's only problem was that he couldn't fool the same people all the time. Very soon his shaky reputation became attached to his name, and businessmen became cautious. They stopped giving us goods without full payment and refused to enter into contracts with the firm of the Martirosyan brothers. They hid, turned off their phones, or "lost" the keys to their warehouses. Some even feigned illness in order to avoid entering into negotiations with Tigran.

As it happened, Tigran tried to draw me into his plots and schemes, convincing me to become his front man so I could take the flak and so he could hide behind my back. For me, it was a line that I could not cross. I expected Tigran to be angry with me, but he accepted my refusal without any noticeable negative reaction. When he saw, over time, that I was ready to defend my position, he came to respect me even more.

His new partner was Konstantin, a ruddy young man with thick, girlish eyelashes and rabbit teeth through which he continuously filtered beer. He was doing the same illegal work as Tigran—but with less talent and success. From the very start, we experienced mutual dislike and even hidden hatred, yet, flung so closely together by circumstances, we couldn't ignore one another.

While Tigran and Konstantin were looking for the innocent, unsuspecting victims of their traitorous strategies, I was assigned the creation of our new office space. The core of it was an abnormally high, spacious room previously used as a production hall. Dismantling the heavy machinery and steel flooring was a laborious task, but it was only the beginning of a difficult, frustrating project. I had little idea how this basketball court–sized space could be used. The unfortunate architect, hired by Tigran, didn't know this either. Only the builders were satisfied, as they now had guaranteed work for many months ahead.

I was now devoting the first half of the day to the construction site, after which I would get back to my office in Makiivka. There I had a secretary, a massive desk, and plenty of time that I didn't know how to use. I didn't receive a salary. Instead, I was given part of the money from the delivery of old machinery for scrap metal, and it was enough to make me happy.

Now and then, Tigran would ask me to sell a batch of Coca-Cola or canned food, which he and Konstantin had received as gifts. He would distribute part of the proceeds to the workers and put the rest in his pocket. No wallet in the world was big enough for Tigran.

I also got some money, but not much, and this kind of business began to bother me. I increasingly thought about quitting my job and ending my career as an errand boy / businessman for the Martirosyan brothers. Memories of my awkward conversation with Samvel still loomed up from time to time, but eventually, my fears of Samvel dissipated as I saw less and less of him. Sometimes he would appear at the construction site, but he hardly noticed me. He would briefly examine the results of the work done and then leave, accompanied by his armed guard.

The workers idolized him. On his rare visits, Samvel would generously distribute bonus money and products, ranging from sacks of cereals to boxes of exotic fruits. He was like a deity descending from his heavenly realm to make a short visit to his earthly minions.

As for me, I received only Samvel's promises to start a big business as soon as the new office was finished. I doubted this would happen in the foreseeable future. I had already learned that the Martirosyan brothers could not be trusted to keep their word.

Chapter 9

So why didn't I leave before I'd become so involved in their affairs? What had kept me close to them? Maybe it was the opportunity to earn real money? Maybe curiosity? Bad karma, the influence of the moon, genetic predisposition, a reduced sense of social responsibility, or the desire to be part of a powerful dark force? There were dozens of answers, and they were all right and wrong at the same time.

I suppose I was wondering the same thing myself on a rainy summer afternoon while sitting in my office in front of the rain-drenched window. My secretary, a petite blonde with a boyish haircut and large brown eyes, was doing a crossword. She had nothing else to do. I didn't even have a newspaper with a crossword puzzle. Each day spent in Makiivka was frustrating and depressing and felt like one more day stolen from my life. I was bored to death and longed to do something new.

I think it was in June or July 1995 when I told myself that I'd had enough. I was going to drink my last cup of coffee in this damn place, then call a taxi and leave forever. I was sure that Samvel had lost any interest in me. If Tigran called me, I would say that I was ill. After a week or two of my absence, the Martirosyan brothers would find another manager for their company. At least, that was my game plan, my rough train of thought. Naïve, eh?

I remember my decision very well, as I remember that I called the secretary to get me coffee. She brought it on a plastic tray with a picture of the Eiffel Tower on it. I was sitting in my leather upholstered chair and returned the smile she gave me. I knew that she had recently divorced, and I didn't want to give her the slightest reason to feel that she was welcome to any special treatment.

Nevertheless, she sat down on one of the chairs across from me and started talking about how lonely she felt at night without her husband. With a steaming cup in my hand, I went to the window. I'd rather I had not done that, considering what happened next.

The windows of my office overlooked the courtyard of the institute. Through the raindrops on the window, from the height of the third floor, I suddenly saw a sight that made me stop breathing, at least, for the moment.

The courtyard of the institute had long been turned into a parking lot for gangsters' cars. They were expensive, mostly black vehicles with tinted windows. Now the trunk of one of them—the black BMW—was open. Three guys in dark T-shirts pulled out a man in a suit and tie. His head was covered with a black bag, and his hands were handcuffed. The man's stiff legs buckled under him, and he fell into a puddle on the landing. Guys in jackets formed a triangle around him and started kicking him viciously, forcing him to get up. Then they led the beaten man across the yard and into the back entrance of the building.

At this point, the secretary was standing next to me, her eyes wide open like a startled tarsier. I turned to her and asked if she saw what I saw.

She looked away and said, "It's none of my business. Samvel knows what he's doing."

Yes, it seemed that he knew *very well* what he was doing and what he was going to do. The problem was that I wasn't going to watch it, nor was I going to get involved in it in any way. Not only because I'd clearly seen the consequences that would result from it but because it went against my nature. I hated seeing defenseless people being beaten. I was ready to put up with the fact that Tigran was cheating people, but Samvel was *kidnapping* them, and that was a completely different matter. It was the final straw that made my presence there impossible—a final warning to leave before it was too late.

To flee without looking back!

I walked back to my desk and yanked open a drawer. The secretary watched in silence as I packed my things. Having finished with this, I looked through the papers to avoid leaving anything incriminating behind. It took no more than five minutes, but those five minutes were fatal. The phone rang. The secretary picked up the receiver and listened. My sixth sense told me *who* was on the other end of the line.

"Tell him I'm sick," I whispered quickly.

Looking into my eyes, the secretary said into the phone, "Yes, Samvel. Maidukov is here. He's on his way to you."

She wasn't a rebel. I also turned out to not be a rebel. Before my mind's eye emerged the battered man from the trunk of a car. I could be next.

Chapter 9

I put my things down and descended to the second floor.

To get into Samvel's office, I had to go through a waiting room guarded by a tall guy with pit bull on a leash. The dog rose from the floor and stood motionless, its muzzle pointed toward me, its nostrils flaring, searching the air for hostile scents. I looked down quickly and saw small drops of blood on the parquet. I stepped over the drops and opened the door.

There were five people in the room. The prisoner stood in front of the couch on which Samvel was sitting—lounging comfortably and in command. The bag and handcuffs were removed from the poor man. Blood trickled from the corner of his mouth and his nose. He held a bloody handkerchief in his hand, which he repeatedly applied to his face. He glanced up at me, and I saw the flicker of hope in his gaze as he realized he was looking at someone who didn't look like a bandit. But how could I help him? He was a complete stranger to me, or so I told myself, and I turned away.

There was no place for me to sit down. All three chairs in the room were occupied by Samvel's henchmen, with their sacred golden chains hanging around their bull necks. Among them was Salim, a round-headed, burly guy, who looked like a Buddha dressed in a loose tracksuit. He was the only one of the three I knew by name, and he struck me as the nastiest of all. His round face with narrow eyes was impenetrable.

Samvel kept sitting in a relaxed position on the couch. It was only the prisoner and I who stood, almost shoulder to shoulder, which somehow seemed to put us on the same level. It was making me nervous.

The tense pause lasted for about a minute. Then Samvel exploded.

"Damn!" he yelled. "Is anybody gonna stand up and give him a fucking chair? Maidukov is head of our firm, and he ought to be treated with respect."

The two guys stood up, one willingly, the other reluctantly.

Salim didn't move. "I thought that dude was some kinda alien to us, huh?"

Samvel squinted his bulging eyes. "Do you want to argue with me, Salim?"

"No, Sam," Salim growled after a few long moments.

As he slowly got to his feet, I knew that I had created an enemy, a vindictive enemy, in whose eyes, my life—any human life—was of no account. I intuitively felt that I saw a born killer in front of me, and in later days, that suspicion would be confirmed again and again.

I never witnessed the killings he committed, but I heard stories about him, and Salim never denied the rumors. Why would he? Creating fear and reinforcing it with death and destruction was a powerful combination. Salim was a rough, thickset boar of a man with a meager vocabulary and a bad temper. When Samvel told me we were going to travel to Kherson together, his words came like a bolt of retribution from the higher forces that protect us from harm.

I mumbled that it was all too unexpected.

"Don't waste my time," Samvel said and tapped the couch, inviting me to sit down beside him.

He put on his little spectacles to show me his power and his benevolence toward me. Throughout the centuries, the principle of divide and conquer has always been actively used by tyrants. By singling out one person at his or her expense—and in the presence—of others, Samvel prevented a possible conspiracy against him. It was unlikely that he was familiar with the writings of Machiavelli; he just acted according to his instincts.

His thugs, looking at each other in silence, sat back in their seats; Salim was the first of them. The prisoner was still immobile, staying where he was. The blood on his face began to clot, so he put the dirty handkerchief in his pocket.

I later learned that his name was Valery. He was under fifty. The eyes on his swollen face were almost turning into slits. I remember that his tie was crooked and a loose button on his shirt showed a chunk of his hairy belly. He tried to carry himself with dignity, though he did it with the grimace of pain.

I learned from Samvel that Valery owed him $45,000. I doubt it was a fair deal, but I wasn't privy to the details. The fact was that Valery could not turn over the money immediately, and Samvel didn't want to wait. For this reason, he was going to take away the most valuable thing that

Chapter 9

Valery had—a fishing vessel anchored in the port of Kherson. I had to go there with him to complete the relevant documents concerning the change of ownership of the property.

"The son of a bitch says his boat costs at least twice as much," Samvel told me, summing up what had been said. "We're gonna send it to the Black Sea for fishing. This will bring us a lot of money. I want you to take care of this, Maidukov. That's what you're here for."

Such a naive approach to business has always been characteristic of Samvel. He never even tried to find a practical use for his utopian projects. He used to think that things would happen as if by magic. He was like a big kid—a bad, spoiled kid, who hurt everyone around him. He wanted everything at once.

It was pointless to explain that the operation of a fishing vessel involves a lot of legal, technical, and organizational measures, as well as relevant experience and funding. Samvel didn't care about such boring details. Like a nasty boy who sees, with wide eyes, an interesting toy in the hands of another boy, he now thought only of how to reach out and take it away.

"Take good look at the boat, and keep your eyes peeled," he said. "I'll be damned if we let this fat vulture screw us."

I thought it was time to abandon this mission. I knew nothing about ships and fishing. It seemed to me that I had a good enough reason. But I didn't even have time to open my mouth, let alone say something. Samvel read my thoughts as easily as if they were written on a display connected to my brain.

He grinned and said slowly, "Maidukov, don't expect to get out of it. You have two choices, only one of which is good. You can either stay where you are, or you can go and join him." Samvel pointed at Valery with his index finger. "Come on, get your brain in the game, and try to count how many choices you have."

Everyone in the room was looking at me. Salim's gaze was disdainful and taunting, while Valery's slitted eyes were filled with hidden compassion.

"When are we leaving?" I asked.

On the way I talked with Valery. We rode in the backseat, while Salim settled himself behind the steering wheel and his companion sat beside him, in the front passenger seat. They listened to thieves' songs, the rough post-Soviet equivalent of gangsta music, written and performed in Russian chanson style. These primitive songs gave me a headache, but the musical torture had its plus side: the guys in the front seats couldn't hear a single word of our conversation.

Valery told me a story as old as the world. A man is about to make a brilliant deal, but he doesn't have enough money to get involved. He borrows money from someone else, but when his deal falls through, he learns with horror that he owes money not to his original partner but to mobsters.

As you can easily guess, this man was Valery. His passion was the sea, and he'd dedicated himself to designing and producing sailing yachts. A year ago, he invested all his money in the construction of a large luxury yacht, which he never managed to finish. He found himself in the position of a commercial fly entangled in the sticky web of debt.

Valery probably told me other stories too—for example, about his family. My memory has not retained them, and I don't remember telling him about myself. We were not friends and could not be. He built yachts. I worked for gangsters. Our paths had crossed by accident, and it was highly unlikely that we would see each other again. To tell the truth, I preferred it that way. He had every reason to think I was a bastard. I was already aware that I, too, considered myself one.

Our Audi was racing toward Kherson at considerable speed, mostly in the middle of the road, and this was somewhat strained. Salim seemed rather a poor driver, and the roads were treacherous, winding, narrow, and full of deep holes. He noticed I was looking at the speedometer on the dashboard, so he tightened his grip on the steering wheel and pressed down on the accelerator. The engine whined; the wheels spun faster.

At a little distance ahead appeared a small herd of cows guided by a lonely herdsman. They were walking along the road until Salim honked his horn. One of the cows startled, stepped to the side, and then suddenly rushed across the road in front of the Audi. Salim's companion shouted at him to look out, but it was too late.

Chapter 9

Trying to stop abruptly, Salim hit the brakes. A moment later, the car struck the cow, and it sounded like a bomb had gone off. Salim cursed and the car veered violently to the right, skidding off the road and bumping across the field before eventually stopping.

Salim was gushing blood from his nose.

"God damn cow ran right in front of me," he said. "Where's the fucking shepherd? I'm gonna kill him."

But the herdsman turned out to be too quick-witted to wait for the bandits to get out of the car. Leaving his herd, he fled across the field at full speed. Salim's companion approached the crippled cow and killed it with a single shot in the ear. He did it in front of passing cars, and he didn't hide his gun. Valery and I exchanged glances.

Until the end of our journey, we kept quiet. Salim and his friend were angry as hell. The Audi had sustained at least $1,500 damage from the collision with the cow. There were numerous dents and scratches on the car's body, the right fender was punched in, and the headlight was smashed.

These men had only recently received the Audi from Samvel, and they both feared that he would not be happy with their story. They agreed that the car should be urgently repaired in Kherson. But a new problem arose when Salim's companion refused to pay because it was not his fault. Salim slowed down and suggested that his friend continue on foot. Suddenly, his companion declared he was joking and promised to kill the shepherd on the way back.

He meant it, there wasn't any doubt. Fortunately, we never saw the fast-moving shepherd again.

We arrived in Kherson on a rainy and windy afternoon, exhausted from the long, nonstop run. Samvel's guys didn't stay at the hotel for more than a few minutes. Instead of showering, changing, and resting, they went to look for an automobile repair shop. Before leaving, Salim instructed me to keep an eye on Valery. I said everything would be all right. When the guys disappeared, I breathed a sigh of relief. The presence of Salim depressed me. His always-half-closed and sleepy eyes harbored something that made me more than a little uneasy, and I dared not look into them very long.

Valery led me to the harbor where his ship, the *Pescarus*, was docked. We walked on foot to stretch our limbs and get some moist fresh air. At a nearby store, Valery bought sunglasses to hide his black eyes. The closer we got to the dock, the more tense he was, and for the first time, I realized that his heightened nervousness was due to something besides the fear of racketeers and regret at the loss of the ship.

The real reason for his anxiety became clear as we approached the *Pescarus*. It was connected to the shore by a rusty gangway and loose ropes wrapped around large iron posts. Even my unprofessional eye easily determined that the vessel was in extremely poor condition and needed extensive repairs and refitting. Once—probably many years ago—it had been painted white, but now the paint had peeled to reveal rusty brown spots along the sides of the hull. Worst of all, the *Pescarus* looked half-submerged, as its deck rose only six feet above the water. This rusty bucket was *not* worth $45,000. I doubted that it could be sold even for $20,000 . . . unless the ship was cut into movable sections for scrap value.

Pretending to be unconcerned, Valery invited me to go up on deck. I politely declined, saying it was risky and pointless. While we were standing on the pier, a grimy tramp looked out from the cabin of *Pescarus* and hid again. I asked Valery if this was the captain. He let out a nervous laugh and asked me not to tell Samvel about what I'd seen at the dock.

"On the contrary," I said after reflection. "We'll tell him right now before he hears it from someone else."

"But why?" Valery exclaimed. "He'll kill me."

"No," I said. "He'll have to wait until you sell your hunk of junk. I know people whose business is delivering ferrous scrap to metallurgical plants. How much does *Pescarus* weigh? What is its length? Displacement?"

After making some simple calculations, I called a scrap metal dealer I knew. He said he could give us exactly $15,000 for *Pescarus* and not a cent more. I asked for a hundred grand. He told me that total costs would be too high because of huge overhead expenses and offered us $25,000. Finally, we agreed on $50,000, and I gave the phone to Valery.

When the deal was concluded verbally, I called Samvel. At first, he yelled at me so loudly that my ear started ringing. I waited patiently, and

Chapter 9

when he was ready to listen to me, I explained the situation to him, and he admitted that having $45,000 in cash was better than floating on a rust bucket in the Black Sea.

Valery was overjoyed that he could liberate himself from debt and gain freedom. He promised to pay me an additional $5,000 for my mediation, but he never did. We never met again. Valery had his nautical business, while I was a slave in the underground empire of the Martirosyan brothers.

I always hoped that he'd managed to break out of the grip of the Mafia. In any case, I never heard Samvel mention his name again. As I later learned, Samvel had a short memory. He was like a predator who notices only the prey that enters its field of vision. At that time, every predator could find enough sustenance in the economic jungle. But times, they tend to change.

The second half of the nineties was marked by the flare-up of the war between the Mafia clans in Donetsk. Samvel was at the forefront of this battle of evil vs. evil. I knew my chances of surviving this bloody grinder were not that great.

Chapter 10

In the Laps of the Criminal Gods

We are all mysterious creatures, inconsistent and incomprehensible. We never know what we can expect from ourselves, what we are capable of, and how far we are willing to go under certain circumstances.

I always thought I knew myself. But during this time, I realized this was an illusion. I never knew myself. Even today, I hardly understand myself, after years of living in bumpy situations. Looking back, it appears rather strange that it was me and not someone else who had sunk so low—to the very bottom of the underground swamp commonly known as the Mafia.

Despite the crooked path I had chosen in the nineties, I am hardly an antisocial or crime-oriented person. By nature, I've never wanted to hurt someone to make myself feel better. I never tried to earn people's respect by intimidating or threatening them.

Indeed, I was softhearted, perhaps too softhearted for a guy who had grown up in Donetsk, where life wasn't always easy and where I, a well-behaved boy from a kind, middle-class family, often dealt with street youth and had to fight my way to and from school.

It didn't make me violent, though once, I split a kid's head open with an iron toy shovel for hanging a cat (it was a favorite pastime of boys in tough areas of the city). Sometimes I stole books from the library and skipped school. Like everybody around me, I drank and smoked and was forced sometimes to use my fists in fights. This was the extent of my bad behavior as a youth. I had never been a troublemaker or a problematic teenager.

Chapter 10

In my childhood and youth, I had many friends and playmates and wasn't averse to having some fun with them, but one of my greatest delights was to stay at home alone. Both of my parents followed steady career paths, each achieving a prestigious and respectable status, so they often went on business trips, which gave me complete freedom to enjoy my independence. From an early age, I got used to being *completely* on my own. It was a real godsend for me. Staying alone, I could read until midnight if I liked and then draw all day long, play the guitar, listen to the music I loved, or do something else—anything else, whatever I wanted.

Once I married, my family became my world, my universe. I had relationships and contacts outside of that, but it was more out of necessity than need. At that time, I did not yet realize that I would become a writer, but my lifestyle wasn't compatible with this intention.

I had my family and my home. Everything else was secondary.

And then, suddenly, a new family entered my life: the Mafia clan of Samvel Martirosyan. It was incompatible with everything I considered the "normal" way of life. The world I knew had collapsed around me, and there was another world beneath it, a much crueler world than that of my former castle in the air with its daydreams—the serene evening with the family and rows of thick volumes on bookshelves. Chris Rea's song "The Road to Hell" turned out to be prophetic. I always get goose bumps when I hear it.

These new circumstances made me a new man, entirely different from what I'd been during my years of marriage and family. My status changed, my mindset changed, and, accordingly, my behavior changed. I gained reliance in myself that appeared to be more like arrogance than self-confidence. I noticed that sometimes I became aggressive and rude, and I tried to restrain myself, but I wasn't always successful. I lost my peace of mind, which affected my behavior at home. I didn't recognize myself at times. I was no longer the gentle husband and father that my family had always known.

Luba, who'd always wanted to see me as a strong, determined male, was not really happy about the changes that had taken place in me. She missed my tenderness. But I couldn't give it to her, at least, not as I'd once done. I was no longer the husband she had known all those years before this transformation.

There were times when we thought about divorce. We didn't actually separate, but we separated emotionally. Sometimes I thought of myself as redundant when I was at home.

At the same time, I always felt like an outsider in Samvel's gang. Although I accepted my lot, I hated the brutal activities of the criminal world and was uncomfortable among tough, ruthless men who were apparently going to be my companions indefinitely. I never intended to spend the rest of my life with them. I couldn't even imagine that this episode of my biography might be extended for so many years.

At this initial stage, I still believed that at any minute, I could jump off the slippery bandwagon I had been riding, but this was an illusion. In fact, I lost my freedom the moment I took the money from Tigran and he introduced me to his older brother. From that day on, I'd been doomed, although at the time, I did not realize how I was in the unenviable position of a fly caught on old-fashioned flypaper strip hanging from the ceiling. If I fluttered, it was not too desperately.

Oddly, the better I got to know Samvel, the more confident I felt in his presence. About once a week, he would send a car for me so we could discuss some matters concerning "our business." Actually, it was never a business—Samvel usually had no idea how to dispose of the property that fell into his hands.

He had a very simple and, at the same time, effective tactic that nearly always worked. First, he'd create a problem for a businessman, and then he'd move in to strike—by offering a solution! Some victims were able to pay him with produce or property. When Samvel got real estate, he couldn't think up anything better to do than to sell it as quickly as possible. Having to maintain an entire army of thugs, as well as their cars, weapons, and hired apartments, didn't come cheap! By my calculations, Samvel spent at least $100,000 a month on this part of his costs, and that didn't include the building, his pompous office, and bribing the police and the judiciary. He never had enough money to invest in anything, and all his business projects remained daydreams.

Chapter 10

Samvel wasn't born for a life of concerted, focused effort. His fiery temper prevented him from rising to a more eminent position in the criminal world, where he might have had more influence. I believe this was the reason for his inability to establish a solid business empire, unlike other mafiosi. Samvel was a classic gangster, like John Dillinger and Al Capone.

The legal existence of mafiosi like Samvel was possible only in the years after Gorbachev's perestroika, which was not a restructuring but a complete dismantling of the state system. The other gangsters who began their criminal activities in parallel with him were either killed and buried under their posh and tasteless monuments, or they transitioned into the country's elite, ultimately becoming respectable businessmen and politicians. They knew that these troubled times would not last forever. Samvel also understood this and tried to follow their example. That's why he kept me around.

When we met, he would ask my opinion on various commercial and legal subjects. But he was both a lousy listener and terrific student. One minute he could be very interested and go in-depth, and the next minute, he could yawn and send me away. One day he might insist that I've been beside him the whole time, and on another, he didn't even think of me as someone with a name.

His mood changed like the weather. In moments of good humor, he was ready to help you with anything, from rare medicines to placing your children in a prestigious university. But most of the time, he tended to be in a bad mood. At such times, everyone tried to avoid him like a gathering storm, because once he got started, his anger would turn into rage. At that point, anything could happen.

Amazingly, one of his fits of rage saved my life.

I remember that it began in early August 1995, as I had just returned from a short family vacation on the coast of the Azov Sea. We'd all had a good time together, and when the week was over, I felt like an ordinary businessman in his everyday life, loving his wife and children, having his little realm of duties, and I was surrounded by familiar things that were precious to me. The reprieve from "work" hadn't lasted long. Before I had time to unpack my things, Samvel had sent a car for me.

My memory has clouded the details of our conversation. I only recall that Tigran was sitting next to Samvel, trying to appear interested but hiding his yawn with his hand. He was bored. He had his own ideas about business and carried them out with the assistance of his companion Konstantin.

Oksana looked into the room and asked Samvel if we wanted to eat anything. He replied that his parents were waiting for him and Tigran for dinner. Hearing this was a relief to me. I had dined with Samvel several times, and each time it'd been a major production.

He normally gathered at the table a bunch of his relatives and associates, all of whom ate a lot and eagerly, talking with their mouths full, their lips greasy, and their hands sticky. Samvel himself ate almost nothing, glancing gloomily at his companions. Sometimes he would yell at someone about something for no reason, but mostly, it was just to get their attention or blow off steam.

A quarter of a century later, during the summer of 2023, I had another conversation about Samvel with my son. Sergiy told me that in his opinion, Samvel was constantly on heroin; he both looked like and behaved like a drug addict—impulsive and nervous. "All the junkies I knew had that same appearance," Sergiy said.

It may have been so, although I'm inclined to think that Samvel didn't use drugs back then. He could not abide the company of people who were drunk or stoned. Once, he beat his closest confederate for simply smelling of marijuana. I also remember the execution of a guy who dared to drink vodka before meeting Samvel. This feature of his nature was known to all who knew him, and I believe that I knew him well enough.

Now, when Samvel mentioned dinner at his parents' house, I was ready to say goodbye and leave with a light heart. To my surprise, Samvel said I would be accompanying him and Tigran. Oksana stared at him in amazement, then at me, widening her eyes slightly. The *real* family of the Martirosyan brothers, unlike their notorious Mafia "family," has always remained out of reach for anyone who was not Armenian.

I knew the father and mother of my bosses. They sometimes appeared in our office. Tigran was similar to his mother, while Samvel largely had

Chapter 10

inherited his father's appearance. The couple were very different people, like their sons. She was a short, chubby, and chatty Armenian woman with flashing coal-black eyes in front of whom both her sons had once been shy. Her husband kept his mouth shut when she made one of her acerbic remarks.

He was a tall, large, and flabby red-haired man whose gaze was always fixed on any woman's legs in his field of vision. His name was George, like my father's. He was a full-blooded Georgian, although he spoke Armenian. He and his wife considered me that rare person who could actually reason with their sons and guide them onto the right path. From the very start, they called me Sergey-Jan, which was the highest degree of respect from an Armenian. In turn, I called them aunt and uncle. I don't remember Momma Martirosyan's name, but her husband, George, was definitely Uncle Jora to me. I regarded him as an older and safer version of Samvel.

I saw no reasons to decline the invitation. How could I? We arrived at the Martirosyan house in the evening. Neither Samvel nor Tigran took guards with them. I was the only one with them, which made the event very special.

Uncle Jora and his wife lived in a two-room apartment on the first floor of a residential building. It smelled of onions, garlic, and spices. The furnishings were modest and cozy. We sat down at the table and started eating. Momma Martirosyan treated us to cabbage rolls, stewed beans, and *basturma*, an Armenian cured meat dish made of beef or lamb. A braided bottle of homemade red wine stood in the middle of the table. There was a lot of cheese, tomatoes, and greens.

At dinner I barely ate anything, politely declining the repeated offers of a second helping. I don't like homemade food in unfamiliar houses and always think about the hands that made it. Where had they been during the process? It didn't help my appetite to wonder what else this dish might have been in contact with.

In the midst of dinner, the Martirosyans surprised me by discussing their family problems. Their voices got louder and louder. Soon they switched to Armenian, making dramatic, emotional gestures such as rolling eyes, exclaiming, walking in and out of the room, and slamming the door with a thud. I said I'd rather wait outside, near Samvel's car. None of the family paid any attention to me—they were busy shouting their heads off.

It was dark outside. Night had fallen while we were having dinner, and I didn't know exactly what time it was, but it was somewhere between ten thirty and eleven o'clock at night. Standing alone in front of the Martirosyan house, I lit a cigarette. I regretted not calling for a taxi before leaving. I didn't have a mobile phone then, so I couldn't warn Luba that I was going to be late. I also could not leave without notifying Samvel, or rather, without his permission. As a result, I found myself in an unfortunate state of affairs, to say the very least. Without any exaggeration do I say that night could have been my last night alive.

It was raining lightly, and the yard was deserted. In order for you to imagine this scene vividly, I will have to describe a Soviet *dvor*, or communal courtyard. As a rule, it was an isolated inner area, a space full of shady trees and flowering bushes, surrounded by apartment buildings—some as high as nine or even ten stories—and equipped with benches, children's sandpits, swings, and tables to play domino or cards. It was customary to leave asphalt driveways free for the passage of cars, but Samvel didn't care. He had parked his car right on the road, blocking the way for anyone else if they wanted to move forward.

Not having my own car nor driving experience, I didn't pay much attention to it. But now my gaze flickered toward the Martirosyan's lit windows, where silhouettes moved behind the curtains, waving their hands wildly. In contrast, the courtyard was a haven of silence except for the muffled voices wafting over from the apartment.

The rain gradually came down more heavily, and I considered looking for a place to take shelter, but I remained standing near the black car, which was wet and glistening from its roof to its wheels. It was a Mercedes—Merc or Messerschmitt, in criminal jargon. About $100,000 was sitting, unattended, in the middle of a narrow driveway.

I said to myself, "Damn it, Sergey, you're not a fucking sentry assigned to guard his master's property." But I moved toward it, tried the car door, and it opened. Neither Samvel nor Tigran closed their cars, assuming that no one would dare steal from them. I brushed myself off

Chapter 10

and prepared to climb into the driver's seat, lured in by that seductive new-car smell, an aromatic mixture of leather and clean carpets. And money.

Suddenly . . . yes, I know well enough that "suddenly" is hardly an appropriate word to use in this kind of narrative, but the whole thing happened just *suddenly*, and not otherwise. So, suddenly, the darkness was illuminated by a flash of headlights! Two cars, one by one, pulled up to the rear of the Mercedes and honked furiously, demanding to pass. I squinted at the bright light and spread my hands to show I was powerless to do anything about the situation. But that didn't stop them from honking their horns, so I shouted toward the drivers that I wasn't the owner of the Mercedes.

This did not reduce the intensity of anyone's passions; in fact, the exact opposite happened. Now I watched two big men get out of the first car. From the second car, three more men alighted. All of them were yelling at me that if I wanted to stay alive, I had better get the hell out of there, along with my damn Merc. All I knew to do was repeat what I'd said before, but it was just a waste of time.

A guy with pale, twisted face stepped forward, holding a shotgun. He looked completely deranged. Staring at me, he racked the bolt, ready to fire.

"Who are you?" he demanded, his voice rising an octave with each question. "What the hell are you doing here? You think you're cool? One move and I'll blow your head off!"

It was useless to explain to him that I was not a driver. He didn't want to hear anything. He'd gotten it into his head that I'd deliberately blocked his path, and he was ready to shoot at any moment. I didn't know about the rest of the guys. I saw in front of me only this one with his shotgun.

As I learned later from Tigran, it was Arthur, the younger brother of Jacob Samson (the same man who had once given me a bullet as a memento before he himself was pierced with bullets on the steps of the Theatre Caffe). Ironically, his mother lived in the same house on Ilyich Avenue where Samvel's parents had settled. From the day Samson gasped his last breath and died in his brother's arms, Arthur had lived in constant fear of an attempt on his own life, so he didn't part with the shotgun and the comforting dose of "nose candy." He gave me ten seconds to move the Mercedes out of his way. And he began to count out loud: "One . . . two . . . three . . . four . . ."

On the count of five, Samvel appeared. It was evident that he had rushed out of the house in a hurry, as he was wearing a pair of rubber slippers on his bare feet. Walking quickly on wet grass and through rain puddles, he approached Arthur and gave him a slap in the face, which was as fast as a blow from a cat's paw.

"How dare you hang around my mother's house with that peashooter, you goat! Get out of here!" Samvel raised himself on his toes to reward Arthur with another slap in the face. "Don't bother my parents with noise—never, never—do you understand me? Put away your fucking gun and gerrout!"

And you know what? Arthur unquestioningly angled the barrel of his shotgun down, hurried back to his car, and backed up. He didn't even snap at Samvel. Both bandit cars remained in the distance, with their headlights off, until we left, which happened only ten minutes later.

Climbing into his Mercedes, Samvel never looked in their direction. He didn't seem triumphant or smug about his victory. It was routine for him. He daily had to prove his power, his superiority over people. Physically, he was not an athlete or a fighter. He had strength within himself, which was much more effective.

In the car Tigran told Samvel that the guy with the shotgun was the brother of the late Samson.

"Arthur Bogdanov?" Samvel snorted loudly and flung his hand as if he were shooing away a fly. "That faggot! What do we care about him for? He's a sissy."

"He lives a stone's throw from our mom," Tigran said. "And he can be a *vindictive* sissy."

Samvel remained silent. But Arthur was destined not to become a threat to the Martirosyan family. Only a few days later, on August 10, 1995, he was shot to death not far from his mother's house at 26 Ilyich Ave.

I think some primeval instinct was warning him that he was being hunted because, on that day, he decided to leave the house not in his car

Chapter 10

but in a taxi. An armed security guard escorted him down the hallway. At about 9:30 a.m., the taxi, an old Soviet Volga, pulled up and honked, and Arthur and his faithful guard got in and rode toward the city's center. Two men in the green Zhiguli car were following them. At the far end of the yard, they overtook the taxi and forced it to a halt at the side of the road.

As a result of this maneuver, the cab crashed into a tree. The dark, tinted windows of the Zhiguli rolled down, and killers began to pour gunfire into the passengers. Arthur and his faithful guard were dead instantly, while the taxi driver was only shot in the left arm. Then the windows of the Zhiguli rolled up, and it disappeared into a side street. Frightened but curious passersby surrounded the taxi with two corpses inside riddled with sixteen bullets.

I don't know exactly how many bullets Arthur got. And I cannot say with certainty whether or not he was killed on Samvel's orders. I was in a situation where it was not safe to ask unnecessary questions.

Did I feel grateful to Samvel for saving me? Not really. It was his Mercedes that nearly cost me my life. He had created this situation himself.

The same goes for Tigran, who often put me in dangerous, vulnerable positions. He, too, was (sometimes) there if I needed protection.

In September of 1996, my thirteen-year-old daughter asked for my permission to attend the first party of her life. Her class had decided to celebrate the start of school at a trendy café downtown. The boys and girls had raised enough money to rent an entire hall for three or four hours. They wanted to dance and have fun, just as adults did.

Luba was against this idea, and Svitlana looked at me with the fervent hope that I would agree. I offered to take her to the party and pick her up (via taxi). Luba frowned. Svitlana jumped up and down. The issue had been resolved.

The café where the party took place was called Krasnaya Shapochka, which meant Little Red Riding Hood. Originally, it was a cinema I had gone to as a child. Later, in the mid-1990s, the building was converted into a small entertainment center, including a café, restaurant, and nightclub. It was always crowded, and cars used to pull up to the Little Red

Riding Hood along the walking alleys and park next to the entrance on the lawns.

The school party started at seven o'clock in the evening. While waiting for Svitlana, I settled down in a nearby open-air café, which gave me a view of the entrance to the Red Riding Hood. Time passed slowly. I drank two espressos and ate two ice creams before I saw that the sky had finally darkened. Fifteen minutes later, night fell. There were still forty-five minutes left of Svitlana's party when I noticed that a group of men were staring at me from three tables away. There were five of them. One man looked at me especially intently.

I suddenly remembered him. Tigran had bought five Sony flat screen TVs with DVD players from him, "forgetting" to pay him for them. I had been present at their deal, and now the man recognized me. He and his buddies looked both aggressive and drunk. I realized that I was in trouble.

I took out a pager from my pocket and sent Tigran a short SOS message. As soon as I had finished writing down my location, the man said something to his buddies, got up, and walked toward me, while the others followed him, spreading out to encircle me on all sides. They were menacing, and I felt cold in my stomach.

I don't remember my conversation with the aggrieved drunk, but he basically demanded his money, while I pretended not to understand what he was talking about. I just played for time, praying for a miracle. Had Tigran read my message? When, if at all, would he come to my aid? Why would he want to mess with it? What would happen to my daughter if I didn't meet her at 10:00 p.m., as we'd agreed? How would she get home alone?

Finally, the group decided to pull me out of the café into the dark night. Two men wrapped their arms around me to lift me from my chair. Café visitors avoided looking in our direction, making it clear that they didn't want trouble. I didn't want it either, but my opinion was worth nothing. According to the men's remarks, they were going to beat me half to death—unless they decided not to stop.

I resisted as best I could, but the forces were not equal. Holding me by the arms and collar, the men dragged me away from the café. In the

Chapter 10

struggle I bit my tongue, and my mouth was full of blood that tasted like copper.

The calm, rather mocking sound of Tigran's voice completely surprised everyone. He greeted me and told my opponents to leave me alone immediately. Behind him were two thugs from Samvel's gang. A dozen more guys stood around the café with machine guns in their hands. It was an unforgettable sight. The gangsters remained perfectly still and silent, but this did not stop them from looking damn convincing.

"They're waiting for my signal," Tigran explained to the owner of the TVs. "Shall I give them the go-ahead?"

The men who had attacked me vanished from the café as quickly as if they had been blown away by the wind. Tigran smiled and asked me if I still needed him. I shook my head, speechless.

"I'm going to the casino, Sergio," Tigran said. "Want to come with me?"

I shook my head again. He patted me on the shoulder and walked toward the car. I didn't even get to thank him.

The people around didn't hide their whispers and looked at me as if I were the hero of some action movie. I didn't feel like a hero. I felt like a bastard who had just narrowly escaped the fate he deserved.

On our way home, Svitlana asked me what was wrong with my face. I touched my broken lip with my tongue and said that I had fallen. She looked at me carefully and shook her head. This was not the movement of a thirteen-year-old girl but of an adult woman.

"Recently, how many times did you fall down, Dad?" she said.

"Too many to count. And too low."

I felt myself blushing and turned to the window. The taxi was driving along a dark street with the lights off. The city, stuck in the impenetrable gloom and hassle which had arrived, filled all the space around us.

"This is life, sweetie," I mumbled. "Sometimes failures happen."

"It's nothing, Dad," Svitlana said. "Anyone who falls can get up again, right?"

I thought she had matured a lot the last year. What about me?

Chapter 11

Wicked Business

Autumn of 1995 was a busy time for me. I struggled hard to get the Martirosyan brothers' company working properly to guarantee them a stable income. I believed that this would shift their focus from crime to commerce, which would lead to a fundamental change in their priorities. Neither Samvel nor Tigran interfered in my affairs, leaving me complete freedom of action. But they didn't give me any support either.

It took a lot of effort for me to find employees who would work for us. Despite unemployment in Ukraine, people were in no hurry to get a job in such a remote place as a former research institute in the middle of nowhere. It was a mile and a half from there to the nearest bus stop, and Makiivka was a poor, seedy town, where few people had cars. They didn't want to travel that far for the small salary I could offer them.

After working in the company for two or three weeks, they would quit, frightened by the situation in the office, where odd things were often happening. The gangsters felt at home there. They could shoot at a target on the wall, where everyone could see it; they could bring prostitutes there and leave them unpaid for their services, ending in noisy, ugly scenes; and the prevailing language was slang and filthy curses. They came and went whenever they pleased, sometimes spending whole days here, waiting for Samvel's orders. It was difficult for ordinary people to accept this.

For me, it was both bizarre and normal. When you have gotten involved in something crazy, you can accept crazy as the norm if you live in it long enough.

Chapter 11

Every morning, I drove to work in a white Lada, which Samvel had put at my disposal. My former driver didn't last long and disappeared without a trace, along with his antique Mercedes. The new driver's name was Alexander, nicknamed Rezany ("Sliced"). His father had been recently released from prison. At night they watched TV shows together and smoked dope. During the day Alexander could not afford to stay home, and that upset him. He dreamed of having such a sum of money that he would not have to work anymore. Then he could smoke weed first thing in the morning, sitting in front of the TV set. It was an occupation to which he was ready to devote his entire life. He spoke of this with a dreamy smile.

The drive to Makiivka took us from thirty-five to forty-five minutes, and during this time, Alexander managed to share all his thoughts and dreams, which, fortunately, weren't that many. Once I'd been delivered to work, he would stay in the car, sleeping from morning to evening. Life without TV and weed seemed an aimless pastime to him.

Our office had a separate entrance. To get inside I went down three steps, then up five. I had done this so often that I clearly remember the route even thirty years later.

The construction of the office remained, of course, unfinished. When Samvel got tired of financing the project, he stopped giving money to Tigran, and for a while, his brother kept the workers from quitting by making promises and threats. But the day would come when they simply didn't appear in the office, along with their foremen and architects.

Of all of them, only Sasha remained, whom I'd hired as our electrician to deal with cables, wiring, switches, lamps, fuses, and other electrical appurtenances, including computers and telephones. He was my wife's nephew. In his early twenties, Sasha couldn't find a steady job, and Luba had asked me to help him. He was short and handsome, with long hair and dreamy eyes. His idol was Jim Morrison (of The Doors). I believed that his kind of work wouldn't bring him into much contact with Tigran and Samvel. And for a while, I was right. But they did notice him when Samvel's leg got caught in a tangle of wires and he yelled at the frightened Sasha. Of course, I stood up for him. Samvel then called Sasha a "fucking dwarf" and that seemed to end the topic.

Except for this episode, my nephew did not interact with the gangsters in any explicit way. He usually scurried around quietly somewhere in the far corner and occasionally joined me for tea and a bite to eat. I took him to and from work in my car. He lived with his young wife in a hostel not far from me. I sometimes felt like his chaperone because he needed to be protected.

To tell the truth, I never really delved into Sasha's work. The electrical equipment of our office seemed to me superfluous, and the huge space we occupied was empty of any furniture or ornamentation. We had only two finished rooms at different ends of the hall. These were Tigran's office and mine, half-furnished and both smelling of cement and plaster.

Tigran installed a large pullout sofa in his room, intending to spend the nights there with his random casino girlfriends. His expectations were not, alas, fulfilled. In autumn and winter, the institute was not heated, and it became very cold there. I had to purchase an electric heater for my office, where I would sit in a warm jacket.

Since November I had made some commercial progress in business. I started by changing the company name. All the commercial firms were choosing catchy names for themselves, like Magic Crystal, Seventh Heaven, Paradise Oasis, or Promising Land. As for the company of Tigran and Samvel, it had the proud title of Two Crowns. It didn't work. Nobody wanted to deal with the crowned Martirosyan brothers, so I changed the name to evoke an association with government agencies. Finally, I came to Samvel and Tigran with a kind of abbreviation—Gossnabsbyt—to hint that we were somehow associated with government purchases and supplies. They weren't happy with my idea.

"A man could break his tongue on that," Samvel muttered. "I like the old name better."

Samvel looked at Tigran questioningly. Tigran nodded. The issue had been resolved. Gossnabsbyt was inscribed on our seal. Well, even though it didn't sound like music to the ears, it was just what I needed to achieve my goal. Thanks to this simple trick, I was able to gain access to the local branch of the Agency for State Reserves of the Ukraine. It was a vestige of the Soviet-planned economy, which would be finally abolished only two or three years later. And it was a real Klondike for any enterprising businessman.

Soviet state reserves were consolidated from an immense fund of commodities throughout the USSR under the direct control of the central government. They formed a major allocation of Soviet reserve stocks of consumer goods—mainly agricultural and petroleum products. These were designated for use for when there was a serious interruption of normal supplies, such as during wartime, when all other stocks have been exhausted. The collapse of the Soviet Union left this giant cornucopia without state control, which many smart people before me took advantage of. I was at the very end of that line of those looting state reserves, but there were still goods to profit from.

After visiting several officials of the institution, I met the head of the planning department. About ten years later, I saw him on TV, when he turned out to be a member of the Ukrainian Parliament. In November 1995 he was a petty official in a cheap suit, who wore a gold watch on his wrist. He listened to me and said that he could sell me a shipment of sugar or canned meats if . . .

"It depends on what you offer me," he said, rubbing his index finger and thumb together.

I chose sugar, as canned beef was already two years out of date. The first shipment was to be one thousand sacks of granulated sugar of 110 pounds each, worth about $40,000. The official only asked for $20,000—in cash—for it. I offered him $10,000, and he readily agreed. I promised to return tomorrow and went to Tigran.

I told him I needed money and a place to store sugar.

"Why do we need a warehouse when we have an empty office?" Tigran said. "Well done, brother. Now you look for loaders, and I'll take care of the finances."

He winked at me. I didn't know then what his winking meant. It all became clear in the following days.

Tigran returned from the Agency for State Reserves with an invoice and a certificate of quality, which made our business completely legal. All documents had appropriate signatures and seals. This was indeed something new! I perked up, but my hope was quickly dashed when Tigran put his hand on my shoulder and told me that his brother was not to be told the true number of sacks of sugar.

"It would be enough for Samvel to know about five hundred sacks," he said. "Trust me, Sergio. I know my brother. He won't count the fuckin' bags. And we will have money to complete the construction. Otherwise, how on earth could this place ever become livable?"

I let him convince me. They are two entirely different things, aren't they? The smell of money intoxicated me, and I expected a generous reward for all the efforts I had made. But I forgot who I was dealing with. Tigran and I shook hands.

The next couple of weeks were grueling. I worked nonstop, trying to get as much done as I could, looking for buyers and loading as needed. Sometimes Tigran's guards helped me. Sometimes I carried hundred-pound bags alongside my buddy, Igor, who had a small, money-losing café on the other side of the research institute. My nephew was too weak to lift sacks that weighed as much as he did. Nevertheless, he hung around, bringing us water and cigarettes. At the end of each day, Tigran gave us small bonuses to keep our enthusiasm going. I came home tired but happy, with pockets full of hryvnias. It was a good time.

Once, Samvel appeared in the office and saw what I was doing, but he did not suspect any deception. The sugar business didn't impress him. He had his own sources of income, and the $10,000 he'd received from Tigran was a drop in the ocean for him. He left without thanking anyone. Tigran, as usual, winked at me conspiratorially. I answered him with a weak smile. The fear of exposure was the only thing that stood in the way of my complete happiness.

Then another circumstance arose that worried me. As it turned out, Tigran gave the official from the Agency for State Reserves only half of the amount and flatly refused to pay the rest. He refused to listen to my arguments that we were losing a reliable and permanent source of income. It was more important to him to dishonestly pocket $5,000 than to legitimately earn $50,000. It was in his blood. He simply could not refuse easy money. He was a born crook.

Eventually, we ended up with a hefty wad of money in an empty office. That day, Tigran and I spoke face-to-face. Sasha was absent, as

CHAPTER 11

he did not come to work with me in the morning. Igor was in his café. Only Tigran and I were sitting at the coffee table in his office, a few thick stacks of hryvnias on the top of it. I asked what share was due to me. Tigran said that he would pay me tomorrow when he exchanged the hryvnias for dollars. On this we parted.

The next morning, my nephew again didn't appear at the appointed place. Alexander and I waited for him for about ten minutes, then drove to Makiivka ourselves. I decided that Sasha was sick and did not attach any importance to it. My head was occupied with other thoughts. I couldn't wait to get my money. I looked forward to returning home with $10,000 and making my family happy. My mood was celebratory, or almost so.

To my amazement, I didn't have to wait for Tigran to come. As a rule, he never showed up at the office before noon or afternoon. This time he was there even before my arrival. He was lounging on the sofa with his legs crossed at the ankle and stretched across the coffee table. Konstantin sat in an armchair with a beer can in his hand. His body was shaking from constant hiccups, and his face was red and sweaty, even though the room was quite cool.

I sat down on the sofa next to Tigran and saw that he was twirling a poker chip in his fingers. It was easy to guess that they'd spent the whole night in the casino. My heart sank inside. I wondered if Tigran had lost all our money—*my* money.

I asked him if he had exchanged the hryvnias for dollars yesterday. He nodded and said, yawning, that now we had enough money to start building the office again. I didn't like the sudden look in his eyes—empty, cold, and without feeling. I asked him if I could get my share of the sugar sold, and he said, "No."

"Haven't you heard?" Konstantin exclaimed, intervening in our conversation. "Tigran told you that the money is needed for construction of the office."

Tigran shushed him and looked back at me. "Sergio, are you sure you want us to finally have a place to work? Well, don't take it hard. Moreover, you are entitled to a consolation prize."

He placed five brand-new hundred-dollar bills in front of me. I didn't move.

"I don't give a shit about the office!" I said. "I need my money, Tigran!"

It was a big mistake. In the heat of the moment, I'd forgotten who I was dealing with. In front of me was a mafioso, the brother of the most dangerous gangster in the area. He was not the kind of man who could swallow his pride too easily or allow others to see him as an equal and not as someone to respect or fear.

In anger, Tigran was almost as impressive as his old brother, but I stood my ground and even said, in the heat of the moment, that Samvel wouldn't be happy to know how the sugar money was distributed. It was a dirty act for any man to do, I admit, but I'm talking here about the person I once was, not who I later became. Then, back in November 1995, I was completely different—everything was different.

Tigran looked up at me, and I thought, "Oops! He will finish me off right now."

During the long pause, Konstantin managed to open a new can. I had no idea how a man was capable of holding so much liquid inside of him. I felt thirsty and licked my lips. Tigran kept looking at me.

"Samvel?" he said. "We don't want my brother to know how you hid half the sweet money from him, Sergio, do we?"

"Me?" I asked mechanically.

Tigran chuckled. He knew he had knocked me out.

"Who runs the firm?" he said. "Who found the damn sugar? Who was selling it? Maybe it was me?"

Konstantin put the beer can on the table, sucked the foam from his upper lip, and said, addressing me, "I wonder who Samvel will believe more? You or his own brother?"

It had the effect of a blow below the belt on me. I caught my breath. It was almost a physical pain, familiar to everyone who had once been devoted to but was then deceived by the same person.

"I was just joking," Tigran said and smiled. His eyes showed otherwise. He wasn't joking.

A storm of rage along with a wave of bewildered resentment swept me. I got up to leave. Tigran grabbed my hand and forced me to sit next

Chapter 11

to him. In one moment he had changed back from the insidious enemy to the caring close friend.

"Listen, Sergio," he said, leaning toward me and putting his hairy hand on my knee. "We're buddies, and we must stick together. You support me, I support you. Our affairs are ours alone, and they don't concern Samvel, right? He has his own business, and we have ours. Come on, bro, don't sulk. Money comes and goes, while friendship remains. Haven't I helped you in trouble?"

Actually, he had saved me from trouble twice. But both times, I'd gotten into danger because of *him*, so I listened to him and said nothing, thinking, "Oh well, let it all go to hell. I will never see you again. This is my last day of work with you."

For a while Tigran continued to assure me of his friendship and protection, and then he yawned and said he needed a nap after a restless night. Maybe I shrugged. Maybe not. All I remember was that I took the five hundred bucks, and the money didn't burn a hole in my pocket, although it could have easily.

When Tigran and Konstantin left the office, I also grabbed the company's seal, a bunch of documents with my signature, and some personal stuff on my way out the entrance. Closing the door from the outside, I hid the keys in a secret place known only to Tigran and me. I didn't intend to go back there. I felt slightly weird and tired, but I was at peace. One might say that I was happy in a way I'd never felt before.

At home, at dinner, I explained to Luba that I was leaving the Martirosyan brothers.

"You're crazy," she said. "You shouldn't do that right now, when things are just starting to get on an even keel."

I didn't tell Luba about my sugar business; I had wanted to surprise her, and now I was glad about it. She didn't need to know that I was deceived again. She received $500 from me and was happy with that. At the same time, I felt like a complete failure.

I had recently celebrated my fortieth birthday and had fewer and fewer chances to get a job. Donetsk was full of young—really young—people with diplomas, ready to do anything for minimal wages. I was too old compared to them, with a bad reputation behind me instead of references from satisfied employers. I also didn't have the capital to start my own business.

Still, I insisted on parting with the past. Why couldn't I become the writer I'd once dreamed of? Luba refused to discuss it—she thought I should have stayed where I was and been happy with what I had.

Gradually, our conversation turned into a loud argument, and our children turned on the music in their room so as not to hear us. I went to bed early, angry at the whole world, though I didn't get a chance to sleep. The doorbell rang. Standing there were two of Samvel's most faithful guys, Salim and Silver. They told me to get dressed and go with them.

I decided that Tigran had complained about me to Samvel, and once again, unease set in. But things were even worse than I thought. The mobsters were looking for my nephew, Sasha. As it turned out, he had stolen a set of police radios that Samvel's men were planning to use to intercept and interfere with the transmission of radio messages by patrol cars or any other police officers. It was very expensive equipment and, most importantly, a source of pride for Samvel. Upon learning of the loss of radios, he had gone berserk. Looking at me gloomily with his slit eyes, Salim said that Papa could easily kill Sasha on the spot for his deed.

I asked why they thought my nephew was guilty. They replied that they had brought the radios to the office and asked Sasha to check out the settings and connections. This had happened about three weeks ago. Since then Samvel hadn't thought about the radios until today.

"Take us to the little thieving bastard," Silver said. "I wanna look this rat boy in the eye."

Silver was a huge guy, a head and a half taller than me. My nephew was a child compared to him. I knew that I couldn't hand my nephew over to the gangsters. In a best-case scenario, they would have crippled him for life.

When we arrived at Sasha's hostel, I said that I would go in and bring him down myself. Salim and Silver didn't like my proposal. They insisted on coming with me. I reminded them that it was late at night and the hostel concierge could call the police. It was a typical Soviet-style dormitory with strict rules. You could only get there from 9:00 a.m. to 9:00 p.m., and you were required to leave your passport at the entrance.

Chapter 11

Samvel's envoys listened to me with gloomy faces. They weren't used to having anyone stand in their way, but they didn't want to make a fuss.

"Okay, man," Salim said glumly. "Go alone. And don't you come back without your fucking nephew."

That was exactly what I did. I returned to the car alone, holding a backpack containing the damn radios.

"They're all inside," I told the guys. "Every one. You can count."

We were standing around the corner from the entrance, illuminated by the headlights of a gangster car. It was cold, and I was shivering, probably from nervous tension. This was one of those moments when my fate as well as my life trembled in the balance.

Salim made a move as if he were going to grab me by the lapels, but Silver barked at him, and he lowered his arms reluctantly, glaring at me.

"Where's this little asshole?" he demanded.

I'd found my nephew in his room, trembling with fear. He'd told me that he only took the radios to get a good look at them, but I knew he was lying. He'd had enough time to do it in the office. Instead, he'd taken the police radios home and hidden them under his bed. I had no doubt that Sasha was going to sell them. That's why he'd stopped traveling with me to work.

I didn't scold him. His wife was seven months pregnant, and I didn't want to scare her and cause a premature birth. I'd silently grabbed the backpack and brought it down to Salim and Silver. They kept insisting that Sasha should be taken to Samvel, but I kept telling them he was sick and couldn't get out of bed. Salim asked me if I understood what I was doing.

"Yes," I said. "I'll go with you to Sam. I will explain everything to him."

"I don't think he will listen to you," Salim said ominously. "All right, jump in the car. Go."

They took me to a remote and unfamiliar area of Donetsk, where Samvel lived at the end of 1995. He was building a new residence, so he had to move from place to place and never stayed anywhere for a long time. It didn't occur to me then that he was doing this from fear for his life. Having expanded the boundaries of his activities, he had acquired many enemies and was now forced to constantly be on guard. This made him even more nervous than he had been before.

When we arrived, Samvel received me in a small room with a round table, a cup of tea between his clenched fists. He sat and I stood in front of him while Salim and Silver breathed down my neck. He wore his usual striped terrycloth bathrobe. His face looked slightly crumpled and puffy. As he listened to my story, he removed a slice of lemon from his cup and placed it in his mouth.

"Shit," he said.

I didn't know if this referred to the lemon or my excuses.

"My nephew is not a thief, Sam," I said. "He was going to return the walkie-talkies tomorrow morning."

"Shit," Samvel repeated, chewing and smacking. "Shittiest bullshit of all shit. I'll fucking kill this asshole dwarf you call your nephew. No one dares to touch my belongings without asking me."

That night is clearly preserved in my memory because all my senses were sharpened, almost to a painful degree. I remember where the light fell on Samvel's face, what color the stripes were on his bathrobe, and what position he was sitting in.

And I remember I said, "Sam, it was me who brought Sasha in here. This is my responsibility."

Samvel rolled his eyes at me. "Do you think that's enough, Maidukov?"

"I don't know," I said. "You once told me that I'm a member of your family. Sasha is from my family. He's my wife's nephew. I have to stand up for him. And I will."

Samvel's silence seemed like an eternity to me. Finally, he slammed his hand on the table and said, "Your stupid nephew is lucky that you're working for me, Maidukov. But his luck may be short-lived. Tell him to stay out of my sight. And remember—you're all mine from now on."

Thus ended this meeting, which radically changed my relationship with Samvel. I was now officially in his debt, and Sasha had unknowingly cemented my servitude.

The next day, I returned to the Makiivka office. Tigran behaved as if nothing had happened. He brought another team of builders to finish the work in the main hall. To tell the truth, reconstruction of the office was

Chapter 11

the last thing on my mind. I caught a cold and was listless and unfocused. The end of the year was approaching, one of the worst in my life. I was not in the mood for New Year celebrations.

I wasn't the only unhappy person at the research center. There was another man with different problems. It was the director, a sickly looking man of about fifty, who had signed the lease agreement with Tigran's company. Knowing he was putting dirty money into his pocket, he had no idea what kind of nastiness was in store for him. Seeing in me his partner in misery, he constantly complained to me about his tragic situation. I had no words to console him. We had both fallen into a quagmire, each with his own reasons. Now each of us had to either drown or swim to freedom.

CHAPTER 12

Family Ties

IN A SENSE EACH OF US WRITES OUR OWN PERSONAL BIOGRAPHY, LINE BY line, chapter by chapter. Sometimes our mental diaries are illustrated with photos, letters, documentary evidences, or even news clippings, and it simplifies our reconstruction of our lives. Yet in most cases, we are forced to rely only on our own memories, which was exactly what I had to do while writing this book.

Memories. The more deeply you dive into them, the more memories will rise to the surface.

I remember January and February of 1996 as one long trail of gray, bleak days, with clouds hanging below the horizon and promising snow that never came. I remember sitting in the dim light of a huge, cold room that was more suited to a half-built basketball gym than a posh office. Typically, there were half a dozen workers busily attaching aluminum profiles to the high concrete ceiling. Some of them would work for a week or two and then leave, having received no money from Tigran. He only showed up at the office to ask how things were going and to take the cash from my desk drawer.

To avoid sitting idly, I organized the dismantling of a mine's massive headframe that towered over the shaft with the idea of selling the scrap iron to a metallurgical plant in Makiivka. This provided a modest monthly income of $5,000 to $7,000. But the profits melted away almost as soon as they were earned. For Samvel and Tigran, this was nothing more than pocket money. Racketeering, robbery, and theft were much more effective and fast than any of my solo attempts. That's why the

Chapter 12

Martirosyan brothers were in no hurry to switch to legal (or, at least, semilegal) business. They strung me along with promises, but they never intended to follow through. I was now in the exhausted stage of our relationship. I had resigned myself to the fact that the brothers Martirosyan had not been created for any grander purpose than the wild beasts—to live upon whatever prey they can get, as that's their mode of survival.

"Let it be," I told myself. "To hell with them all, as long as I can withdraw money from the company account without having to answer to anyone. Sooner or later, Samvel will get tired of waiting for big income from me, and he will tell me to fuck off."

That was my plan. In other words, I had no plan at all, having only enough energy to go with the flow. Such tactics can save you energy—but you won't necessarily end up where you need to be.

When the money raised from the sale of the headframe ran out, the Gossnabsbyt business shrank to nothing. I didn't care. I was now in a kind of stupor. In the mornings, like a windup toy, I set off to the hated Makiivka and the building I called my "workplace," not clear why I was there or what I was supposed to do. Sometimes Igor joined me—a tall, handsome young man with jet-black hair and unblinking raven eyes. His café had suffered losses because Tigran considered its cash register as his personal piggy bank. This left Igor without any income. He saw me as a fellow sufferer, and this made him speak frankly to me.

I remember how we sat in my semidark office and complained to each other about our situations. This was in early spring of 1996, as it was still chilly at nighttime, though, in the afternoons, the sun would shine brightly outside. We did not see the sun and did not feel its warmth. The office had no windows, and its marble floor stayed cold all year long.

Igor was in a black coat and a turtleneck sweater, his nose slightly red and wet around the nostrils. His round eyes were sad, and his face was filled with anxious concern as he told me about his newborn second daughter and his need to be earning more to keep up with expenses. However, Tigran had robbed him of his lifeline to success—his café.

"This is not the best place for a café, you realize," Igor said. "Nevertheless, we have visitors, mostly local drunkards who would bring us about five or six hundred bucks a week. You may say that it's not that bad, but I can barely make ends meet. I have to buy new goods again and again, which leaves me without any money. Tigran takes everything he finds. And he forbids me to tell Samvel about it."

"Your story sounds similar to mine," I said, nodding.

I think we discussed this topic for a while, having no other topics to talk about. And I remember that we were surprised to find that we were not alone in the office. Several men in plain clothes walked toward us silently and deliberately, as if they knew not only where they were going but what they were going to do.

I stood up, intending to ask them who they were and why they were here. I didn't get the chance. The man who walked first, with the others following behind him, was already a step away from me. Without a word, he punched me in the stomach. The air was knocked out of me, and I felt so sick I couldn't speak or even breathe. I doubled over in pain and saw a police ID in front of my nose; however, my vision was blurry, so I couldn't read the man's name or his rank. Then he hit me on the back of the head, and I fell hard to the floor, landing on my knees before tumbling to the side.

I tried to rise and was knocked over again. The policemen beat me and Igor without any malice, as if they were just doing their boring, daily job: thump, thump, thump. They didn't hit us in the face and didn't try to injure us. They only sought to demoralize us and deprive us of the ability to resist. And they achieved their goal. Within a minute, our will was broken. We didn't protest or show any resistance. As far as I remember, we didn't even yell at the police that they had no right to treat us like that. They *had* the right, and we both knew it.

The beating was followed by a brief interrogation. I cannot remember their questions or my answers. Then it was Igor's turn. He was sitting on the floor, curled up in a ball, when they asked who he was and what he was doing here. He identified himself and said that the two of us had entered the office by accident.

"Sergey works in my café," he muttered, licking his lips. "Release us, please."

Chapter 12

His attempt to shield me from the police failed. He was cursed and beaten again, and then I was told to call Tigran. I understood that I would have to obey, but I still asked, "Why?"

"You're going to tell him your office is closed, Maidukov," the police officer said sternly. "I'm giving you one day to pack up your things and get the hell out of here. Twenty-four hours, not a single minute more. Call now. If your boss has any objections, then tell him to come here and say them to my face. I swear to you he'll regret it!"

Tigran did not come. He listened to my confused story and said that he was far away.

"Hold on, Sergio, hold on, my friend," he said. "I'll be there soon, and I'll kick anyone's ass who tries to mess with us."

He didn't. Neither he nor Samvel came. They weren't so reckless as to risk war with the police merely to get one man out. Tigran never showed up at the office, nor did he rush to the police station where I was taken.

When the cops were dragging me out of the building, I had a distinct feeling we were being watched from somewhere above. I raised my gaze and saw the director of the research institute standing at his window, looking down at me. After he noticed that I saw him, he quickly retreated from the window and disappeared from my sight.

I realized that he had been the one who called the police. Despite this, I bore him no ill will. Turning to the police for help was the only way to cleanse his institute of the criminals who had taken it over. Things had gone too far. The director was forced to defend himself, his reputation, and his freedom.

As I found out later from Tigran, the director's son-in-law was actually the captain of the police, the very one who had hit me first. His involvement had saved the director from the revenge of the Martirosyan brothers. Many years later, I ran into him by chance at a Crimean resort. He strolled along the seaside promenade, surrounded by his family, looking tanned and happy. I walked toward him with my grown-up son. When the director saw me, he promptly averted his eyes and walked faster, leaving me to stare at his back.

Sergiy asked me if this man was my friend. I shook my head and replied that I may have mistaken him for someone else. That man and I, we both had memories that prevented us from being friendly.

Back in 1996, I spent the rest of the day at the police station, where I was taken to a certain room with two or three cops surrounding me; firing, in one breath, a number of questions at a time at me; and jumping from one subject to another. Several times I thought they were about to give me another thrashing, but they just shouted and shook their fists at me.

In the evening, I was taken to the police captain, who showed me surveillance footage in which I appeared in the company of Samvel and his mobsters. I looked pretty weird among them, with my nineties curtain haircut, wearing my blue jeans and denim shirt. Enjoying my bewildered reaction, the captain tore the lease agreement used in renting office space into small pieces, threw it into the wastebasket, and asked, "Do you understand how things are? You forget the way to the institute, and I forget about your existence. You appear on the horizon again, and I unleash all the devils of police hell on you. Now get out of here while you still can!"

My ribs and insides hurt from the beating, but I felt almost happy. Freedom had arrived from an unexpected source. My days and night of slavery were over.

The next day, I filed an application for the liquidation of the Gossnabsbyt, burned all documents having to do with my businesses, and dropped the seal into the sewer well. I informed Tigran about this by phone and received no objections from him. He and his older brother were already left behind—two pale ghosts of the past.

For two or three days, I rejoiced over my freedom and idleness. Luba did not share my joy and was alarmed by my unemployed status, but I kept telling her that it could not be worse than my previous existence. I felt like a man escaping from a sinking ship. Those days of relief and recovery were probably the highlights of my adult life.

The spring came early, shining and bright. The air was sweet and clear. The color of the sky had that peculiar hue found only in Southern Ukraine and only on certain days. It was cold yet warm at the same time,

Chapter 12

like the partly cloudy/sunny skies in René Magritte's painting. You had the feeling that at any moment, the blue air would part like a stage curtain to reveal a new path, another way of being and a different destiny, a kind of "stairway to heaven," as sung by the English rock band Led Zeppelin. "And a new day will dawn for those who stand long, and the forests will echo with laughter."

But the magic curtain did not part. At the end of March, the sky was overcast with clouds, and fate reminded me that it can be cruel. Early one gray morning, my mother called me and said, "Momma is dead."

Then she broke down and wept bitterly.

It was dawn, sometime before six in the morning. I stood at the gray window, staring dumbly out into the slow rain, and wondered what my mother meant by that. At first, I thought she was referring to herself in third person, slipping into "Mommy this" and "Mommy that," as if she were talking to a small child. But I wasn't a kid anymore, and she was alive. Dead people can't call you up in the morning and say they're gone. And they don't cry either.

"What did you say, Ma?" I demanded.

She sobbed, repeating, "She's dead. She's dead."

"Momma," I said. "Please stop crying, and tell me what happened. I don't understand a thing."

She kept crying, making weeping sounds that had a distinct tone of despair. I stood there in the morning twilight, pressing the phone to my ear, and I could feel my heart pounding in my chest because I knew that something awful happened, yet I could not find out what it was as I stood barefoot on the cold floor of my flat, listening to the mournful wailing of my mother.

"Get yourself together, Ma," I said. "Will you at least tell me who's dead?"

"Ama is dead," she said at last and stopped weeping.

At first, it was a huge load off my shoulders. Ama was my parents' pet—a black-and-white American cocker spaniel named Amanda. Actually, her full name was Domino Chelsea Elcos Amanda, and it always seemed to me that the dog was aware of her ancient royal lineage. I remembered Amanda's clever chocolate eyes, her delicate way of laying her head in my lap, her silky hair flowing through my fingers, and I felt the pain of loss. It hurt more than my rib being cracked by the cops.

"I'm sorry," I murmured. "I'm so sorry."

By dog standards, Amanda was a very old lady, sick and weak, but this did not make her death any less tragic. My mother was in despair, as if she had lost her daughter. I tried to comfort her, but how dull those words of soothing were, as though they were made of wood! Putting them together, I constructed sentences that made no sense, similar to bridges leading nowhere—you know, "It's over," "Please don't cry," and "Tears will not help tragedy," the meaningless set of remarks that are customary to utter in such cases. People have come up with millions of words, but sometimes that's not enough.

Mom listened to me and continued to cry. The lump in my throat was too hot and large to continue speaking. I just said that I was going.

The trip to my parents took me half an hour on empty morning roads. They met me in their hall, both overwhelmed with sadness and guilt.

"She started collapsing," my mother told me in a tone of apology. "She suffered so much, our poor, dear Ama."

"She was so brave," my father added, and his voice cracked like that of a young boy.

All three of us looked down simultaneously. Amanda's body lay a few feet away, motionless and mute, the tongue between her teeth, her dull eyes open. This was her favorite place, next to the door, where she had spent a lot of time waiting for my parents to return from work to take her out for a walk. When I would take her out, she'd quickly do her business and hurry back home to lie on the floor and listen for footsteps outside the door. I didn't own her. My father and mother were her gods.

They told me that they were unable to watch their dog suffer. They had to call a veterinarian who performed euthanasia. Guilt was tearing them apart now. My father looked miserable and confused when he asked if I would help him bury Amanda.

"That's why I'm here," I replied and leaned over to stroke Amanda, as if she needed it.

Chapter 12

It wasn't until I touched her matted fur with my palm that I realized that Amanda was indeed dead. Her fur was lifeless. The whole body was entirely lifeless, from nose to tail.

Sometimes Amanda would lick me lightly in gratitude, but even at such moments, her eyes were always fixed on my parents if they were around. An animal's love is permanent. This is what sets them apart from us humans.

I asked myself when was the last time I'd visited my parents and found that it was a very, very long time ago. Amanda had always been with them. Her death made them lonely.

My mother brought a light-green checked blanket, and my father started to wrap it around Amanda. When he had done, I took the roll and carried it to the garden. Mom stayed at home, while Dad went along with me. He carried a shovel.

The garden was a hundred yards from our house. The farther I walked, the heavier the burden got. Being stretched forward by the weight, my hands became numb. Amanda weighed no more than a two-year-old child, but she was dead, and maybe you've heard that deadweight is twice as hard to handle. This is true.

"Is she heavy?" my father asked. "Give her to me."

"No, I can manage, thank you," I said through the clenched teeth.

I never saw my father so devastated and broken. He looked much older, with his bent shoulders and his eyes sunken in darkened sockets. Before leaving, he hadn't put on his hat, so the wind ruffled his gray hair. I felt sorry for him. I felt sorry for my mom. I felt sorry for Amanda, myself, and the whole world. But what I could do?

Dog graves are not as deep as those dug for humans. Digging in the wet ground was easy. Everything else was difficult. While I was heaping the loose soil over Amanda's body, which was wrapped in the green blanket, my dad turned away so as not to see this. His hair was completely white against the gray sky. All these years, I'd lived without noticing how my parents were turning gray and aging. The thought of it dug into my heart like a sharp splinter. I was probably a bad son. I could not say that they were ideal parents, but that didn't ease the weight on my soul.

At the funeral dinner, my mother never cried, and I was grateful to her for that. As we drank tea, I asked Mom how her business was doing.

Not too long ago, she'd started running her own shop, called the Tulip. She and my father had put all their savings into this. In the recent past, they'd both had their PhD degrees and prestigious positions in scientific research institutes, but the state did not want and could not provide them with a decent existence. It was a time when everyone had to take care of him- or herself.

My parents had bought a basement room in the building next to their house and hired two salespeople. My father made the shelves for the goods with his own hands and covered the floors with linoleum. Mother went to Moscow every month for wholesale consignments of bijouterie and jewelry. The store was not only a source of livelihood for my parents, but it also provided a new meaning for their lives.

With my question, I'd intended to distract my mother from gloomy thoughts, but it had the exact opposite effect. She burst into tears and told me that she would probably have to close the Tulip. Four weeks earlier, racketeers had come to the store and demanded a huge amount of money for my mother's right to engage in trade. The deadline they'd set expired in a few days. I looked at my crying mom, I looked at my frowning dad, and I asked if the racketeers had identified themselves. This was common practice. Gangster names were like business cards. The one who didn't have a big name didn't have authority.

My mother said that the chief racketeer introduced himself to her as the Goblin. I went out into the hallway and called Samvel. It was an impulsive decision. I could not leave my parents defenseless and helpless in the face of impending danger, especially at such a dramatic moment in their lives.

Samvel listened to me and said that the Goblin would no longer come close to my parents' store. I asked what to do with other recruiters if they appeared.

"You know my name," Samvel snapped. "Use it."

Then he just hung up.

CHAPTER 13

A Failed Millionaire

I THINK IT WAS LITERALLY THE NEXT DAY (OR CLOSE TO THIS) THAT Tigran called me at home and said that Samvel was inviting me and my wife to his birthday party. It was impossible to refuse. By solving my parents' problem, I had created more of my own. I did not want to see Samvel at all, and I didn't want to fall into his field of vision again. Also, I was very worried that Samvel had invited me to his birthday with Luba, as I hated the very idea of introducing her to the society of criminals. My wife was forty-two then, but she looked much younger. She was thin and very attractive, with blonde hair and large breasts. I wanted to keep her as far away from Samvel and Tigran as possible.

However, Luba accepted the invitation excitedly. We were rarely in public together, and Samvel's birthday party would give her the opportunity to show off the new scarlet dress that I had given her only a couple days before, for her own birthday.

Late in the evening on April 5, 1996, we left our children alone at home and took a taxi to the city center. By a strange coincidence, Samvel gathered his entourage in the Little Red Riding Hood, where, not so long ago, Tigran had saved me from the company of drunken businessmen. The weather was warm, and I remember that the birthday party took place in the open air, on the terrace of the restaurant. I also remember that, closer to midnight, I had to give Luba my jacket because the air had grown chilly.

It was an unforgettable party in every way. About thirty persons—the entire color of the Donetsk Mafia, guarded by armed bodyguards—were

Chapter 13

seated at the tables and partook of the feast. The tables were arranged in the form of a giant letter T, at the head of which was Samvel Martirosyan, flanked on either side by associates. Tigran sat at his brother's right hand, and Luba and I sat at his left hand.

It was unlikely that this was a sign of Samvel's special disposition toward me. Most likely, he was afraid of being stabbed in the back or shot at close range. I was his human shield in case of a sudden attack.

Samvel sat at the table without body armor. He wore a silk white shirt with an Orthodox golden cross on his furry chest. All bandits wore crosses. They were hardly devout Christians, but the constant threat of death taught them not to neglect the slightest chance of salvation.

Some of them looked at me and my wife with curiosity, some with disdain, and some looked through me, preferring to see only Luba in her bright-red dress. I had known many of them by name or by sight for months, and we would shake hands when meeting, but that meant nothing. To all these mobsters, I was an outsider, a stranger, the white raven in the flock. That night I felt it more acutely than ever before.

When I toasted Samvel, he offered me a classic Mafia kiss on the cheek, and I noticed a few nasty looks directed at me. Most dissatisfied were Salim and Marat, two faithful companions of Samvel. I thought each of them would rather see me dead than sitting next to their boss.

Luba did not notice this. She enjoyed everyone's attention and felt like the heroine of *The Godfather*. Until that night, she had never tasted oysters, roasted pheasant, or sturgeon on a skewer. Sparks flew from her eyes, and red highlighted her cheeks. Pleased that she could see him in all his splendor, Samvel leaned toward her and said in his heavy Armenian accent, "Luba, we're just getting started. Very soon I will make your husband a millionaire."

His words affected her like champagne. She became very animated and was on the ninth cloud of happiness. She received many compliments that night. In honor of the holiday, Samvel removed the taboo on alcohol, letting his guests drink plenty of their favorite liquors. I couldn't afford to relax. Samvel drank nothing but mineral water, and I wisely followed his example. At some point, he looked at me and said, "The right thing to do, Maidukov. Tomorrow you'll need a sober head. I want you to start a new firm. Very soon, a million dollars will drop into your bank account."

It was his exact word: "drop." And I felt despair. New firm? A million in a bank account? This did not promise me anything but new troubles. Luba thought otherwise. She'd heard my conversation with Samvel and was especially gentle with me that night. She dreamed of a millionaire husband. I dreamed of a quiet, orderly life away from the gangsters with their blood money. We were moving along the same road, yet in opposite directions.

In bed we didn't make love, but we did have a discussion. I was telling Luba that I should find a way to get away from Samvel. She was insisting that I should stay close to him. I said that swimming next to a shark is life-threatening. Luba didn't reply to that. She was fast asleep.

As for me, I lay in bed, staring at our bedroom ceiling and wondering if tomorrow I would be under the ceiling of a prison cell or that of a coffin lid.

In the restaurant I had exchanged a few words with one of Samvel's bodyguards, named Cowboy. He was a lanky blond fellow with red lips and spade-shaped palms from which grew long fingers, slender but strong, like nails. His appearance was more rustic than urban, and he seemed dull and good-natured, which set him apart from the mobsters. One of his duties was to walk the pit bulls that guarded Samvel. Since I had recently buried Amanda, I asked Cowboy how his "doggies" were doing.

He told me that Samvel had decided to get rid of the pit bulls, as they had been attacking his numerous Armenian relatives. In addition, the dogs had brought a lot of headaches with the constant moving of the "family" from place to place. One day Samvel woke up in a bad mood and ordered Cowboy to kill all four dogs. I asked him if he did it. He shrugged and said he'd had no choice. "It was either them or me," he said. "You can't disobey Papa's orders. You do as he says, or you're dead."

Cowboy had spoken of this as a kind of irrefutable fact that did not need confirmation. The sun rises and sets. Summer is a hot time, and it's cold in winter. Samvel killed those who did not please him. Simple

Chapter 13

truth. Terrible truth. With this realization, I fell asleep and woke up the next day.

Samvel's new business plan—if it could be called a business plan—was to take out a $1 million bank loan. He gave me money to open a company and introduced me to a young man whom the gangsters called Boris the Banker. In fact, Boris was not a banker, as I soon found out. He was a young man with a red beard and shifty eyes. His happiness—or misfortune—was that he had a father who managed one of the commercial banks in Donetsk.

In those days, a so-called commercial bank could be opened by anyone with about $50,000 and connections in the state financial system. These private banks did not bear any responsibility either to the government or to depositors. Usually, these were ordinary offices where people came, believing that they would receive a 100 percent return on their deposits. They deposited money in bank accounts, and then their banks declared bankruptcy and closed. It was a simple circuit that worked like clockwork. Deceived depositors went to another bank, where the same story was repeated. Television advertisements served as bait, luring thousands and thousands of naive people into the net. About three-quarters of them were seniors who'd grown up in the USSR and blindly believed in law and order. In the nineties these concepts were empty words.

As far as I know, Boris fell into the clutches of the Mafia through his own stupidity. He had met Tigran in a casino or restaurant, where they discussed business. Boris blurted out that the easiest way to get rich is to take a big loan from the bank. Tigran became interested and asked how to do it. Boris was probably drunk because he boasted that he could provide a loan of up to $1 million.

Could the Martirosyan brothers miss this opportunity? When Boris came to his senses, it was too late. Tigran introduced the braggart to his older brother, and that was it. Samvel pressured Boris into promising to provide the loan. (Most likely, it was a scene accompanied by rolling eyes and the voice raised to a scream.) Samvel was the master of this kind of show. Boris got scared and repeated his fable about $1 million. He should have known what it meant to give his word to a gangster, but he underestimated the significance of his promise and fell into a trap. It was just the same as if he'd invited vampires into his life.

When I met Boris the Banker, he looked like a very unhappy, very frightened young man in a checkered tweed jacket with leather arm patches. He had good manners, owned his own company, and came from a Jewish family, so his office was located on the second floor of the Donetsk branch of the Sakhnut. Its mission originally was to encourage Soviet Jews to emigrate to Israel, but it was later transformed into a cultural and educational center.

Boris's office was a spacious room full of booklets and brochures with views of Jerusalem, Nazareth, and other sights of Israel. There were four desks, three of which were occupied by Boris and two of his employees—respectable middle-aged women, one with spectacles, one without. The fourth table was for me. Samvel wanted me to be inseparably close to Boris and to control his activities in taking a loan from the bank.

Once or twice a week, mobsters came into the office to ask poor Boris when he would finally bring them a million bucks. They hung a dartboard on the wall and had noisy, emotional marksmanship competitions. On such days Boris let his employees go home and remained alone in the office.

I remember how Marat suggested that he stand close to the target, and the guys would throw darts around his head. Boris managed a smile and said it was a funny. Without a shadow of a smile, Marat replied that this was not a joke at all. Suddenly, he jumped up to Boris and hit him on the ear with his fist.

"When are you going to finally get a fucking million?" he yelled. "Why the hell are you sitting here, damn Yid? Run to your daddy, and ask him for money!"

He was swinging for the next blow when I asked him if he wanted Samvel to know about it. I told him that Boris would not be able to show up at the bank with a damaged face and that this would delay the loan. Marat looked at me with hatred and ran out of the room, along with his henchmen.

He had special reasons to hate me. I knew him from his school days, when he was a frail, undersized teenager, a whipping boy for anybody.

Chapter 13

Marat was his real name, I think. We didn't know each other personally; I'd seen him only from a distance and I'd had no desire to approach him. At school he was nobody; he was nothing. He couldn't play ball games or fight and preferred to crush caterpillars and beetles with his fingers instead of playing sports. I didn't notice when he'd appeared in our school, and I didn't pay attention when he disappeared. Marat probably also recognized me, and his dislike was likely caused by how I remembered him as a lonely little schoolboy, sulking in a corner of the playground. People do not like there to be witnesses to their humiliation—especially those people who'd like to forget their miserable pasts.

I don't know and will most likely never know what life path led Marat to a criminal environment. Be that as it may, he'd gone this way and become what he'd become—one of the four or five then-closest associates of Samvel. And this was another reason for Marat to hate me as his competitor. He left without a word, yet he slammed the door with such force that pieces of plaster fell to the floor.

Until that moment Boris had considered me one of the gangsters. After the incident with Marat, he saw me as an ally. I read it in his eyes and asked him if he really hoped to get a $1 million bank loan. He answered evasively, not knowing how much he could trust me. I told Boris that sooner or later, his deceit would become apparent. The sooner this happened, the easier the consequences would be.

"Don't let Sam finally believe in the success of the idea," I said. "Otherwise, he will feel that you took away that damned million from him. Tell him the truth, and tell him the truth right now. Don't delay. If you've got a painful tooth, extract it before you develop an abscess, and the pain will be quickly over."

"Samvel's guys will beat me to a pulp," Boris said plaintively.

I asked him if he was married. He replied no.

"Then drop everything and run," I advised. "Call Samvel when you are far away from here. He'll be furious, but in a few weeks, he'll get you out of his head, and you can return to your normal life."

Boris looked at me and asked why I should not do it myself.

"'Cause I'm in too deep," I said. "And I have nowhere to run, having my wife and children all around me."

As far as I can tell, Boris followed my advice, because my "watch" in the Sakhnut office stopped. The next time I met him was in the early 2000s, when I was already a writer. He limped forward, using a cane. We said hello, and I told him, "Samvel got really mad when you disappeared. I hope he didn't find you."

"Who is Samvel?" Boris asked coldly. "I don't remember any Samvel."

Of course, this was a lie. Samvel was unforgettable for everyone who got in his way. The cane in Boris the Banker's hand and the ugly scar across his forehead were proof—at least, to me.

After Boris' escape, Samvel didn't immediately abandon plans to take a prize bank loan. His next attempt was through another local businessman, Petya, who was quite successful in delivering wholesale cheese to shops in Donetsk—until the truck with the goods was stolen. This brought Petya into debt, and then his story was the same: the agony of a deer caught in a quagmire. As soon as he could get out of one debt, he had a new one. The borrowers intimidated his wife and threatened to take away his apartment. Ultimately, he was forced to turn to Samvel for protection and sign a contract with the devil. The gangsters used him as a cash cow, pumping out all the profits from Petya's company.

He tried to be stoic about his position, even though his eyes were those of a hunted beast. His parents were deaf and dumb, which didn't affect Petya mentally or physically. He was a good businessman, able to turn profits easily and with a minimum of fuss. And he was smart enough to figure out Samvel's plan.

He and I were sitting in his office when Petya said, "If a miracle happens and I get a loan of a million bucks, I will be killed. Gangsters need a financial kamikaze. I'm not that kind of man. Today I told Samvel that my company went bankrupt, so he can't count on me."

I thought that maybe he was not a kamikaze but a suicide attempter who'd committed hara-kiri.

Soon Samvel called and told me to come to him along with the "fucking cunning." The meeting was scheduled for late evening. As soon as Petya heard the news, he poured pure Royal alcohol into a glass and mixed it with Coca Cola. I shook my head and reminded him that Samvel can't stand the presence of drunk people. Petya said that he knew,

Chapter 13

prepared himself a second drink, and downed the glass in a few gulps. He was pretty drunk when Salim and his partner came to pick us up.

In the hot summer evening, our car left Donetsk and rushed along the highway. After a while, Petya put a cigarette in his mouth. Salim's partner turned to him, grabbed the cigarette, threw it out the window, and made a threatening gesture. Petya promptly jerked his head back. I realized that Samvel was very angry, and the mobsters were charged with his anger.

Late at night, we rolled up at a two-story country hotel with stunted firs and a flower bed opposite the entrance. Bugs swarmed around a lone lamppost. Judging by the abundance of guards and cars, I guessed the hotel was occupied by Samvel's entire gang.

Petya and I were taken upstairs. There were chairs in a large hotel room with a massive couch, heavy curtains, and a tiny palm plant in a big flower pot. I sat down on the couch. Two guys put Petya on a chair in the middle of the room and stood behind him. He asked for water and was told to shut up and wait. I felt sick. I knew something bad was going to happen very soon.

Samvel entered the room with a quick step. He was taut and ready to release his pent-up anger at his latest victim. He began to shout at Petya in falsetto, demanding that he complete the loan business. Petya explained that banks do not lend to bankrupts.

"My company's dead," he said, "because my account went into a negative balance. I can't help it."

"Balance, balance," Samvel shouted, mimicking him. "I don't care about shitty balance. Let this eat into your jaded brain, man. I ain't working for you, but you're fucking working for me, that's how I see it. You don't get it, do you?"

While Petya was repeating his story about bankruptcy, Samvel stepped close enough to smell the odor of alcohol on his mouth.

"Bastard! How dare you come here drunk like this?" Samvel yelled. "From now on you keep your trap shut as tight as you can. Otherwise, you'll regret it." Then he turned to me. "Tell me, Maidukov, can we get a loan from a bank? I need a million bucks. Urgently."

I felt a chill in my chest, as if I were on the edge of an abyss.

"No banker will even talk to me, Sam," I said carefully. "We don't have anything to bail. Don't you know that our company is fake? No money, no real estate."

"Why do we have no money and real estate?" Samvel quickly asked.

He no longer stood in front of me but sat on the couch. He looked completely insane. He'd gotten it into his head that he would be able to gain a million of the US dollars and wasn't able to give up this idea. I thought that now I would be finished. Samvel was not ready to accept arguments and reason logically. Failure drove him crazy.

At this moment, Petya drew Samvel's attention to himself. If he had been sober, he would have restrained himself and kept silent. But the alcohol had gone to his head. Drunk people are rarely discreet.

"May I smoke, Samvel?" Petya asked.

I could hear a gnat itching in the room.

Samvel rolled his eyeballs at Petya.

"Forget about it," he snapped. "Sit where you sit, and don't open your stinky mouth."

"I can go out if the smoke bothers you," Petya said.

He got up. The guy behind him put hands on his shoulders, forcing him back down to the chair.

"No, you can't," Samvel said.

"But—"

Petya made another attempt to get up. Samvel gave a sign. The guy hit Petya with his palms over both ears. This insidious trick made Petya scream in a high hare voice, as the air that rushed into his ears had damaged his eardrums.

"It hurts," Petya complained, covering the sides of his head. "I hear nothing, nothing!"

You don't often get to see men cry, especially impressive, bearded men like Petya, and it was not a sight to behold. He was breathing in harsh gasps, tears running down his hairy cheeks. His parents were deaf, and I think he was crying not only from pain but also from fear of going deaf too.

While he swayed from side to side, clasping his ears with both hands, Samvel looked at me.

Chapter 13

"It's time to act," he said. "I want your company to start making money—I mean big money, and I'm gonna take care of that. This is all clear to you, Maidukov?"

I looked at Petya. His eyes were closed in pain. A trickle of blood flowed from his left ear. The guy behind him was ready to repeat the execution.

"All clear, Sam," I said.

Part III
Resolution

Chapter 14

Violence Virus

During the summer of 1996, the legal gathering place for Samvel's "family" was the Chance Café, or more precisely, the café's terrace under open sky. There were no umbrellas or sunshades, yet most of the small tables stood in the huge shadow cast by the nearby building, the first story of which housed a kitchen, bar, and a small shop selling beer, chips, nuts, and various snacks. It was located in the right wing of the same research institute where I had started my career under the Martirosyan brothers, and I hadn't progressed anywhere since.

The director of the institute had left us without an office, but part of the premises had been bought out by the owner of the café, Igor. Since Tigran and Samvel were Igor's owners, the Chance terrace served as my office. I'd spent enough time there to be able to mentally reconstruct that scene even now. The picture still stands before my mind's eye as something that will always live within me, like my tongue or teeth or tonsils.

Let's look at the Chance Café together.

All tables are occupied by mobsters and numerous relatives of the Martirosyan brothers, which most often coincide with each other. Many of them, with rare exceptions, are men aged twenty-five to thirty-five years. None of them wears shorts, even in extreme heat, for fear that it, in some way, detracts from their masculinity. They do not remove their sunglasses under any conditions—even in the shade. Everyone smokes. Ashtrays are filled with dead and smoldering cigarette butts.

When Samvel's father visits the café, he's always accompanied by one or two girls who are dressed extremely lightly, if not frivolously. Then the

Chapter 14

eyes of those present turn to them, coveting and flesh-eating. Uncle Jora enjoys everyone's attention, though he doesn't spend much time in the café to avoid being caught there by his wife or eldest son. Samvel dominates his father, but one of the few people in the world who can influence Sam is his mother. However, she rarely appears in public since she has a weak heart and doesn't tolerate heat well.

Samvel is invisibly present in the café from morning to night. Everyone is waiting for Papa, to receive instructions from him or to turn to him with a request. There are usually more requests than instructions. Someone is going to ask Samvel to get a rare medicine, someone is waiting for money, or someone is looking for patronage. No one knows exactly when he will appear or what his mood will be. This makes the waiting both intriguing and tedious, like waiting for the hero to enter stage left. In this drama Samvel is the protagonist and antagonist in one body. All the others are extras, with the possible exception of Tigran.

He appears daily in the afternoon, a little drowsy and lethargic after another sleepless night. He never pays for drinks and snacks, and everyone tries to follow his example, but Igor is relentless. He can't afford to treat the whole crowd at the establishment's expense unless he wants to go bankrupt, and he definitely doesn't. Amazingly, he somehow manages not only to make ends meet but also to gradually increase income. His staff includes the seller, the bartender, and the waitress, Irina, who attracts increased male attention.

As a rule, Igor sits down at the table with me in his spare time. When I have told him about the $1 million loan and the businessman Petya, Igor concludes, "The man went deaf in one ear and won his freedom. The game was worth the candle. He was smart enough to get drunk, even though it was a risky move."

I don't remember anyone drinking anything stronger than beer at Chance Café. And I don't remember a single day when I felt relaxed there. I did things that I shouldn't have done, and I wasn't where I wanted to be. Staying in an alien environment was burdensome. Around me there were constantly a lot of hardly familiar people, whose interests and aspirations seemed, to me, primitive and boring. They did not read books but listened to trashy music; their speech was illiterate and rude.

Forced to associate with them, I involuntarily lowered myself to their level. Mimicking them, I had changed, and the changes were not for the better. Gradually, little by little and imperceptibly, I became one of *them*. It was a period when I abandoned the business, and I was glad to do so.

The gangsters looked at businessmen like cash cows. You stop giving milk money, and you are sent to the slaughterhouse. I didn't want this fate for myself. I remembered clearly Valery, with his nose smashed; Petya, with his eardrums damaged; and many other businessmen who were brought to Samvel in car trunks, beaten, handcuffed, and demoralized.

Sometimes there were the recalcitrant ones among them, and their ultimate fate was covered in darkness. I could only guess what happened to them next from the fragmentary remarks of the mobsters, from their grins and the expression of their faces. They didn't know pity or doubt. None of them would show mercy to me if Samvel ordered them to kill me.

The realization of this fact prompted me to come again and again to the damned café and sit there from morning to evening in the company of men from the Martirosyan brothers' entourage. I had few errands and responsibilities, and I received a couple of hundred bucks a month for this, which was not enough to support my family, but I wasn't going to change anything in my life. I had come to terms with my position. I wanted nothing and aspired to nothing. It was moral lethargy, if not death.

Tigran occasionally turned to me with small tasks, although he no longer involved me in his machinations. Konstantin accompanied him permanently, looking down at me with lazy superiority. If not for the mandatory can of beer in his hand, he would have looked like a fat cat, squinting in the sun.

Most of the days were alike, indistinguishable and tedious in their monotony, but sometimes something would happen that would make everyone but myself slightly happier.

One afternoon a luxury car with its windows rolled down and speakers booming pulled up to the parking lot in front of the café. The eyes of everyone present focused on the two young men behind the windshield. The music from the car was loud and defiant. For some reason, it seems

Chapter 14

to me that it was a hit by Swedish rock band Europe from their album *The Final Countdown*. The troublemakers looked at us like animals or a bunch of monkeys in a zoo. The most amazing thing was that I felt like a part of this bunch.

"Turn off the music!" George shouted.

He was a tall Armenian in white trousers and a white T-shirt with the Levi's logo on the front of it. A massive gold watch glittered on his wrist. He had appeared in Samvel's gang recently and had, for some time, held a privileged position. I didn't know who he was, a bandit or a relative—probably both.

The guy from the car leaned out the window to tell him to shut up and then called him an ape, maybe because of George's excessive hairy growth, which the Armenians usually exhibited with pride.

Grumbling, George took off from his chair. The two strangers inside the car did not take this as a threat, continuing to sit in their seats to the sound of the music. I think they were mobsters from some other crime group. To their misfortune, they weren't aware of where they were and who the boss was here. It took only a few seconds for them to realize their fatal mistake.

No one had time to react. It was as if the world suddenly froze, leaving only George to act. In a couple of leaps, he reached the alien's car. From my seat I could only see his broad, bending back that was shaking from the vigorous movements of his right arm and shoulder, up and down, back and forth, as he punched the driver's face with his fist.

It was the fastest fight I have ever seen. How long did it last? Two seconds? Three? When George straightened up, the guy behind the steering wheel leaned back helplessly, his face swelling rapidly, his lips bleeding like crushed cherries. His companion hastily turned off the music and shouted that they were leaving. George waved his hand to signify that the both of them had better hurry. The split-lipped guy rotated the steering wheel and reversed the car before spinning it around and heading away at full speed. The crowd in the café erupted in triumphant cheers.

All over the world of criminal groupings, there was always a cult of force. Everyone wanted to prove their superiority. Weakness was equated with mortal sin. Physical strength was regarded as the most important virtue. But an even more important quality was personal courage. A real bandit could not afford to hide behind the backs of others. He was obliged to fight himself, to escape from the imputation of cowardice, or, even worse, a "lack of balls" when it comes to a direct clash with the enemy.

By beating the stranger, George raised his own rating by several points at once. He returned to his table as a winner. The rest of the men in the café returned to their conversations and drinks as if nothing extraordinary had just happened. This was their everyday life. *Our* everyday life.

That long, mad summer of 1996, I had the opportunity to witness another savage beating—and even take part in it.

Tigran had a nephew, named Robic, who constantly hung around in the Chance Café and in the nearby residential area, not knowing what to do with himself. For a long time, it never occurred to me that the thirteen- or fourteen-year-old teenager was the son of . . . Samvel. For me, he was an ordinary Armenian boy, rather plump, pimply, and a little dense. I suspected that he was mentally retarded and much more mature than others said, as his face was bristly with black stubble and he always tried to look under the skirts of passing women.

Robic often approached me with stupid questions, and I had to politely answer him because in front of me was his close relative, Tigran (not to mention Samvel). It was hypocrisy, I know. I was terribly hypocritical then. It was my way of survival.

One sunny afternoon, Tigran and I were driving from somewhere to Café Chance in his red Cherokee, when Robic ran out into the middle of the road in front of us. Tigran hit the brakes. His nephew was sobbing loudly like a baby, smearing bloody snot across his face. As far as I could understand from the boy's incoherent speech, he was offended by some men—"big, big fellas," as he put it.

Tigran grabbed him by the shoulders, demanding him to name the offenders. Still sobbing, Robic pointed in the direction of the only grocery store in the area. They spoke Armenian and did it so emotionally that I understood them without knowing the words. At the end of the short conversation, Tigran pulled a baseball bat out of the trunk of his car and ran toward the store. Without thinking, I followed him.

Chapter 14

It was a natural impulse, instant and primal. I should have thought twice before getting into a fight, but I didn't. What was it? A tribute to friendship? Team spirit? Herd mentality? All that I knew then was that I should be at Tigran's side in a moment of danger.

A group of men stood on the porch of the store, passing around a bottle of wine. Their heads turned promptly in our direction. Of course, they saw the bat in Tigran's hands, but none of them moved. They were drunk, and there were four of them against the two of us, not taking into account Robic, who was mincing far behind.

One of the men stepped forward to meet Tigran. Maybe he was going to rely on his physical strength. Maybe he was going to sort things out with us verbally. But Tigran was not going talk to him or anyone else. He came to punish those men, whether his nephew was right or wrong. It didn't matter how and why the conflict between Robic and them occurred. For Tigran, only retribution mattered.

His bat swung down on the head of the first man. Knock! Have you ever heard a hardwood club strike a human skull? This is a very characteristic and extremely unpleasant sound, believe me. It stays in your memory for a long time. As for me, I am able to reproduce it mentally, even after so many years.

After that Tigran's swinging blows followed one after another, on the men's shoulders, arms, and hands that were covering their heads. Two of them took off running fast, as if their lives depended on it, and for now, they did. One man fell off the porch and onto the pavement, his face bleeding from ears and mouth, a large gash on the left side of his forehead. The last one tried to hide in the store. I caught up with him in a moment, grabbed him by the scruff of the neck, and then rammed his face against the door. Blood gushed from his nose. Pinching his nostrils with his red fingers, he jumped off the porch and staggered away down the street.

Instead of chasing him, I rushed to Tigran. I saw that he was ready to beat the lying man to death. I grabbed the thick end of the baseball bat, persuading Tigran to stop. He tried to wrest it from my hands, growling something inarticulate. I never thought he could be so strong. He was a beast full of rage.

Cursing and roaring, Tigran pushed me away and again swung his heavy club, but at that moment, his relatives and friends arrived on the battlefield, and together, we managed to pull him away from the bloodied man.

After this incident, the local men were afraid to even look in the direction of Robic, no matter how drunk they were. Robic himself also received an important life lesson. As a teenager, he developed the habit of bullying passersby, and as an adult male in his midthirties, he killed a man with a knife on the orders of his father, Samvel. But this was a completely different story, so I suggest that we return to the year 1996.

Over and over, I witnessed violent scenes, and I slowly realized that it no longer turned me off. I remained indifferent at best, but the spirit of violence is poisonous and contagious as hell. Today you watch someone being beaten, and tomorrow, you yourself are ready to use force against anyone you consider aberrant, adversarial, or insulting.

My family wanted to see me return home as a loving husband and father. However, as a member of a Mafia family, I was used to being treated very differently, and this affected my behavior. I was changing so fast that I could hardly keep track, becoming less and less myself.

At times I was unrestrained and despotic. One nasty deed followed another; one harsh word paved the way for other harsh words. It was like an avalanche that, once triggered, gets carried along down the slope by its own mass, growing larger and heavier.

One day my son and I got into an argument, and I pushed him away so hard that he fell—a sixteen-year-old teenager who dared to go up against his father, a strong and aggressive man of forty. It was a heinous act that still torments my conscience. I felt the same way after yelling at my sweet daughter and taking a swing at Luba. Every line, every word, of this confession is accompanied by well-deserved pain because I was hurting those I loved, being driven by my own frustrations.

When quarrels with my wife were becoming too long and heated, I didn't bother myself with looking for conciliation but flatly packed my things and left. As a rule, that took only a little time, and because it was summer, I didn't need a lot of things.

Chapter 14

When going downstairs and walking to the car, I usually avoided turning around and looking up at the windows of our apartment on the seventh floor. It would be painful for me to see my wife there. Or my son or daughter. It would have caused me much heartache, and I avoided heartache. Life is hard when your soul is soft—that's how I thought. My character had hardened into that of an uncaring and selfish man, and I was glad of it.

During such murky periods, I lived with my parents for a few days or with my nephew Sasha, in his hostel, or somewhere else where no one would look at me with reproach and bother me with questions like "What's going on in your office?"

In my parents' house, I felt uncomfortable and superfluous. My father and mother were upset by my family troubles, and they constantly told me that it's time to make up my mind. I spent a day or two with them, then went looking for another shelter. The worst was the hostel, with its only bathroom on the floor. Sasha's wife and their newborn son lived with her parents in the countryside during the summer, so their room was at our disposal.

But living conditions there were terrible. The room was a living room, bedroom, and kitchen at the same time, and you couldn't take a step there without stepping on a cockroach. Furthermore, it wasn't equipped with air-conditioning, so it didn't protect us from the summer heat. I would stay in Makiivka until late and then arrive at the hostel no earlier than 10:00 p.m., most often irritated and tipsy. Sometimes I got so drunk that I didn't remember the previous night. But one of those nights stuck in my memory.

I was driving back home or to Sasha's when a thought came into my boozy head that seemed wonderful to me. I decided to meet Eugene, whom I had not seen for a couple of years. It was the same friend of my childhood who'd refused to help me in my hour of need. I was eager to visit him in my new role as a mob henchman. I didn't mean to scare him or get revenge; I was just going to show him what a "big shot" I'd become. It was just drunken bravado on my part. Such wrong decisions often have bad consequences. This one was no exception.

Having learned from Eugene's mother his new address, I told Alexander to take me there. We drove up to a one-story house behind a high wooden fence, standing in a row with other small shacks behind the fences. The area looked unkempt and poor. It was deserted. Dogs barked in the yards, alarmed by the appearance of strangers.

Alexander asked me what I had forgotten in this hole. It was a reasonable question. The small brick house did not look like the home of a successful businessman with a luxurious office and leggy secretary. I thought that perhaps Eugene's career was not as brilliant as I'd imagined. As I looked inside the gate, I saw that the windows of the house were lit. This meant that my old friend was at home. What made me think that he was *still* my friend? Alcohol. The worst consultant ever.

I told Alexander to come pick me up in an hour and entered the narrow courtyard. There was no dog, so I went up to the porch unhindered and pushed open the door, which was not locked. Muffled male voices reached my ears; when I opened the second door, the voices grew louder, and I saw before me several men at a table under a single bare lamp. They fell silent and looked at me. The table was filled with vodka bottles. Eugene sat in the center, like the main figure of a caricature of *The Last Supper*. I said hello and took two steps forward, smiling. He sat motionless, staring at me.

"I don't know why in the hell you're here," he said slowly, "but how can you fucking come in like this without permission?"

I suddenly saw that he was dead drunk, like his stoned companions. Compared to them, I was sober as a whistle, and it occurred to me that I'd found myself at the wrong time and place. My last meeting with Eugene hadn't been friendly, and I shouldn't have come to him unannounced. I'd just made another big mistake—but why not? My whole life at that time was one grievous mistake.

Eugene's gaze was dull and persistent when he said in a drawl that was both arrogant and alcoholic, "Maidukov, weren't you taught manners? You must knock on the door before entering. Come on, go out and do it. Show us you're a very well-behaved boy like you used to be."

I should have silently walked out of this gloomy house. Instead, I decided to express to Eugene what I thought about his proposal and

Chapter 14

about him. He listened to me for a while, and then everyone jumped up from the table and rushed me.

It was a miracle that I managed to break free and run out the gate into the street, toward the headlights of my white Lada. The second miracle was that Alexander hadn't gone somewhere to indulge in his favorite pastime—smoking dope in front of the TV. To give him his due, Alexander showed real dedication in this brawl. With one hand, he pushed me toward the car while brandishing his baseball bat with the other.

Eugene fired at us twice with his gas gun—I remember I somehow noticed that it looked like the Charter Arms Undercover .38 Special revolver by which John Lennon was shot to death—but the shots had no effect in the open air. Overall, it was a chaotic fight that didn't cause any serious wounds or bruises to anyone. Yet as Alexander and I drove away, one of our opponents threw a stone after us and broke the rear window of the Lada.

"Okay," Alexander muttered, "you asked for it, assholes."

Around the corner, he pulled his phone out of his pocket and made a call. Help arrived an hour later. When Salim and his guys broke into Eugene's house, there was no one there except the sleeping owner and his cats. It took extra effort for me to persuade the mobsters not to maim my former friend. Eugene escaped with a bruise under his eye and a couple of broken teeth.

I noticed that, leaving the house, Salim's guys had taken some loot with them: a gas pistol, a VCR, a TV, and a computer. I asked them if they had to include robbery with their rescue, and Salim answered curtly, "Hey, we don't work for free! Never. That's not our style."

Of course it wasn't! Robbery after assault was one of the basic rules of the mob. I saw it happen again when another ill-conceived idea popped into my head. The encounter with Eugene reminded me of my early, desperate times, when I was brazenly deceived and robbed by Grousko. Having secured Samvel's permission, I took three strong guys with me and made a second excursion into the past.

In the autumn of 1996, Grousko's company shrank to the size of a one-room office, where he and two of his employees did their work. The export of rolled metal I had organized for him had not lasted long.

Instead of getting rich, he'd turned into a small businessman in a cheap suit and an awful tie. He had lost the luster of being a successful young man, although he'd retained the nasty habit of biting his nails.

The mighty tall guys were standing behind me when I reminded Grousko of his debt, so he didn't argue. He resignedly gave me all the money that was in his safe: something like $1,000. When my support group and I left his office, the guys received half of the take for their services. As Salim said had pointed out before, they didn't work for free.

They asked me how much Grousko owed me in total, and I lied, saying he had otherwise paid me off. Even at this low point in my moral life, I couldn't let them return to this miserable office and take the last money from this loser still nervously biting his nails. I was fed up with this game, and it was making me ill. I yearned instead for a shot of moral strength so that I could move on.

I had reached rock bottom. Now I needed the strength to climb back up.

One day in October, I went to the nearest church and tried to pray, standing right in front of the crucifix. But I couldn't get through my confession, and Christ didn't hear me. I left the church with an empty soul and a feverish head.

For several days I lay ill at my parents' house, suffering from sudden bouts of fever and nightmares. I even spent my birthday in bed. When I woke up, my mother handed me a box containing a pair of gorgeous white sneakers. It was Luba's gift, which she had left for me while I was sleeping.

"Are you happy now?" my mother asked me.

"And how!" I answered.

My voice sounded muffled because I'd had to turn my face to the wall before speaking. Those white sneakers meant more to me than anything else, more even than a heavenly sign from God proclaiming that I had been forgiven.

I returned home that same evening, and the first thing Luba asked me was "Are you sure you really want this?"

"Absolutely," I replied with a nod.

Chapter 14

She looked into my eyes for a long time, checking whether she saw there what she expected.

"Mind you, I can't take your damned comings and goings anymore," she warned me.

"Neither can I," I said.

Luba shrugged, as if saying, "Do whatever you want, and we'll see how it goes."

And that was that.

CHAPTER 15

An Inevitable Partnership

SINCE 1997 I'VE TRAVELED TO WORK BY BUS RATHER THAN BY CAR, AND my work location has also changed. My driver, Alexander, was drafted into the army, and our Lada was placed at the disposal of Samvel's lads. Every time I read in the Donetsk newspapers about murders for hire committed by killers in their Ladas, I wondered if this was the car, only repainted. I could only hope that it wasn't.

During this period my contact with real gangsters was reduced. About once a week, I met with Tigran and Samvel, but I no longer had to spend all my days in a criminal environment, and this was a great relief for me. I felt as if I once again belonged to my home, my family, and myself. Once again, I could rewallpaper rooms and read philosophical treatises. I chanted mantras and listened to rock and roll. Schopenhauer, Lao Tzu, and Socrates shared their wisdom with me instead of Salim or the Cowboy, and it was a real treat for me, a true celebration for the soul, you know.

The problem with celebrations, alas, is that they don't last.

Once, Samvel called me and said he wanted to see me for an important conversation that afternoon. We met in the open air outside the city, by Samvel's armored Mercedes. He was guarded by armed guys in four cars. Tigran's Cherokee was sixth in the row. I pulled up in a taxi that sped away as soon as I got out. Every resident of Donetsk knew that such gatherings along country roads were fraught with danger. Gangsters constantly arranged meetings in deserted places, where no one could sneak up on them unnoticed. Approximately a third of these meetings ended

Chapter 15

in gunfire, providing local newspapers with front-page headlines about gang wars, burnt vehicles, corpses riddled with bullet holes, and pools of blood on tar.

On that day, Samvel wore a bulletproof vest under an open jacket, and he was carefully watching every passing car. He looked like a man suffering from lack of sleep. A cold wind blew. Tigran's hands were in the pockets of his light trousers, and his nose was reddened. The trees had already shed their leaves, and the crows sat on their branches in black clusters.

When I stopped in front of them, Oksana got out of the Mercedes to join us. I'd rarely seen her after our first meeting at Samvel's house. She had changed her hairstyle and become brown-haired, but her face remained the same, like the wedding ring on her finger. We said our hellos, and I looked at Samvel.

"Do you remember her?" he demanded, nodding at Oksana.

"Why?" I asked cautiously.

"Because both of you are gonna work together," he said. "Oksana once worked in a clothing store, so she knows the business, and there's no point for her to sit idle at home. Women need to do something, or they'll go mad from boredom."

I thought Samvel was acting like a typical guy avoiding his annoying girlfriend. The prospect of getting an attractive young woman as a partner didn't seem exciting to me. My wife would be even less happy about it. She was too jealous and hot tempered a woman to tolerate other women around me. It hadn't been long since the day we had finally made up, and I hated the very idea of starting over. Keeping my eyes down, I began to explain to Samvel that I intended to retire for family reasons, but he abruptly cut me off.

"Family?" he exclaimed. *"Your family is us!"*

I reminded him that I also had my parents, my wife, and my children.

"Who else but me takes care of them, Maidukov?" he said. "Who else, huh? You're all safe only because of me. Think about it. Think about your mother and your dumbass nephew. Don't you want them to be safe?"

His last words made me look up. Samvel's eyes told me more than his tongue. His gaze was menacing, while Tigran and Oksana looked at me as if I were a capricious child who had tried to run away and now feared the ultimate punishment.

I did not answer Samvel's last question. There was no need for this, so we just got down to business. He softened his tone and asked if I had heard of Janusz Krantz. I just nodded. Not long ago, Kranz had been considered one of the richest people in Ukraine, not to mention Donetsk. He owned a luxurious restaurant, several factories for the production of paints and varnishes, sea ships, and a few grocery stores.

After he was killed outside his office by machine guns, the Kranz-color company was passed on to his wife. For several years she had bravely striven to maintain control of the company, but she was just a lonely widow, a young woman surrounded by a pack of criminal predators. Piece by piece, they tore the company apart. Samvel was the last to get a taste of this feast: he'd bought a store in the very center of Donetsk, at Pushkin Boulevard, a stone's throw from the Donbas Hotel, where I had once been the president of Globalinvest.

It appeared I had made a circle and was now back where I'd started. How much longer did I have to keep on going round and round, like a rat in a wheel? After all those years of ups and downs, managing a store seemed like a trivial pursuit to me. Since 1993 I had learned how to make big deals and knew that I was capable of more. Although Samvel's proposal didn't appeal to me, I thought, "Hmmm. Grocery store? Why not?"

Meanwhile, Samvel ended his speech with these words: "This damn shop will bring us a lot of cash. I want you and Oksana to take care of this. And remember, this is the start. In less than a year, I will put you in charge of a whole store chain all over the country. How do you like that, Maidukov?"

I would be a complete fool if I believed Samvel. The store was just another toy to be used by the Martirosyan clan. I suspected that this would not last long, and that soon, I would be free as a bird.

"It will be great," I said.

Indeed, the start was not so great. First of all, I had to meet Kranz's widow to redo the paperwork. It was a difficult moral test. I had to stand face-to-face with a woman ruthlessly robbed by gangsters, including those members of my so-called family.

Chapter 15

Our meeting took place in a tiny perfume boutique—the last piece of real estate the widow had preserved in her possession. I went in there with a heavy heart. The mixed smell of perfumes, deodorants, and aromatic oils gave me a vague association with a funeral, when the sealed coffin is adorned with floral tributes before it leaves to the cemetery.

The wife of the late Janos Krantz was an elegant blonde in a black business suit. Dark circles under her eyes prevented her from looking as young as she would have preferred. She met me standing up, with a cardboard folder in her crossed hands. She didn't return my greeting; she just handed me a folder and said that she had already put her signatures where required.

I should have left silently, but at that period of my biography, I would do everything wrong. I told the widow that I remembered her. She looked at me mutely with her clear gray eyes.

"That was four years ago," I said, smiling. "I tried to get a job at Kranzkolorit. It was you who did the interview."

"Anything else?" she asked coldly.

I muttered something unintelligible and started toward the exit.

"Wait," she called out to me unexpectedly. "I've got something to say that may be important to you. My husband was a bandit, and he ended up badly. You're all bandits, and you'll all end up like him. Now you can go. Good luck!"

With her parting words deep in my brain, I went to the city administration office, where Oksana was waiting for me. She had an envelope with five hundred-dollar bills from Samvel to be used as bribes for officials. We spent $300 on registration. When we left the administrative office, Oksana handed me one bill and said that from now on, we would share everything as equal partners. I didn't take the money. She assured me that Samvel would not know. "But I will know," I said. Oksana looked at me like I was crazy and hid the money in her purse.

At first I was afraid that she would turn out to be a capricious, agitated woman who had always abused Samvel's patronage, but she showed herself to be an extremely self-motivated and energetic partner. She told me that her husband was serving time in prison, and Samvel was taking care of her and her son.

Oksana's husband still had about five years left to serve his sentence, and she admitted that she was no longer waiting for his return. Having finished her story, Oksana looked at me, waiting for my reaction. I wisely kept silent. It was her personal life, and I didn't want to get into it. Partners do not have to show mutual interest and sympathy. This only hinders their joint business, especially if they are a man and a woman.

I had to remind Oksana of this when she made it clear to me that we could be partners not only in the store but outside as well. I shook my head. No. Impossible.

"Are you afraid of Samvel?" she asked boldly.

"I'm sorry, but you're not my type," I replied.

She laughed, throwing her head back so high that I could see the gold crowns on a pair of her upper teeth.

"It was just a test," she said. "Forget it."

That was exactly what I did. But she didn't. Without realizing it, I had acquired another enemy in the Martirosyan family, although I did not suspect it at the time. I still saw Oksana only as my business partner. Yet she was also a woman whose pride was wounded. This made her dangerous.

Outwardly, Oksana did not betray her resentment. Every working day passed according to the established schedule. Early in the morning, we went to the wholesale warehouse for goods. For this we had hired a middle-aged family man, who served as both a driver and a loader. As he had no connection to the Mafia, this created the illusion of "normalcy" for our business. I tried not to think about who owned the store, how we had obtained it, and what we did there.

Until noon Oksana arranged the goods on the shelves and stood behind the counter while I dealt with invoices, quality certificates, payrolls, and numerous other papers. Then I went home, leaving Oksana with the saleswoman in the store. It stood at a busy intersection, where big crowds gathered on Saturdays and Sundays. On weekdays the street was also crowded, so we made good profits.

Approximately three hundred people passed through our store daily, and each one of them left at least five dollars there. Cigarettes, lighters,

Chapter 15

drinks, chewing gum, condoms, sweets, and coffee—everything would be sold at an unfathomable rate and needed to be replenished every day.

Oksana and I set our own salaries ourselves, and it was good money. Once a week, we collected all the proceeds, exchanged it for dollars, and took that money to Samvel.

In the spring of 1997, he settled into his brand-new house that looked more like a fortress. It featured bulletproof windows, six-meter walls twined with Bruno's coil under high voltage, watchtowers in the corners, and searchlights and surveillance cameras, which were, at that time, an amazing curiosity. Surrounded by small, one-story houses and narrow streets that were traversed more by bicycles than cars, it evoked associations with a medieval castle. In fact, that's how it was. Samvel was a modified version of the feudal lord, living by his own laws, invisible and inaccessible to ordinary people. They looked at his stronghold with reverent horror and tried to bypass it by the tenth road.

The house wasn't that far from my own home, which didn't contribute to my peace of mind. It seemed to radiate violence and cruelty. I almost physically felt it. And I have never been relaxed during visits to Samvel.

He usually received me and Oksana in the yard under a giant military-style camouflage net. It was a precaution against a grenade thrown over a wall or a sniper in a helicopter. There was a long wooden table under the canopy, at which we sat waiting for Samvel. When he left the house and sat down across from us, we put a pile of money in front of him. If he was in a high spirit, he would ask us about business and give us a generous sum to purchase goods. But most of the time, he was in a bad mood. He was tense and restless. His gaze wandered constantly as he sat across from us, with one or two bodyguards behind him.

He had every reason on earth to be nervous and fear for his life. As I learned later, this was the time when Samvel had turned into a hunted beast. Throughout 1997, Ukrainian guardians of the law tried three times to bring him to criminal responsibility—for robbery, illegal possession of firearms, racketeering, blackmailing, and theft on an especially large scale. But every time, Samvel had managed to get away with it or get off with minimal formal punishment. Freed from short-term imprisonment, he usually found that his rivals and partners had time to appropriate pieces of his pie, as well as arrange bloody revenges. Many his opponents were killed or missing.

With his cruelty and vindictiveness, he had turned against himself all the local Mafia leaders. They eventually gathered in an underground meeting and sentenced Samvel to death. The situation was all the more dangerous because his closest associates were also dissatisfied with his dictatorial manner; these associates were rumored to be Grisha and the previously mentioned Marat. There was a high probability this was true because, one day, the two of them just disappeared without a trace from Samvel's entourage.

Forced to be constantly on the alert, Samvel lost his peace and sleep. Although he fenced himself off from the outside world with high walls, this did not save him from assassination attempts by accomplices and relatives. I had the impression that he allowed himself to relax a little in the presence of Oksana and me. Sometimes Samvel took advantage of our arrival to crack a joke or tell a story or two, but after a minute, he might frown and tell us to get lost. And there were days when I left his house alone because he'd told Oksana to stay with him for an "important conversation." It made me very, very careful in dealing with her.

Still, I wasn't vigilant enough.

Having received relative freedom and a lot of leisure time, I focused on things far from the Mafia and business. In the first months, the store brought me enough money not to worry about my daily bread. I read a lot, helped Luba with the housework, and enjoyed being with my children. Growing up, Sergiy and Svitlana became more and more bright personalities, and we had many common interests. We studied Castaneda together, we drew and painted, we listened to music, strummed the guitar, admired distant stars, and looked at water droplets through a microscope. It was a great time for my mental rehabilitation. I believed that the worst was over and looked to the future with hope. I was like a man who enjoys life while sitting on a powder keg with a smoldering fuse.

In the meantime, strange things started happening in our store. Throughout the fall of 1997, daily revenue began to decline until it was below half of what it had been.

Chapter 15

As our cash register emptied, the shelves and refrigerators were full of goods. We stopped going to warehouses for batches of food, packs of beer, and boxes of cigarettes. I didn't understand what was the matter. Oksana assured me that the reason was a decrease in the flow of customers, but as far as I could tell, that was not the case. I spoke to our saleswoman face-to-face and suspected that she was hiding something. Then I decided to conduct a private investigation. Instead of going home as usual, I took up an observation post across the street from the store and started to wait.

It was vital for me to unravel this riddle. Samvel became more and more indignant when counting the money brought by Oksana and me. He had not yet directly accused us of stealing, but he was close to it, and he has never been distinguished by restraint. During our last meeting, he didn't look at me directly even once, and this was a very bad sign. Arousing Samvel's suspicions was like teasing a hungry beast.

On my second day on duty, a van pulled up to the store accompanied by a red Jeep Cherokee. I immediately realized that I was about to see Tigran and Konstantin, and they appeared in front of me at a distance of fifty feet. While the van driver was unloading the goods, they entered the store. I got up from the bench, followed them, and found them counting money together with Oksana. They all three looked at me simultaneously. Oksana was clearly taken aback. Konstantin looked at me with hatred. Tigran smiled and made an inviting gesture.

"Join us, Sergio," he said. "You're entitled to your share."

Their scam was simple and effective. Tigran and Konstantin were finding unaccounted goods somewhere else and then would bring them to Samvel's store. Since they were accustomed to getting goods for nothing, this allowed Oksana to trade in drinks, food, and cigarettes at dumping prices. These shenanigans took place after dinner, while I was away. Thus, our standard assortment was gathering dust on the shelves while the store was having giveaways. Afterward, the illegal income was distributed among the three partners, and the saleswoman also received her reward for keeping her mouth closed. Everyone was fine, except for me. It was not about money, it was a matter of life and death—*my* life and death.

An Inevitable Partnership

I told Tigran that I didn't want my share, which could cost me my head. "Samvel will burst with anger when he finds out," I told him.

"*If* he finds out," Tigran corrected me. "You're not going to tell him, are you, Sergio?"

His voice was purring like a cat's. But I clearly remembered the name of this big, menacing cat: *Tigran*—the one who always keeps his fangs and claws at the ready.

"What am I supposed to tell your brother if he asks?" I muttered. "Sam already suspects I'm stealing his money."

"I'll tell him you're an honest fella," Tigran said. "Or I'll tell him the opposite. Your choice, Sergio. Don't take the wrong step."

I told them that I was out of the game. I wasn't going to be responsible for a store run by others. Tigran caught up with me on the street and once again warned me not to spill the beans. He said otherwise I would regret it, and he meant it. His parting look was full of cruelty.

I left depressed. Whatever I did would take me out of the fire and into the frying pan. I couldn't tell Samvel that I was leaving and *why* I was leaving, but at the same time, I couldn't stay. It was an insoluble dilemma. I got completely confused in these relations with the Martirosyan brothers and felt like a fly between two spiders.

For several days I puzzled over what to do and came up with nothing. On Friday evening Samvel called me and said that he would be waiting for me to come tomorrow afternoon with store receipts. It sounded like a warning shot. He spoke to me nervously and abruptly. I decided that this was the end.

At dinner I did my best to keep my family from noticing my condition. They couldn't help me, and I didn't want to involve them in my problems. It was my fault, not theirs. And it was only my responsibility. My son, with his Kurt Cobain haircut; my daughter, with her first love affair; and my wife, with her dream of a car, were not involved in my personal drama. I myself was the author and the main character of this. And it was I who'd brought myself to such a deplorable ending.

When I thought about it, I wanted to cry, but I didn't. Adult men have problems with their tear glands.

Chapter 16

Waiting for Judgment Day

On the last Saturday of December 1997, I went to the store and found only the saleswoman there. She told me that Oksana didn't show up for work and gave me an envelope with money. There was about $2,000—about a quarter of the original weekly profit.

I got into the car and told the driver to take me to Samvel. It was like going to an execution. Today it's hard for me to imagine what state I was in, but I think I was close to panic. My driver didn't notice my state, but he drove without speaking. Maybe he felt something crooked was going on. Or maybe he was totally preoccupied with his own thoughts, as was I. People do not necessarily have to be involved in a conflict with mob leaders to be preoccupied. They have plenty of other reasons for this.

On the road to Samvel's fortress, about two hundred yards away, there was a car flashing its headlights at us. Igor looked out from there and gestured for me to join him. His Café Chance had closed a few months ago, and he'd become something of an adjutant for Samvel, acting as both housekeeper and messenger at large. It made him perpetually anxious and thin as a rail. I noticed the dark shadows under his feverish eyes. He told me that he was on duty here so as not to let anyone in to Samvel's house. Such posts were placed on all three access roads.

Early in the morning, the police had arrested our Papa and taken him to prison. They had to storm the building using fire escapes, and they'd shot a guard who was trying to resist. Samvel was going to barricade himself in the basement, but he was captured and handcuffed. Before leaving,

Chapter 16

he ordered Igor to collect money for his release. I gave Igor the store proceeds and felt as if I had lifted a heavy burden from my shoulders.

Igor told me that the police had arranged an ambush in the house, so I better stay as far as possible from there. I replied that I would gladly do it and asked about him. He looked at me with his raven eyes and said, "I was stuck in this shit too deep, Sergey."

"It's never too late to wash," I said.

"Then try," Igor said. "Good luck."

He stayed, and I left.

Returning home, I sat in front of the TV and, one by one, began watching all the local news reports. Late at night, the official spokesperson for the Donetsk Police Department acclaimed that the Mafia boss Samvel Martirosyan was arrested and placed in a pretrial detention center. Newspapers wrote that a criminal case was opened against him, which threatened him with a long prison term. By a mysterious coincidence, our store on Pushkin Boulevard had burned down. When I saw footage of the smoking black ruins, I brought home cake and champagne. For the first time in a long, long time, I felt free.

Samvel tightly sat in a pretrial detention center and no longer bothered me with his crazy ideas about what he imagined the business would be like. Tigran allegedly had flown to Armenia. His smart-assed partner, Konstantin, was attacked by unknown men, savagely beaten, and had to be taken to the intensive care in Makiivka's hospital. Samvel's gang ceased to exist, and I got the long-awaited opportunity to start over. It was like a breath of fresh air after being underwater for so long.

For a whole week, I lazed around, lying on the couch in front of the TV with the remote control in my hands. I felt like a character in The Beatles song "I'm Only Sleeping," who, half-asleep, was keeping an eye on the world going by his window. Ice storms hit northeastern America, causing widespread destruction; massacres took place in Algeria, where hundreds of people were killed; vandals decapitated the famous Little Mermaid statue in Copenhagen; Pope John Paul II visited Cuba and condemned the US moves to isolate the country; the Spice Girls won their American Music Awards; and the Supreme Court of Ukraine rejected the petition for pardon filed by Samvel Martirosyan's lawyer.

When my eyes began to tire from viewing all the news releases, MTV clips, and TV series, I bought myself a thick newspaper with job advertisements and unfolded it, giving my eyes some rest. I had awoken to my new life.

In February or March 1998, I passed an interview at the biggest insurance company in Ukraine and was appointed as its regional manager. I got a modest office in a student dormitory with a dozen agents at my disposal. On the very first day, I realized that my new job would be monotonous and boring. All this juggling with insurance policies didn't seem too exciting to me, but I was glad to get away from the risky path of crime. I'd been walking on thin ice for too long, and I wanted to feel solid ground under my feet. Boredom and monotony were the best adventure for me.

My new employees created the familiar atmosphere of a classic Soviet institution. They were cheerful retirees, housewives with knitting tucked away in their desk drawers, and recent college graduates who couldn't find a more profitable place under the sun. They came and went, replacing each other with kaleidoscopic speed. The profession of an insurance agent required people to be as sneaky as a traveling salesman and as pushy as a merchant from an oriental bazaar. Only a few had these qualities. I hadn't.

Our office was located in three adjacent rooms, one of which was occupied by me alone, with no one else. There I had plenty of free time to read books and find something to do in front of the ancient computer that made a boiling-kettle noise. With my rather inert attitude toward work, I didn't earn too much, but I had some savings from the time spent with the Martirosyan brothers, so my family did not experience any financial difficulties.

Months passed, about which I have nothing to tell, except that they really passed. We don't notice when we are happy. We dream of happiness only when we are unhappy, and this is the greatest stupidity in the world.

From time to time, I thought about changing jobs, but I stayed where I was, in my spacious office with a rickety desk and a humming computer. The insurance company was like a rehab clinic for me—a kind of psychotherapy that enabled me to extinguish memories of recent traumatic

Chapter 16

events. I was sure that my stay in this serene oasis could continue indefinitely. That was another big mistake of mine.

I was returning from a traditional Monday meeting at the main office in the central part of Donetsk when I saw a black car coming slowly behind me. I remember it was a damp gray afternoon. Huge drops of cold autumn rain fell from the clouds above and splashed into puddles on the pavement. I also remember that I was without an umbrella. Having reached the tram stop, I jumped inside. The black car was not far behind. It stubbornly continued to follow the tram until it was time for me to get off.

Stepping down onto the boardwalk, I looked at the car. A man sat in the front seat behind the wheel. He wore a beard, and he was looking right at me. It was Tigran. He rolled down the window and waved.

I stopped to notice the cold rain spattering on me, as well as the drops running down my sleeves and behind my collar. Tigran waved again. Before approaching him, I made sure that my knees did not bend as I walked across the street. Tigran was very pale, with dark-blue circles around his eyes and an untidy beard that looked like it had been painted loosely in charcoal. He said, "Get in, we need to talk."

He was alone in the car. It was an old Volkswagen with a cracked windshield. It didn't correspond with the usual posh appearance of Tigran. Apparently, the affairs of the Martirosyan brothers were bad, if no worse than simply bad.

I climbed into the car next to Tigran and asked him how he knew where I worked. He replied that he'd met me by chance, and of course, I didn't believe him. I was being followed. For what? While I was thinking about it, Tigran told me to fasten my seat belt.

"I'm not going anywhere, Tigran," I said, holding the car's door open.

He didn't get angry, just shook his head reproachfully. The centuries-old sadness of the entire Armenian people accumulated in his eyes.

"We were good friends before, Sergio," he said, "and I always helped you with your problems. And money? Didn't I share with you everything that I had, down to the last cent?"

This was clearly an exaggeration, so I shrugged my shoulders and told him that he got ten times more from me than he gave. So what?

"Buddies don't count money between them, do we now?" Tigran said. "So, what's up? Aren't we buddies anymore?"

I wasn't sure how to answer the question. My thoughts went back to the very start of our partnership, to that accursed room full of armed mobsters, where Tigran had introduced me to his brother. I searched my memory, searched the events. He'd always used me as a pawn in his cheating games. Was he again trying to take advantage of me? I proposed to him that he say directly what he wants from me this time.

"It's not me but my brother," Tigran said.

My muscles tensed involuntary. Mentally, I'd buried Samvel long ago in the dark depths of my memory. Now he seemed to have risen from his grave, still incorporeal and invisible but already quite real. I wasn't happy about this resurrection at all, and I listened to Tigran with growing anxiety.

He explained to me that Samvel would appear before the court in two or three weeks. His lawyer suggested that several credible defense witnesses be prepared. Samvel chose me among others. According to his plan, I was to testify in his defense, characterizing him as an honest, law-abiding businessman—and not a gangster.

"Your speech is going to make a favorable impression on the jury, Sergio," Tigran said. "You're respectable, you have a well-hung tongue, and you know how to convince people, so we believe that you can do it."

"I don't think so," I said.

"Sergio, do you know that my brother has high hopes for you? Don't let him down. You know what happens to people who upset Samvel, right?"

Tigran's voice took on a menacing intonation. I forced myself to overcome my fear and stubbornly stood my ground, saying over and over that my testimony meant nothing and that's no reason for me to take part in the trial.

"You better think about it properly," Tigran said. "I bet you'll change your mind."

On this we parted, but the next day, guests appeared in my office. These were three guys from Samvel's personal guard, led by a giant nicknamed Silver. They greeted me familiarly and said that they would guard

Chapter 16

me so that nothing would happen to me before the trial. In the evening they accompanied me home, and in the morning, they met me at the entrance. My office has turned into a gangster hangout, just like it used to be in Sakhnut. All day long, my "guards" crowded around the place, eating hot dogs, playing cards, and throwing darts at the target hanging on the door. Arguing about the championship, they raised a terrible noise, and they didn't let the girls pass without saying some vulgarity to them. My best insurance agent, sixty-year-old Velichko, couldn't stand this mess and complained about me to the company's management. They fired me, putting in my place the conscientious Velichko, who, no doubt, deserved it more than I did.

After leaving the insurance company, I spent several days at home not answering the phone or doorbell. On the eve of the court session, I nevertheless lost my vigilance. It was a dead night, and I didn't expect a dirty trick. I was having a bright dream when the hallway telephone awoke me. In the dream I was a little boy, drowning in the sea on a sunny summer day while the people on a beach watched me. Before I jumped out of bed and left the bedroom, I looked at Luba, who opened her eyes and stared at me. She told me I'd better not pick up the phone, but I was thinking about my elderly parents. The green glow of the digital figures on the small clock on the bed table showed 3:30 a.m. You can't stop answering late-night phone calls when your mother is sick and your father is in his late sixties.

It wasn't my parents who'd called me. Standing in the dark with the phone to my ear, I heard an unknown male voice, raspy and low.

"Listen to me, Maidukov," the voice said, "I want to warn you. Make no mistake, or you will regret it."

"Who are you?" I demanded. "And what the hell are you talking about?"

"You know what I'm talking about, Maidukov," the voice said. "Go where you're told, and do what you're told. Otherwise . . ."

Suddenly, I realized who was on the other end of the line, but before I could say a word, he cut off the call.

When I returned to bed, Luba asked who it was. I replied that I didn't know. But I knew. I was sure that it was the voice of Salim, a narrow-eyed, heartless killer accustomed to carrying out his threats. I hugged Luba and closed my eyes.

"Your hands are icy," she said. "And you're trembling."

"It's grown cold, hon," I mumbled. "Fall is upon us."

Luba snuggled closer to me and soon fell asleep. I was awake. I needed to make a decision.

Chapter 17

Crime and Punishment

THE COURT HEARING IN SAMVEL'S CASE TOOK PLACE IN NOVEMBER 1998, in the city of Luhansk, about ninety miles from Donetsk. I got up early to have breakfast with my family. The four of us sat at our small table and chatted about this and that. There was a bright light in the kitchen, and the window was dark. Outside, it was pouring rain, a cold autumn shower without lightning and thunder, which made it especially grim and dull. I didn't want to go anywhere. I wanted to stay at home and read some thick, boring novel, then doze off, waiting for my children to return from their studies.

Sergiy was a second-year student at the same Institute of Soviet Trade that I'd graduated from twenty years earlier. Recently, he'd cut his long blond hair and thrown all his Nirvana relics into the closet. Meanwhile, Svitlana was still going through her neopunk period and dying strands of her hair bright blue. Luba and I didn't like it too much, but we kept our opinions to ourselves. There was nothing like a generational conflict in our family. There was nothing like the forty-year-old crisis. We were all very close, and I think we loved each other as much as was possible. My duty was to save our wonderful family, even if it doesn't count four, only three, without me.

Neither Luba nor Sergiy nor Svitlana knew what decision I had made. On top of this, they didn't know why I was going to Lugansk for a court hearing in the criminal case of Samvel. I told my family it would be a normal business trip, so they weren't worried and devoured our breakfast with gusto.

Chapter 17

Meanwhile, time inexorably devoured my life. I looked at the watch and advised my children to dress warmly. They looked at each other as if saying, "The hell we will, no matter what!" I ran my hand through Svitlana's blue hair and got up from the table. It was time to say goodbye. Luba kissed me on the cheek and asked me not to be late for dinner. I promised, although I was not sure that I could keep my word when I'd carried out my plan—*if* I could make it happen.

The car was waiting for me downstairs. I climbed into the back seat, lost in my thoughts. Like I said, I'd already made up my mind, and my decision was to testify not in favor of Samvel but against him. This was my only chance to get rid of him once and for all. I wanted him to get the punishment he deserved. To some extent, my belated repentance took place here, but on the whole, my considerations were purely selfish. I had a future only as long as Samvel Martirosyan was locked up. His lack of freedom presupposed my freedom. And vice versa. There was no third option.

Throughout the hour-long trip to Luhansk, I mentally prepared my speech in court. The two guys accompanying me were unfamiliar to me, so they didn't bother me with questions or chatting. We drove along the wet highway at breakneck speed and in complete silence. With a high degree of probability, the car radio was playing some songs, but they were definitely not "The Road to Hell" or "Stairway to Heaven."

So nothing and no one stopped me from thinking.

And I was thinking . . .

I was thinking hard . . .

The Ukrainian judicial system had its own characteristics that are hardly understandable to foreigners. By law, the country had a jury trial, although, in practice, the situation was different. Professional judges were opposed to the involvement of outsiders who could prevent them from delivering "ordered" verdicts, so they rejected jurors under all sorts of far-fetched pretexts. Nonetheless, Samvel had insisted that his case be considered properly. Thus, I had to appear before three judges and three jurors. My first task was to convince these six to give Samvel the harshest possible sentence. My second task was to leave Lugansk and return home alive.

What was I going to do next? To be honest, I had nothing more than waiting to see how it all would end. For several hours I carefully weighed my chances and came to the conclusion that I was unlikely to be subject to vengeance. I was sure that all Samvel's mobsters had become disunited and disorganized without his ruling power. Whenever he'd gone to prison, they'd all run away in all directions and tried not to get into trouble. In addition, I was going to ask the court to protect me as a witness. Such protection was unlikely to be effective in Ukraine of the 1990s, but the fact itself could prevent gangsters from taking decisive action. As long as their Papa was behind steel bars, I might feel safe—relatively safe.

These were my thoughts at that time. If I were to describe more than what was on the surface, then, in fact, I was not definitely sure that I would dare to openly oppose Samvel. So far it was just a plan that was not put into execution. And to tell the truth, my resolve wavered when we drove up to the Luhansk court, whose grey building stood dismally against the cloudy sky from where small rain drops were falling. I saw at least two dozen cars with tinted windows in the driveway, all of which could have belonged to Samvel's associates or his Armenian relatives. Do I dare to challenge them? Or will I prudently pronounce the words that the gangsters expect from me? Both hemispheres of my brain gave exactly opposite answers to these questions. When I entered the courthouse, my steps were a couple of inches shorter than usual. I felt as though in a dream. My thoughts and impressions were confused and fleeting.

While the lawyer explained to me at length and in detail what I would do and how, I pretended to listen to him, but his entire speech was unrecognizable to me. I heard only separate words not connected by a single meaning. I was dumb and numb.

In the corridor Tigran approached me and offered me his cheek for a traditional Mafia kiss. Kissing him, I felt like Judas, although Tigran was not Christ, like his older brother. He asked if I was ready. I looked at him and replied, "Yes, sure," and that was true. When I saw Tigran, all my memories and feelings came flooding back to me, and I realized that I wasn't going to keep my mouth shut and wouldn't lie when I was called to testify. Doubts disappeared. I became cold-blooded and concentrated, or should I say, I *decided* I ought to be cold-blooded and concentrated.

Chapter 17

Tigran told me that he'd returned from Armenia specifically to attend the event and that it was extremely risky on his part.

"No risk, no gain," I said, thinking not of him but of myself.

Tigran tapped me on the shoulder and asked if I had prepared my speech. I nodded. My speech had to be extremely concise and precise. From the start I had to say was that Samvel was the leader of a criminal gang. Just a few very simple words . . . very difficult words.

A judicial clerk led me into the courtroom and sat me down in the seat assigned to me. There were so many people in the room that one had to be careful of oxygen deprivation. All four windows along the left wall were closed. There were no bars on them, but I associated the place with a jail. This impression was probably triggered by the iron cage to the right of the judge's table. The construction was preparing for Samvel.

A narrow aisle had divided the courtroom in half: at the end of the aisle, there was a wooden platform for speakers with rows of chairs in front of it; the chairs had flip-up seats that had to be pushed down before you could sit on them and were connected to each other, like in a cinema, so that they couldn't be moved. The first rows were reserved for the Martirosyan parents and relatives, whose voices sounded like the buzz of an orient bazaar or an audience waiting for the show to begin. As far as I could tell, no newspaper reporters or TV journalists had been allowed inside the courtroom. There were one hundred people or so in the audience.

I was sitting in the third row on the left, among the other witnesses: Igor; Oksana; Konstantin, who was with his wife; my former secretary; and some people who were strangers to me. As for the true bandits, there were fewer of them in the courtroom than I expected to see, but this did not bring me any relief. All these people constantly inhaled and exhaled air, filling the enclosed space with carbon dioxide. There was nothing to breathe, so at times, I felt like I was close to fainting. I hadn't heard the term panic attack in the nineties, but I think I was experiencing something like that back then. My heart was ready to jump out of my chest, my head was spinning, and my face was covered with perspiration.

Igor leaned over to me and asked what was wrong with me, but I could not utter a word in response, fearing that I would vomit. He handed me his handkerchief. I rubbed it across my wet forehead and looked around. The mobsters sat back in their chairs, chewing their gum and exchanging remarks. It seemed to me that they were all looking at me. I turned away.

The secretary came up and asked me to sign some document. I hardly understood what she was saying to me and forced myself to take the pen in my stiff fingers. As usual, I signed with my left hand, changing my signature. The secretary walked farther down the aisle. I heard one of the mobsters call her a chick behind me, and the clicking of her heels quickened.

Streams of sweat trickled down my back. I looked longingly at the window, as if hoping that it would open by itself and let a portion of fresh air into the room. Outside, part of the neighboring building was visible, surrounded by primitive scaffolding. There, at the level of the second floor, sat two men in construction helmets, hunched over in the pouring rain. Their jackets shone with water. "Why do they work in leather jackets?" I thought. "And why don't they wait downstairs for the rain to stop?"

The jury was brought in, and they took their places. Looking the jury over, I noticed that all of them avoided looking at the audience. It seemed to me that they looked rather scared, and I thought that, most likely, Samvel would escape punishment again, being found not guilty. Will my testimony change anything? I swallowed several times to moisten my parched throat.

The judge and his two associates entered the courtroom, and everybody rose in deferential silence. The judge's black robe was short and didn't meet on the belly. He didn't look like a man capable of dealing with a Mafia boss. It was easy for me to imagine him in a store with a cart or in a garden, watering flowers, but not as a conquering hero. He was a tired, middle-aged man, wearing glasses and a tight robe, who had no intention of saving the world or even a small part of it.

When he and his two associates had taken their seats, Samvel was brought into the room. He wore a green tracksuit and white sneakers. His hair was cut so short that his scalp looked bald. He sat down on a chair

Chapter 17

in the middle of the barred room for the accused and spoke in Armenian to his mother and father. The judge had to reprimand him three times before he fell silent. The two wards behind Samvel stood motionless, like the stone idols of Easter Island. They were afraid of him, I saw it clearly. And I heard the judge's voice when he addressed Samvel. It was not an authoritative, confident voice. There was almost a pleading intonation in it.

I have often read books in which prisoners are compared to caged animals. In the case of Samvel, this analogy did not work. As a child, I used to go to the zoo and stand for a long time near enclosures with wolves or tigers to meet their gaze. When this happened, I saw nothing there except a feeling of being hunted. I can assure you that Samvel didn't have this *caged look*. He behaved like he was in charge of the situation, and he most likely was.

Our eyes met and remained locked for a second or two. Then Samvel turned his gaze to someone else, but I managed to understand everything he wanted to tell me. I also realized that he would definitely be released from prison, no matter how this trial ended. My testimony couldn't change anything. What was the point in calling Samvel a crime boss publicly? Everyone already knew that and could not do anything about it. They didn't even try. Then why should I try?

We so easily justify our weaknesses, indecision, and cowardice. It is so difficult for us to show our strength, perseverance, conviction. In any case, these words apply to me.

Applied. This is the more accurate word.

While I sat in stupor, tormented by doubts, the moment of my vital test inexorably approached. As soon as everyone was present, the proceedings began. First, Samvel's attorney started his plea to find his client not guilty, because he felt the police had arrested him on false charges. Then the prosecutor came forward and made the exact opposite statement. He said that the charges were not false and included mayhem, extortion of money, exploiting the helpless state of victims, blackmail, and robbery. He took a pause and continued: "Samvel Martirosyan also indicted for murder in the first degree . . ."

A single gasp filled the room. Then the resonance of indignant voices spread. The choir died down as the judge banged his polished yellow gavel, calling for silence. Samvel jumped up from his chair and screamed at the prosecutor in a high voice close to a treble: "You bastard, don't you dare slander me! My hands are clean! There's not a drop of blood on them!"

The judge stood up and raised his gavel, preparing to knock on the table again.

These were unusually loud and frequent bangs, one following after another.

Bang-bang-bang-bang!

Along with this, the two windows of the courtroom cracked and crumbled to the floor. Machine gun shots at close range, a splintering of glass, and a scattering of plaster on the opposite wall made a sudden and dramatic interruption to the trial proceeding.

In a somewhat incomprehensible way, my field of vision expanded and acquired supernatural vigilance, allowing me to watch everything and everyone at once.

I could see the judge throw his arms up to cover his face as a hail of shattered glass pelted him and, the next moment, fall heavily backward . . .

. . . and the attorney promptly jump over the desk, looking for cover behind it . . .

. . . and the secretary, writhing in hysterics . . .

. . . and each of the public in the first rows of seats—screaming . . . running . . . ducking . . . hunching . . . crawling . . .

But Samvel was the first to react to the shots, falling face down on the floor so that the bullets would not hit him. He did this before his wards had their weapons ready to return fire. But the shelling of the courtroom had stopped. The men in the wet leather jackets had disappeared from the scaffolding outside the windows. There was nothing now visible there except the gray rain.

Not realizing that the assassination attempt was over, people made their way to the doors, which were blocked by police. I saw Igor in the crowd; he was helping Momma Martirosyan. I saw gangsters there,

Chapter 17

hurrying to leave the place. Only two or three of them rushed to the windows to cover their Papa. He himself continued to lie on the floor of the cage, not daring to raise his head.

He was taken out of the courtroom as soon as the panic subsided. The judge was carried out on a stretcher, his bloody arm hanging lifelessly down. After that we were all kept in the hall for about an hour. The investigator asked me a few banal questions and told me to sign a protocol. I did it with my trembling left hand and left the courthouse.

The rain had stopped. The parking lot was cleared of cars with tinted windows. The area in front of the two broken windows was surrounded by yellow caution tape, shaking in the wind. A half-dozen police officers wandered under the scaffolding around a nearby house, searching for shell casings and other evidence.

The show was over, yet there was no happy ending. There was no ending at all.

I returned home by bus and spent several days in bed with a high fever. I drank gallons of raspberry tea and a linden decoction. When my bladder was about to burst, I forced myself to get up and trudged to the bathroom. Then I would come back and fall face down on the bed. My strength left me. I didn't want anything.

It was pneumonia—very severe but not long-lasting. While I was fighting the disease, a couple of reports about the incident in Lugansk flashed on television newscasts. It said that the judge was wounded, while the crime leader, Samvel Martirosyan, having understood from the first shots that it was an assassination attempt against him, prudently sprawled on the floor, which saved his life. The killers armed with machine guns fired at the windows of the court from a car as well as from the scaffolding of the building being repaired opposite. After such an extraordinary event, the hearing of the case was moved to Donetsk, where Samvel was sentenced to fourteen years in prison and was transferred somewhere in Western Ukraine.

The news was more healing to me than any medicine. Looking back, I found it a miracle. As if somebody above me just clapped their hands, and it was on. I didn't have to act as a witness, and Tigran disappeared from my horizon again. No one bothered or threatened me. Left without a leader, Samvel's gang went deep underground or on the run. He himself was in custody, trembling for his own skin.

For about a month, I walked the streets looking around, but once the new year arrived, I started a new life. As soon as 1999 started, I found myself a quite-decent and promising new job of a regional manager for a large company that sold equipment for shops and restaurants. Specializing in fridges, freezers, and refrigerated counters, it wore the title Iceworld and was based in Odessa, with a network of branches throughout Ukraine.

Since the company's headquarters along with its management were located 350 miles from Donetsk, I was left to my own devices most of the time. I had an assistant and a trading floor the size of a tennis court. It was registered as an exhibition center to hide the proceeds from the tax men. We sold refrigerators, counters, and freezers for cash, but we didn't have a cash register. For what? There were many hiding places in the sales area.

Twice a month I put money—from $20,000 to $40,000—in my bosom and went by the night bus to Odessa. These were perilous journeys, with stops at bus stations full of drunkards, vagabonds, and bullies. One can't sit on a cold bus for ten hours without visiting the loo. Each such sortie carried the risk of being robbed, and a couple of times, I was very close to this.

Another difficulty of my work was that my assistant and I would unload trucks full of refrigerators with our own hands, as this allowed us to save considerable money, which we divided in half. As for the discount system, here I managed it myself, playing with percentages at my own peril and risk. I considered this my rightful reward for the prosperity of the outlandish firm in my hometown.

The Iceworld exhibition center occupied the right wing of the Youth Sports Palace, which stood, isolated, about two hundred yards from the nearest street. It was on the edge of the rather-deserted park, where occasional joggers and couples walked about along leafy tracks and alleys, holding each other by the hand or other parts of the body. Every week a corpse was discovered there, and most often, it was women who had been raped and murdered. This did not stop more and more new couples from

Chapter 17

entering the park in search of romance. Essentially, it was a small forest in the center of Donetsk—the maddest and wildest version of New York City's Central Park one could create. In my childhood we kids often ran there to play (a secret to our parents) until we came across a dead man hanging from a tree. In short, it was an ominous and deserted place where I lured customers through billboards along the street.

We usually functioned until 6:00 p.m. In winter it was already dark at this time. Visitors were rare in the evening, so both my assistant and I rejoiced at the appearance of each buyer. In February 1999 one such visit reminded me of what time and place I was in.

That buyer entered the Iceworld exhibition center just before closing. He was a young man with an absentminded smile and a wandering look, in which one could read complete indifference to shop equipment. He pointed to the first refrigerator he came across and asked the price of it. Then he pointed to several other units and said that we could load everything into the van parked near the entrance. I told him the total cost of his purchases. He replied that I don't have to worry about money, turned to the glass display case, and waved his hand invitingly.

In the next minute, three more guests entered the hall and positioned themselves in such a way that my assistant and I were surrounded and pressed against the wall. I immediately realized that things were bad—or even worse than that. In front of us were standing a row of real bandits; I'd seen enough of them to determine their social status. They didn't threaten us with weapons, yet I knew they were armed. Their leader checked the cash register and took some cash from there, which I kept there for such occasions. Then he repeated his order for us to take out the freezers and load them into the van.

It was not a prank, not a stupid joke. Everything was happening in reality very quickly and realistically. Something clicked in my brain—some kind of toggle switch that turns on inside us in moments of threat.

"I'm working for Samvel," I said in a voice so calm that it surprised me. "The store belongs to him."

The four exchanged speedy glances among themselves.

"Your Samvel is now in the slammer," their leader said.

"Anyone can end up there," I said, looking into his eyes. "In the same prison, even in the same cell with him."

It wasn't courage. It was some kind of inspiration. I didn't choose words. I played my part ad lib.

The robbers exchanged glances again and then left the hall, without saying a word. Samvel's name still had weight in the criminal world. It was like casting a magic spell. My assistant looked at me questioningly and asked what would have happened if the robbers had not believed my bluff.

"It wasn't a bluff,' I answered. "I really know Samvel—closely."

"Wow," my assistant said, shaking his head.

Although Samvel's name saved me one more time, I immediately threw him out of my brain, longing to forget him, as I tried also to forget Tigran and all those last years, saturated with adrenaline, violence, danger, and constant feelings of guilt. Recently, I'd started a new life, calm and measured, and I didn't want to look back at what hurt me. Who needs pain?

The devastating consequences of the collapse of the USSR gradually faded away. Dust settled, shocking quakes stopped, and people rubbed their eyes and found that the ground no longer slipped from under their feet. The dead economy was coming back to life, gaining strength like a zombie. The circulation of money accelerated, trade gained momentum, and there were more and more shops and cafés everywhere.

The Iceworld's owner, Antonov, saw this boom in the economy and was eager to seize the moment. He insisted that I visit all the new supermarkets in Donetsk, offering them complete sets of equipment, from racks to freezers. When I'd collected an extensive list of potential clients, Antonov came to negotiate with them personally.

On the day of his arrival, I had a business meeting, so I showed up for work late. Antonov greeted me dryly and said that we needed to talk. I caught my assistant's eye and sensed something was wrong. I listened to Antonov warily, not expecting anything good, and my worst expectations were realized. Antonov told me that he valued his company's reputation very much and couldn't allow it to suffer because of my compromising connections with the underworld.

Chapter 17

"Sergey, you are casting a shadow on our image," he said at the end. "You'll have to leave. I hope you understand. Do you?"

He was a smooth young man with a round, red-cheeked face and shiny brown hair parted precisely in the middle. You could tell at a glance that he was successful and always would be successful.

I nodded and asked, "My assistant will take my place, ain't he?"

"Definitely yes," Antonov replied. "I need dedicated people."

We both looked at my assistant. He lowered his gaze and pretended to read the instruction manual for the refrigerated display case.

I took my monthly salary and left. The dismissal from the company was an unpleasant event, but not a tragedy. I knew I would find another job. I knew I could do things that were not taught in commercial colleges. And I had balls enough to get up again and again when I was knocked down or I'd fallen.

It was a lot.

Chapter 18

An Offer I Couldn't Refuse

It was May or June 1999. Or maybe July. During the day the city heats up in the sun so much that it does not have time to cool down during the night. It's only early morning, but I'm already hot and sweaty. I carry two huge nylon bags in both hands, trying to keep them off the pavement. This is a difficult task. The damn checkered bags are not only big but simply huge. Each one can accommodate an adult man inside and weighs about one hundred pounds. Okay, fifty. Well, okay, okay, let it be forty—but it's still a very heavy burden.

I carry my bags to the clothing market. It's about a mile from my house. The market is on a spacious asphalt area, fenced on all sides by a continuous concrete wall that is twice the height of a man. There are no awnings, no counters, no toilets, nothing. This operates only on weekends and does not offer any amenities. Crowds of people gather there—about one-third are sellers and two-thirds, potential buyers.

Stacks of banknotes change hands here to be stuffed into wallets, bags, and pockets. Pickpockets, swindlers, and gypsies prowl the square—you need to keep an eye on them if you don't want to be left without money or things. Once, my bag was stolen, and once, I'd brought home two hundred counterfeit dollars. I'm a bad market trader; I have no soul for this.

I know it now, and I knew it then.

At first my wife was selling in the market, while my responsibility was to bring and take away bags filled to capacity with goods. Now Luba comes to relieve me only at noon, when she finishes her household

Chapter 18

chores. This is only fair. After all, I am an unemployed man who has a lot of free time.

After leaving the Iceworld, I was unable to find a decent job. Was my being almost forty-five years old the reason? Or did I have "Crime" written on my forehead? Be that as it may, company heads didn't consider me a suitable candidate. Finally, I found myself in the market square, and I didn't know where I would be tomorrow.

Getting to work, I usually spread large plastic sheets on the asphalt, carefully pressing their corners with bricks or stones. This was my counter. Sun, rain, and dust could quickly spoil goods, so trade had to be nonstop. Luba and I bought men's leather jackets in Istanbul, women's clothing in Krakow, unisex shoes in Moscow, and children's clothes in Odessa. These were tedious journeys on which our survival depended. At that time the market fed us.

In the foreseeable future, Luba planned to open her own clothing store, and I was looking forward to it. The bazaar business was real torture for me. I suffered not so much physically as mentally, as I was deeply ashamed to sell cheap jeans and dresses in front of hundreds of people passing by. I would lower my eyes and turn away when I saw familiar faces. But they still recognized me and came up to me, asking how my business was and how much these Chinese socks cost, and this faded Polish sweater, and these Adidas sneakers, which didn't look like Adidas sneakers at all. For me it was humiliation. I felt like a pathetic loser, looked upon with contempt by others.

On one of these painful weekends, I noticed some unusual activity in the part of the market where all the merchants stood in the rows, forming passages for customers. At the beginning of my "corridor," a large procession appeared, attracting everyone's attention. People turned their heads, craned their necks, and even stood on their tiptoes to see better. I thought that some deputy or mayor had honored us with his arrival, but it was someone more significant.

I saw Samvel approaching me.

He walked next to Oksana, with two tall bodyguards on either side of them. He was wearing a black shirt, which made his face pale, like that of a dead man. They were followed by a retinue of two dozen men of varying ages. Two guards walked ahead of the procession, clearing the way for Samvel. He behaved like a king among the mob. He really was a king. A criminal one.

I bent over, pretending to move my goods from place to place. This was done to hide my face from Samvel, and it was as if I were making a deep bow to him. The procession approached. As it passed by, a bill with a portrait of Benjamin Franklin fell right in front of my nose, which was a generous donation to a beggar. I straightened up and looked after Samvel. He didn't turn back, considering it beneath his dignity. But a few minutes later, his messenger approached me. It was Cowboy, whom I had known from the very beginning of my criminal odyssey. His thick Mick Jaggerish lips were pulled back into a grin.

He lived somewhere in the neighborhood, and every time we met by chance, Cowboy would complain about how the Martirosyan brothers had left him and their other "foot soldiers" without any means of livelihood. Now he was beaming with happiness, saying, "Our Papa got an early release."

"He got really mad when he saw you here," the Cowboy said. "Told the guys to bring you to him in the evening. He wants to talk to you, and I bet he's going to take you back. Now everything will be hunky-dory!"

"Mm-hmm," I repeated automatically. "Hunky-dory. Just terrific."

Cowboy looked at me in bewilderment.

"Hey, aren't you happy, bro?"

I told him that I had decided to retire. I guess I wanted to test the reaction of an ordinary gangster before expressing my intention to the boss. Cowboy frowned.

"You can't just walk out on Papa like this," he said. "Unless in a coffin—or even worse, no remnants or coffin at all."

Lowering his voice, he told me that behind Samvel's house, there was a barn where a cast-iron bathtub and large glass containers with hydrochloric acid were stored.

"Whoever is bathed in this fucking bath will not need a funeral," he said. "There was a man and—whoosh!—there's no man, only rags of meat and skin, floating in acid. You better keep your mouth shut, bro.

Chapter 18

Papa came out of prison as mad as hell. Don't be looking to get your ass kicked."

Cowboy's caution sounded like a scary campfire story, but deep inside, I knew it was true. I spent the whole day, the whole evening, and the whole night in anxiety, waiting for the doorbell to ring. Then several more days and nights passed without any further incidents. Samvel seemed to deliberately let me worry longer. He sent a car for me only a week later, when my nerves were like violin strings.

It was a Friday evening, I think, because Luba was putting things into our "shopping" bags. It was not an easy task. When I tried to do this, I usually couldn't fit the last pair of shoes or jackets. I didn't interfere with or help Luba, but most likely, I was lying on the sofa with a book—it might have been Stephen King's *Bag of Bones* or something like that. If my children were at home (I'm pretty sure that's how it was), then Sergiy was probably playing the guitar, using vague jazz chords, and Svitlana was listening to rock music through headphones while drawing sketches of outfits for nonexistent models. In any case, it was a normal family evening, with cozy lighting in the living room and delicious smells in the kitchen. When the doorbell rang, this whole idyll collapsed. The ringing was sharp and demanding. I looked through the door peephole and saw two tall male figures on the landing. "Come on, let's go," said one of them. I didn't need to ask where. I got dressed and went out.

As I approached the elevator, Luba called out to me and asked when I would be back. I looked at her standing in the doorway. More than anything, I wanted to be home again instead of driving through the night to a bandit's lair. But I had little choice. Taking a sulfuric acid bath did not seem like a worthy end to my life's journey.

"Let's see how it goes," I said and stepped inside the elevator car.

It was cramped for the three of us there. Samvel's guys were large, so my eyes were at the level of their chins. I felt small and helpless. Why on the earth did Samvel cling to me? Aren't there enough other businessmen in Donetsk? Why me, always me? Why did I deserve such a fate?

These were meaningless questions. I myself was to blame for what happened to me. There were many roads in front of me, but I'd chosen the one that led me to Samvel. And it now depended only on me for whether

I would be able to get through this or whether I would remain there until my death. As far as I knew, lifetime in a criminal environment was short. I should have found a way out before this ended.

The car brought me to a familiar house, which looked rather like a military fortification under a camouflage net. The gate opened and closed behind me as though it was the jaws of a leviathan. I got out of the car, crossed the yard, and entered a hall with half a dozen men who were watching TV, playing backgammon, or just lounging in a chair. They looked at me indifferently. Silver returned my greeting with a lazy wave of his long hand. Salim sat motionless, staring at me. His look reminded me of the existence of a secret barn with a cast-iron bathtub, even though this detail had not left my mind since I'd heard about it.

The house smelled of oriental cuisine and male socks. It was so large that it could comfortably accommodate at least two dozen people, mostly men, half of whom were Armenians. Tigran didn't live with Samvel, nor did his parents. If I were in their position, I would do exactly the same. This was not a home for family life. It was home to a constant war—a war with the whole world. It was a barracks-like environment, with pornographic magazines scattered everywhere and television screens showing boxing matches or unassuming karate films starring Bruce Lee: *bonk! bang! clang!*

As I sat among those tough guys, awaiting an audience, I noticed that the surface of the coffee table in front of me was covered in cuts and realized that somebody had played the favorite gangster game here: stabbing a knife in between fingers that are splayed wide. Chewing-gum wrappers and torn packages of salted nuts were scattered on the carpet under my feet. Unwittingly, I overheard a conversation between two guys sitting nearby. They were discussing some businesswoman who had recently been held in a garage while her husband collected money to pay off her debt to Samvel. As far as I understood, the captive was subjected to gang rape in a perverted form. Among the rapists was the same Robic whom Tigran and I had once defended against drunk men in Makiivka. She vomited on him, and he became the butt of friendly banter after that.

Sitting there, I told myself that this time, I would not let this scummy quagmire suck me completely into its depths. That evening, I decided I

Chapter 18

needed to escape from Donetsk with my family. I didn't know exactly when I would do this or how, but I started looking in this direction. You may say that I should have thought about this much earlier, and I agree with you—although this was not as simple a task as it might seem. My children studied at their educational institutions, my wife had begun to build her own business, we were entangled in numerous kinship ties, and we did not have sufficient savings to buy us an apartment in another city.

How long did it take me to realize my plan? One month? Two? Three? The most difficult thing was convincing Luba and our children of the need to move away. They hardly wanted to ruin and rebuild their lives because of me. But alternatively, I couldn't leave them and go alone, because that meant I'd be left without a family. I wasn't going to do it. The "family" that Samvel offered me could not replace the real one. It was just a gang, and I didn't belong to it. All my former illusions had been dispelled. I was surrounded not by friends but by enemies. It was time for me to get the hell out of this environment.

When I appeared before Samvel, the first thing he did was reprimand me for disgracing him and his family by selling "tattered rags in the fucking marketplace"—that's how he put it. "How could you stoop to shit like that, Maidukov!" he exclaimed in his high voice, ready to break into falsetto. "Why didn't you come to me for help?"

I didn't say that I was tired of living on his handouts. And I didn't mention that he would hardly have remembered me if I hadn't caught his eye in the marketplace. I only told him that no one had notified me of his release.

"It was a fucking big surprise for everyone," Samvel said smugly. "They thought they locked me away for the rest of my life, but here I am again."

He spread his arms to the sides, as if inviting me to admire him. He was wearing an emerald tracksuit and snow-white running shoes that had certainly never been used for jogging. A golden cross glittered on his chest, as unchanging as the dark semicircles under his eyes. His office had a low ceiling and was decorated with a giant globe made of polished mahogany. On the floor was a handwoven oriental rug with tassels. Samvel and I sat on massive mustard-colored velour chairs. On the wall behind him was a poster of a tanned blonde in a white bikini. The shade of the palm leaves made her body zebra striped.

I don't know if these details are important. I don't think so. But I retained them in my memory for many years, and therefore, they had meaning for me. Like, for example, the fact that Samvel's cheek, offered to me for a kiss, always felt like sandpaper to my lips. Or his way of giving money. First, he would show it to me, waiting for me to extend my hand, and then he'd throw the bills in front of me. That's what he did that time, too, and I took the damn money. I used to do it every time and then curse myself, but I never refused, never said no. Samvel not only subjugated me, but he'd also bought me. And I was sold. This was the truth that I'd hid even from myself.

Five hundred bucks was enough for me to ask Samvel what I had to do. He looked at me for a long, unblinking, basilic glance and asked me about my cooperation with the SBU.

It was a bold, unexpected stroke that completely stunned me for a while. How did he know about this? What will happen to me now? Is Samvel going to finish me for being a traitor? I remembered Salim's hateful gaze . . . and the special bath in the barn . . . and my children, whom I did not hug before leaving home . . . then, in the flow of these panicky thoughts, a guess arose that gave me the strength to maintain external calmness.

Tigran! He must have told his brother about my former work with Momot. That I was the president of a company that enjoyed the patronage of officers of the Security Service of Ukraine, which didn't make me a spy or informant. And yet I had to lick my lips before answering.

"It was only an episode, Sam," I said. "I hardly knew these people. I had met them two or three times only, so I wasn't very familiar with them."

"But I s'pose you're *still* familiar with them," Samvel said insistently. "And they probably remember you, right?"

What was it? An examination? A test of my loyalty? Did Samvel suspect me?

I shrugged. "It was a long time ago, Sam. We haven't met since."

Chapter 18

Samvel's reaction was absolutely unexpected. He told me that he was looking for a secret meeting with SBU officers. He wanted to cooperate with them, as Momot had done before him. In his opinion, Andrew Andrewich and Ivan Ivanovich could have saved him from criminal prosecution. He viewed the SBU as his protection from the police. And he was confident that this cooperation would be mutually beneficial.

"I can be helpful to them, and they can be helpful to me," Samvel said quietly. "Together we'll achieve a lot. Call your friends from the SBU right now, and make an appointment with them."

I told him that they were not my friends and that I didn't have the opportunity to call them, because their phone numbers had long been thrown out of my head. Samvel said that in this case, I would go to them personally. He was always impatient, like a child. He wanted everything to happen instantly, as if by magic. He never knew how to or wanted to wait. For nothing. For no one. Under no circumstances.

I began to explain to him that this was impossible, because a person cannot just go to the Security Service from the street and offer his services, but Samvel cut me off sharply.

"You're not a man from the street," he said. "You're one of *my* people. Those security men, they've surely heard of me, 'cos everybody knows me in the city, so I tell you they'll accept you. Maidukov, I want you to be my representative in the negotiations, got it? I can't go there myself. You're gonna do it for me. Tomorrow."

My jaw dropped. I tried to convince Samvel otherwise, telling him that such meetings should be done advisedly, not from any sudden whim. He refused to listen to me and repeated that he intended to send me to the Regional Department of the SBU tomorrow—there'd be no postponing my visit until later.

Samvel personally took me there in his black armored Mercedes. It was the first time I saw him behind the steering wheel. And for the first time, I saw him without an escort cortege. It was just the two of us inside the car. Despite the mortal danger that awaited him at every step, around every corner, Samvel didn't take a single guard with him. Everybody was told that we were going to visit his sick father in the hospital. The secrecy of this kind was justified. Cooperation with any law enforcement agencies was regarded as unacceptable in a criminal environment. By making contact with the SBU, Samvel was violating the unwritten law of the Mafia, which could have cost him his life. However, his life was always hanging by a thread.

We pulled up to the SBU building on Shchors Street, and I got the feeling that we were being watched from the windows as if every one of them had eyes, looking and waiting silently. And there were undoubtedly surveillance cameras that were recording our arrival. The headquarters of the former KGB organization was known to every citizen of Donetsk. Since Soviet times, people have always tried to avoid the building, or they've lowered their heads and quickened their pace when passing by. It was always quiet and deserted there. The entire street seemed haunted: no children playing nearby, no passersby, and not even animals—just cars.

"Go," Samvel said.

I wanted to say something like "I'd let sleeping dogs lie," but he repeated urgently, "I said, 'Go, Maidukov, go.'"

Feeling like a complete idiot who voluntarily sticks his head in a noose, I got out of the car and headed toward the four-story gray building surrounded by a concrete fence. Before entering inside, for some reason, I buttoned the top button of my shirt. Maybe I wanted to look as formal as possible.

The lobby was silent and gloomy. The armed sentry stared at me as I entered through the door. The duty officer at the glassed-in counter asked me what I needed. I asked to be let in to see Major Andrew Andrewich.

"Surname?" the officer demanded.

"I don't know. I think his name is Andrew Andrewich."

"This is not enough."

"Then Ivan Ivanovich," I said. "He's a colonel."

"Surname?" the officer demanded one more time.

I spread my hands in a gesture that said, "I don't know." The duty officer gave me a stern look, picked up the phone, and spoke to someone, covering the receiver with his hand.

Five minutes later, a man of thirty or thirty-five in a plain dark suit appeared in front of me. All I remember about his appearance is his weird Julius Caesar hairstyle. He jerked his head, inviting me to follow him.

Chapter 18

We crossed the lobby into a narrow corridor and entered the small room behind the door he had opened. I noticed that the door did not have a sign or any identification marks on it. The man stepped aside, allowing me to look past him. There was a table and two chairs, but he did not invite me to sit, making it clear that our conversation would not be long. I thought that this room was intended to receive anonymous visitors and would be thoroughly bugged.

"I'm listening to you, Sergey Georgevich," the man said in a neutral tone.

How did he know my name? I didn't introduce myself to the duty officer. It finally dawned on me that I shouldn't have come here with questions about Andrew Andrewich and Ivan Ivanovich. They might not like my initiative. There were no windows in the room, but there was another door in the far corner. Where did this lead? Maybe to the basement? If they took me there, no one would know where I'd gone or where to look for me.

"It was a mistake," I mumbled. "I just was looking for some of my old mates . . . and, you know, mm . . . " I stumbled, not knowing what to say.

"Your mates?" the man in the dark suit asked. "*Here?*"

His voice was full of poisoned irony.

"It looks like I've had the wrong address," I said, squeezing it out of my throat. "May I go?"

"No, you cannot, Sergey Georgevich," the man said. "First, I'd like to ask you a few questions."

Looking at me searchingly, he asked if I wished to make some kind of statement. When I answered in the negative, he inquired if I had any information that could be used for the benefit of national security. Again, my response was "No, I haven't." The collar was choking me, and I hoped that the man didn't see the perspiration on my forehead. It was too hot a day to be in a room with no windows and no air-conditioning.

In a voice as monotone as rain, the man in the dark suit explained to me that withholding information of this kind is tantamount to committing a crime. "Are you sure that you've nothing more to say?" he asked at last, still watching me. Having received an affirmative answer from me, he said that in that case, he had something to tell me.

An Offer I Couldn't Refuse

I listened to him, looking into his eyes. He advised me not to play with fire and then added, "We know who owns the car you arrived in. Now go and tell your boss to never come back around here ever again. He'd better stay away from our organization like the devil from a cross. When required, we'll find him ourselves. And you, too, Sergey Georgevich."

With that, the man in the strict dark suit left the room, leaving the door open. This meant that I could be free, and I didn't stay in the stuffy room for one damn extra second. The officer's farewell words rang in my ears. There was a threat in them, which promised nothing good for either me or Samvel.

I left the gray building in dismay, but I forced myself to collect my thoughts and then steeled my gut and my face to prepare for the next round of my game. I wasn't a particularly good businessman, but I was smart, and it wasn't like I could stop being that. At any rate, I knew how to get out of difficult situations, that was for sure. In the short time it took me to walk from the SBU headquarters to the black Mercedes, I'd managed to come up with a version of the conversation that would suit Samvel. I gave him only those fragments of the dialogue that he would like. After listening to my interpretation, he nodded thoughtfully.

"Are you saying they will contact me?"

"That man said so," I confirmed.

For a few moments, Samvel's face expressed self-satisfaction, which was suddenly replaced by suspicion.

"No one must ever know where we were or why," he said in a low, menacing voice. "Otherwise, I'll rip your tongue out and feed it to you. Remember this, Maidukov."

"I will," I muttered.

How else could it be? Such things are not often heard. I still remember Samvel's words and the way they were said. I would like to forget, but I've not been able to.

Isn't that what he wanted?

CHAPTER 19

Between Three Fires

IN THAT SUMMER OF 1999, I RECEIVED A NEW JOB FROM SAMVEL THAT was no less strange and uncertain than all the previous ones.

His reasons for keeping me with him may seem a mystery, but the explanation was quite simple. The reason for his attachment to me was not a special value of my brain. The fact of the matter was that Samvel had no other candidates—if he even thought of replacing me. No decent businessman would risk his good name and everything, including life itself, to collaborate with him. I was the only one left at his disposal in the business field—his best card, his ace of trumps. Okay, maybe not an ace but a jack or ten. A feather in the hands better than a bird in the air.

Outright banditry had lived out its last days in Ukraine. Cool mafiosi one by one became respectable businessmen (the luckiest of them is Rinat Akhmetov, who was destined to soon become the uncrowned king of Donetsk, then the country's richest person, according to *Forbes*' wealth tracker). Samvel was in hurry to jump on the latest bandwagon of whatever other clans were doing in Ukraine at the time. In a sense he was the last of the Mohicans. His competitors and yesterday's buddies bought up factories, set up production, captured markets, and gained political influence and considerable prosperity. Samvel watched them with envy. He dreamed of a high status in society. It finally dawned on him that he would have no future if he remained who he was—a reckless gangster who knew how to act only by force and coercion.

With that in mind, in the summer of 1999, Samvel decided to make up for lost time. I was not able to find out how he managed to lay his

Chapter 19

hands on an entire shopping complex in the center of Donetsk, but he got it. The complex was called Miner, which was in accordance with the city's mining specifics but had a "foreign flavor." To my ears it sounded like a German or Jewish surname.

The Miner building was located a few steps from the Central Market, where the transport routes converged, which ensured a constant flow of visitors. About a month before this, the owner of the market had been shot to death by killers, so the transfer of Miner to Samvel's ownership could have been connected with this. The building housed a bar, a café, a grocery store, and a women's clothing boutique.

Having informed me about his prize acquisition, Samvel said that from now on, my place would be there. He also told me that Tigran had been appointed manager of the Miner. I saw this as a loophole for escape and said that in my opinion, Tigran could cope with the task on his own. Samvel looked at me from under his brows.

"Who cares about your fucking opinion here?" he snapped. "You're going to the Miner, that's it. I want you to look after my brother, Maidukov. Tigran fished a whole lot of cash from me for reconstruction and all the stuff. We can't let him pour it down the drain. Tigran and Konstantin, they are a cunning pair that need to be looked after, got it? I don't want my money to be spent on chicks and casinos."

I shook my head and told him that Tigran would not allow me to control his expenses.

"You will find a way, Maidukov," Samvel said, lowering his voice. "In fact, it's you whom I see running all this business shit. But I can't suspend my brother, because it would offend him, see? This is purely a political thing, don't let me be misunderstood."

That last maxim sounded so unusual coming from Samvel's mouth that I looked at him carefully, as if expecting to see someone else in front of me. But it was still the same old Samvel whom I'd known all these years. And I didn't believe that he himself or the situation around him had changed for the better. When a person makes the same mistakes, how can he or she achieve a different result? Samvel had no chance of establishing a stable business. Tigran was his fox in the henhouse, while I was no longer his hen that would lay the golden eggs for free.

Times, they were changed.

When I appeared in the Miner, Tigran greeted me with open arms, like a best friend. To tell the truth, I was glad to see him, too, despite all our past tensions. He was a good man in his own way—as long as you didn't have to share money or business with him. He had a great personality and was able to make noble gestures.

As if nothing had happened, he put his arm around my shoulders, and I smelled the scent of his favorite cologne filling my nostrils. I sneezed, and Tigran laughed his trademark hissing chuckle. He patted me on the back and said, "Welcome back, Sergey. Welcome, my friend."

As always, he was dressed in the best fashion of glamorous movie gangsters in his own Hollywood iteration. His hair and beard were perfectly trimmed, and the white collar of his shirt was spotlessly clean. But something had changed in his posture and the expression in his eyes. As I soon learned, Tigran began to have problems with his spine, which forced him to wear a medical corset under his clothes. He attended massage sessions and carefully hid his illness but sometimes suffered so much that he could not get out of the chair without assistance. However, this did not stop him from being as energetic and active as before.

After exchanging the latest news with me, he gave me a tour of the premises, showing me everything from a marble bar counter to a large-scale commercial oven in the kitchen. Konstantin followed us like a silent shadow (assuming that shadows can drink beer and rely on a cane to walk). The beatings he'd received last year didn't go without consequences. Konstantin no longer looked as smug and self-confident as before. I thought that not only had his bones been broken but also his will.

The building placed at Tigran's disposal was two stories and had a large basement with utility rooms, which had to be reached through narrow corridors and stairs. His office contained a large sofa, a coffee table, and a huge plasma TV. My office only had enough space for a desk and a flimsy chair.

Tigran was plotting a grand renovation of Miner, intending to turn it into an elite nightclub, the best in the entire city. This meant that the scale of his theft would be enormous. I was almost sure that the nightclub

Chapter 19

would never be completed. I knew Tigran's habit of squandering thousands of dollars and leaving staff without salaries. The sight of money drew him in, like a shark smelling blood. Konstantin circled around him in the manner of a pilot fish feeding on scraps. No, the nightclub had no chance of ever opening.

Our tour ended in a women's clothing store that occupied the entire right half of the building. Among the mannequins, racks of dresses, shoes, and accessories placed on shelves, about a dozen guys wandered around, examining, groping, sorting, and taking things away. Tigran called them "my lads" and said that he'd allowed them to take gifts for their girlfriends before the goods were sold in bulk to some other store. They were all strangers to me and did not look like athletes. The oldest of them was no more than twenty-five years old, so they were unlikely to cost Tigran dearly.

In his usual boastful manner, he said that soon his "personal guard" would outnumber that of Samvel. I thought that the competition between the Martirosyan brothers for leadership was unlikely to benefit them, but I kept my opinion to myself. I didn't intend to stay with them that long and didn't want to get involved in anything.

Tigran put two white fur coats on the counter and said that I could take them for my wife and daughter for free. He said the fur coats were made from arctic fox and cost a lot of money. And guess what? I took those damned fur coats and thanked Tigran for the generous gift. In fact, these were stolen things, and I should not have even touched them, but I didn't find the strength to refuse. It was not a matter of my greed, it was a matter of my desire to please Luba and Svitlana, but it was one of those actions of which I am still ashamed.

When I proudly put my acquisitions in front of Luba, she wrinkled her nose and said that this was not an arctic fox but a cheap fake. Neither she nor my daughter ever wore those faux fur coats, and they collected dust in our closet for a while until I tossed them in the trash. Such was my price in the eyes of Tigran.

But he bought me not only with money and gifts. As I already wrote, he was a master of grand gestures. When we left the clothing store, he said that day was the day he would treat me to a real, home-cooked dinner in honor of our meeting. I responded with a polite refusal, citing urgent matters at home, which was a lie. Tigran looked at me shrewdly and said that Konstantin would not be with us.

"Just you and me, Sergio," he said. "Like good old days."

Particularly for me, those "good old days" weren't so good at all, and I didn't remember that we'd ever had dinner together, he and I, but I thought it would be wise to accept the offer. In the end it was I who depended on Tigran, not the other way around.

In fact, we had dinner for three, not for two. Sitting behind the wheel of his new car (now it was the Ferrari F355 Spider, also bright red), Tigran said that he was going to introduce me to the mother of his son. This was a complete surprise to me. I asked him if she was his wife.

"I told you she's my son's mother," he answered. "It's too early for me to get married while there are so many cool chicks around. But the time will come, and I will marry Rita. She's the only one whom I truly love and whom I can trust completely."

He didn't mention Samvel, Konstantin, me, or one of his many girlfriends. He named Rita, and I thought she must be an extraordinary woman.

She turned out to be the complete opposite of the image I'd conjured of her in my mind. Rita was an inconspicuous little woman with an unmemorable appearance and colorless, shoulder-length hair combed straight and tucked behind her ears. She received us in slippers and a dress that looked more like a dressing gown (perhaps it really was a dressing gown). The sight of Tigran made her eyes shine like two opals, and she seemed almost beautiful to me. She smelled of food being cooked—the whole house was scented with the roasting lamb and the aroma of apple pie. A minute later, I smelled it all over myself, from my hair to my socks.

Rita lived in a one-story house behind a green board fence at the edge of the narrow street. Old-fashioned lace curtains hung on the windows, and the walls were decorated with magazine posters of French movie stars and Italian pop musicians. I didn't get to see Tigran's son, as he was on vacation with his grandmother. I found out that he was four years old and a very handsome and brave boy.

"Just like his dad," Rita said, looking at Tigran.

Chapter 19

Her gaze directed at him was filled with such adoration that I understood why he was attached to this shy and quiet woman with colorless hair. She loved him as though he were the only man in the world. He was a god to her, no less. Or maybe even more.

We sat down at a table covered with a cheap nylon tablecloth that featured a shining main dish of fried trout, each fish with a little heap of greens, and a surrounding bank of stuffed peppers. While Rita put more and more new dishes on the table, Tigran proudly told me that she had mastered the recipes of Armenian cuisine to perfection.

I remember that the cabbage rolls and stewed lamb with walnuts were amazing. We drank sour red wine from a wicker bottle and talked about everything except business. It was a sweet, intimate evening during which I recognized a Tigran I had never known before. But this was a short-lived transformation. The next day, I saw in front of me the same, familiar Tigran: wily, cunning, and selfish.

Once the money came into his hands, he could not stop until he had spent every last cent. He was a gambler by nature, and this affected his approach to business. He played, not worked. And he stubbornly refused to make any calculations, as I repeatedly suggested to him. He hated numbers. In vain I came to him with price lists and business plans. He would take the papers from my hands and put them aside or throw them in the trash. Under his leadership, the Miner was a bottomless pit for Samvel's financial investments.

Rolls of carpet, miles of laminate, oak flooring, marble slabs, German plumbing, Spanish tiles, and more—and much more—were delivered to us every day. Tigran got some goods cheaply, and some he received for free, but Samvel was always told the full, if not double, price. And this was far from our only expense item.

I would come to my office in the morning and find a bunch of girls waiting for an interview. These interviews were personally conducted by Tigran, who was recruiting future waitresses, croupiers, and dancers. He didn't show up for work until noon, so we were all treated to watching the girls hang around the building for hours. It was dusty and dirty there because of the construction work, and the bar was occupied by Tigran's young thugs, so my office and the bookkeeping areas were their only refuge.

They would swarm around me, asking when they were going to start work, and I honestly told some of them it was unlikely to happen, but they preferred to believe Tigran, not me. He changed girlfriends every day, and each was given a gift or a luxurious dinner in a restaurant, which also cost a lot of money. This doesn't even include the freeloaders and slackers who circled around Tigran, waiting for another handout. Money flowed through his hairy fingers like water.

My office was at the center of events, so I saw all this, knowing that one day, the deception would come out. The project of building a nightclub devoured huge sums and was moving forward very slowly. It couldn't end well. Samvel trusted Tigran less and less. Every now and then, he called me to ask pressing questions. How justified is the investment in the club? When will spending end and income start? Why is the renovation going so slowly?

My good relationship with Tigran and the damned fur coats he gave me were preventing me from being frank. I had ironed out difficulties and avoided delicate topics, though the lie could be revealed at any moment. How would Samvel react if he knew about his brother's embezzlement? Would he blame me too? In this case, I had no excuses or hope for forgiveness.

We were saved only by the fact that Samvel sat in his fortress without getting out and didn't appear in the club in person. His life was in constant danger. After the shooting in court, another unsuccessful assassination attempt was made on him. The circles around his eyes were so dark and distinct that you could see the sockets of his skull. Outwardly and mentally, Samvel was terrible. His outbursts of rage became more and more frequent, inexplicable, and violent. Everyone tried to stay away from him at such moments.

Whenever he called me to him, I expected that his anger would fall on me in full force and that this would be fatal for me. Being next to him was like sitting on an awakening volcano.

Be that as it may, I was doomed to look into Samvel's bulging eyes quite often, and during our meetings, he would insistently ask me when

Chapter 19

men from the SBU would contact him. Having heard from me once again that I had no idea when this might happen, Samvel would begin to boil, then continue with the next traditional question: "Then maybe you can tell me clearly when your fucking club will be up and running, eh? I'm tired of throwing money away. I want money to flow to me instead."

In response, I just mumbled something unintelligible, trying to delay the inevitable collapse. I couldn't convince my family to move, and I didn't see a way to escape. My fate, my future, and my life were in the hands of Samvel.

My days and nights were filled with anxiety for myself and for my loved ones. I don't know why I remember so clearly an early morning in 1999, when I was awakened by the faint whistle of a jet aircraft vibrating the silence of the gray of dawn. The sound grew, and it quickly became a roaring whistle that resonated through the window's glass until the plane flew out of hearing. I tried to picture myself up there, sitting in the passenger cabin of the long-range jet aircraft, somewhere across the Atlantic or the Pacific, surrounded by my happy little family, among the relaxed people setting out to meet new adventures, business projects, and much-awaited meetings . . . I tried, but I couldn't.

I remained lying where I was, and I suddenly realized clearly that I wasn't going anywhere until the very end of this drama. The scenes were planned out ahead of time, the roles were assigned, and the possible activities of each player were determined. I prepared for the worst. Perhaps this helped me survive the whirlpool of events that would go on to suck me down.

As usually happens, the storm was preceded by some calm. A few days later, when I met with Samvel, I noticed that his mood had changed dramatically. He no longer asked me about the SBU officers and the reconstruction of the nightclub. He looked energetic and inspired, like a man who saw a new attractive goal in front of him. He gave me some money and said that he would have a lot of things to do in the near future.

For several weeks in September and October 1999, I didn't see him, which was a great relief to me. Tigran and I had successfully completed the renovation of the Miner and were preparing the nightclub for its opening. The bar and café began to make a profit, which was encouraging.

Yet I did not delude myself into being too optimistic. After being in that business for a relatively long time, I'd become irrevocably aware that all of this apparent prosperity could be extremely temporary, depending on how the situation would pan out over the next few weeks and months... or days and hours. By this time I knew for sure that the clouds were gathering over Samvel's head and his best times were behind him, as the world was changing around him faster than he could keep up.

He felt this, and it made him hurry even faster, preparing a new field of activity for himself. Realizing that the competition in Donetsk was too tough, Samvel turned his gaze south, toward the Sea of Azov. There, one hundred miles away, was the small port city of Berdyansk. In the nineties there'd been no large gangs or influential oligarchs there who could repel the invasion of Samvel's mighty and close-knit "family." By changing Donetsk to Berdyansk, he killed two birds with one stone.

Firstly, he expected to gain control over the vast flow of goods passing through the seaport. Secondly, he was leaving the place where, by that time, there were too many hunters for his head. Strategically, it was absolutely the right move. As for tactics, Samvel acted according to a repeatedly tested and proven model.

While Tigran and I were busy organizing the Miner club, Samvel, along with a couple dozen armed thugs, made several visits to Berdyansk. The head of the local police was showered with lavish gifts and assured that the crime rate in the city would drop sharply. The mayor of Berdyansk was bribed, as were some other officials. The most intractable ones were intimidated or beaten. In October 1999 Samvel actually took the city by storm. The only bastion that still did not fall was the port itself, the last and most delicious piece of the Berdyansk pie. Early the next morning, Samvel was going to break into the office of the port chief and force him to sign documents transferring the terminals and warehouses to the ownership of a company called the Seagull.

In other words, to me!

Me...

I heard this stunning news in the late evening as I sat in front of Samvel in his house, which looked like a defending fortress. The first thing I could say was that I needed to think. Samvel, who was watching

Chapter 19

me like a cat watching a mouse, replied that he had already thought about everything for me.

I put forward to him all the counterarguments that came into my head. My family and I were not ready to move so far—at least not yet. My children couldn't interrupt their studies. We didn't even have a place to live.

"Who is talking about your family here, Maidukov?" Samvel exclaimed impatiently. "At first you go alone. I'll put you up with me."

I learned that he'd built a new house in Berdyansk, three times larger than the current one. For this, Samvel had bought an entire kindergarten with its territory and surrounded it with a high wall. I vividly imagined gangsters sliding down slides and swinging on swings, but I didn't laugh. This was no laughing matter for the person who'd gotten a black mark just recently. It was handed to me personally by Andrew Andrewich.

Two or three days before the meeting with Samvel, I'd had another meeting that showed me the precariousness of my position.

I was walking down the street when a man in a flat checkered cap and a cheap dark nylon raincoat, the kind worn by half of the middle-aged folks in Donetsk, called out to me. In his right hand, he held a pie in oiled paper, while his left hand was stuck in the pocket of his raincoat. He stood at the crossroads in plain sight, but he was as inconspicuous as an invisible man. The collar of his raincoat was turned up and the peak of his cap, turned down, concealing his face, so I didn't immediately recognize him as Andrew Andrewich.

"Good afternoon, Sergey," he said, eating his pie as though he hadn't eaten in days. "Were you looking for me?"

His voice sounded casual while his face looked almost bored as he addressed me, yet I could see that my visit to the SBU directorate still angered him. I glanced around to see if Ivan Ivanovich was nearby, watching.

"This was a mistake on my part," I said.

"A big mistake," Andrew Andrewich said. "You can't even imagine how big it was, Sergey."

"I'm sorry," I muttered.

He put the rest of the pie in his mouth and chewed it. Then he crumpled the oiled paper into a ball, threw it on the pavement, and said, "Soon you will be even more sorry than you are now. You're in shit, Sergey. You're up to your ears in it. Do you even realize who you're dealing with? Samvel is not just a bandit; he's a potential dead man, whose days are numbered. What awaits you next to him? Think about it, Sergey. Think carefully, and run before it's too late. There's not much time at your disposal."

I cannot vouch here for the accuracy of every word spoken by Andrew Andrewich, but the general meaning of his speech was as I shared, and it made a dismal impression on me. Perhaps I tried to say something in my defense, but Andrew Andrewich didn't listen to me. He only repeated his advice to me to immediately leave the gang, then left.

Although I took his message very seriously, I underestimated it. And as a result, I sat in front of Samvel, who told me that tomorrow I would become a direct accomplice in his crime. He didn't care that I had my life, my family, my plans, and my desires. This did not bother him at all. He was going to use me like oiled pie paper, rolling me into a ball and throwing me at his feet.

Tomorrow.

I thought I would pack my things and run away that night. But Samvel looked at me like a rooster looking at grain and told me that I would spend that night in his house. I didn't even have a cell phone to warn Luba, and I told Samvel that. He grinned dismissively and said that he would call her himself.

It was a disaster. A Complete wreck. There was no escaping for me. I felt like a man who was sentenced to death and had to go to the scaffold in the morning. I thought I wouldn't sleep that night, but I passed out as soon as my head hit the pillow.

I woke up early, moved up to the window, and looked out into the yard below, which looked like a prison yard, with no trees or flowers or grass. On the concrete parking lot lay a dove, surrounded by three crows. They took turns pecking the poor half-alive bird with their sharp beaks. The pain caused it to twitch agonistically, and then the crows froze, watching the twitching. As soon as the dove fainted, the crows resumed their attacks, devouring their prey alive.

Chapter 19

I understood the futility of my attempt, but I ran down the steps from the second floor to drive away the crows. The front door was locked and guarded by Cowboy, who had a shotgun in his hands. He shook his head and said that it was forbidden to go out.

When I returned to the window of my room, the dove below no longer moved its wings or raised its little head, so the crows now pecked at him without any hindrance.

Did he remain conscious until the very end? If so, it was a terrible death. It was easy for me to imagine what the dove felt and what the crows felt. I walked away from the window.

Chapter 20

The Last Chance

The cavalcade of cars heading to Berdyansk stretched for a good three hundred feet, so it was more like a military operation than a business trip. Samvel was not driving in his armored Mercedes but sharing the backseat of another car with me. I think it was a precaution against assassination. Every predator one day turns into prey, and Samvel realized this.

On the way he asked me many questions but listened to the answers with an absentminded look while his eyes were darting around the landscape. During our two-hour journey, he licked his lips at least a hundred times, although they still remained dry and sore. He was like a gambler who had put everything he had on the line, including his life. His feverish excitement was transmitted to me. Perhaps no trip has ever seemed so long to me.

Before heading to the port, we stopped at the Berdyansk winery. The director and chief technologist came out to meet us. Samvel introduced me to them and said that from now on, I would control their activities, which was a big surprise to them as well as to me. The director gazed at me with his narrowed eyes and muttered, "Welcome, partner," but his look told me the opposite.

After a short tour of the vineyard and workshops, Samvel and I left the factory. About a dozen armed gangsters escorted us to our cars. Factory workers poured into the courtyard or leaned against the windows to watch the show. I thought that they were probably discussing my candidacy and were unlikely to find kind words for me.

Chapter 20

I told Samvel that I didn't know anything about winemaking and that it wouldn't be wise for me to go into this business. Without turning his head in my direction, he jumped in his Mercedes and drove off so fast the tires squealed. As I, still standing there, watched him go off, I thought about how the farther he was from Donetsk, the safer he seemed to feel. This was paradoxical, considering that not so long ago, Samvel had called Donetsk "his" city. Actually, there was no place on earth where he could settle for a long time. He was like the Flying Dutchman, the captain of the cursed ghost ship that never made port, and his entire biography confirmed that impression.

I made the rest of the journey on my own, in the company of ordinary bandits, called "infantrymen" in criminal jargon. The car smelled pungently of men's sweat. Suddenly, I realized that these big, armed guys were scared as hell to attack the port. But they feared Samvel even more, and this predetermined their future fate. Those who study statistics have never examined the number of young people who died in gang wars on the territory of the former USSR in the 1990s. I believe the losses were much greater than during the Soviet Union's invasion of Afghanistan. These young men longed to have everything at once. Some of them didn't even have graves or tombstones.

They and I got out of the car in front of a gray building: the Berdyansk Seaport Administration. We all slammed our doors extra loudly, as if to encourage ourselves. Samvel was the last one to step out of his Mercedes. Looking at the gray building in front of him, he put on his sunglasses. It was his own way of gaining courage . . . or boldness . . . or determination . . . whatever it was called.

He was the first to enter the port authority building, which he did through the front entrance. I followed him a few steps, then stopped, unsure of whether or not it would be wise to continue. The mobsters marched past me without halting and disappeared, one by one, behind the heavy double doors.

I found myself still standing outside the building, pressing my shoulder against the rough plaster wall, not moving, not making a sound, not even breathing. I could not make up my mind about whether to go in or to leave. I looked around to see if anyone was watching me. Oksana stood in the parking lot next to the gangster's car and looked at me. She was wearing one of those cheap fur coats from the Miner store. I didn't know that Samvel had taken her with him to Berdyansk. He was probably going to introduce her to a new business. This was the last straw to break my patience and make up my mind for me on the decision that had long been gnawing at me.

"Run, Sergey, run! Run before it's too late!" I thought.

Yet it *was* too late. Too damned late.

A muffled shot was heard from inside the seaport building. My heart galloped, while my feet were rooted to the concrete. About five seconds later, the door swung open, letting out Silver along with a choir of voices shouting, "Atas! Atas!" (a criminal yell meaning "Run away!"). Following on his heels, the other men of Samvel's gang appeared, one after another, flying through the door and straight down to the cars.

As numb as a pillar of salt, I watched the police catch them and throw them onto the pavement. I didn't know where these cops in masks and helmets had come from, but now the place was swarming with them. There were police sawhorse barricades on both sides of the parking lot, and vans were rushed to the scene, their cobalt-blue lights flashing in the daylight, their sirens howling loudly. There was even a helicopter hovering overhead, indicating the enormous scale of the operation.

I had no doubt that this time, Samvel would end up in prison for a long time. At least a hundred cops and special forces officers were involved in detaining him and his gang. This meant that Samvel has crossed not only the law itself but also the path of someone from the highest echelons of power in Ukraine.

Subsequently, I heard rumors that Rinat Akhmetov was interested in the massacre of the Martirosyan "family." To tell the truth, for me personally, these rumors were more than plausible. The future Ukrainian oligarch number one was then clearing his way to the top of the political and economic Olympus. The rebellious and headstrong Samvel prevented him from achieving his goal.

For the Martirosyan brothers, this turned out to be a fatal circumstance. But what about me? The liquidation of Samvel's gang meant my liquidation, too, though not necessarily physically. I could simply be put

Chapter 20

in prison under any article of the Criminal Code of Ukraine: forgery of documents, tax evasion, or aiding and abetting. It was a logical end to my career. I'd moved myself toward this with enviable tenacity and consistency. I'd refused to listen to the voice of reason and even to the voice of Andrew Andrewich, who'd directly warned me about the consequences. Now it was too late. Or was it?

In the chaos that was seething around me, I still stood unnoticed and untouched. My age, my nongangster appearance, and my aloofness made me invisible to the cops who were catching the "big bad wolves" and twisting their muscular arms.

Oksana got into the car and huddled there, trying to be as unnoticeable as possible. I thought it was an instinctive and justifiable impulse toward self-preservation, and then I began to slowly retreat from the entrance to the seaport administration. My steps were small, and I kept a neutral expression on my face. With all my appearance, I seemed to be telling the police, "Look, I'm not running anywhere, because I don't feel any guilt about me. I have nothing to do with this. Don't mind me."

I was fifteen feet from Oksana's car and considering myself almost saved when a man in a blue padded jacket blocked my path and pointed me to a white van, near which Andrew Andrewich was standing, talking with a helmeted officer of special forces. The two of them wore bulletproof vests with a logo reading SBU.

Andrew Andrewich sent the officer away and ordered me to come up. His face was stern and hostile. He asked where to take me: to the SBU department or to the bus station. I chose the second option.

"This means that you agree to cooperate with the Service," Andrew Andrewich said, both asking and clarifying.

I glanced toward the car where Oksana was hiding and said that my conversation with the SBU officer made me a traitor in the eyes of the gangsters.

"Ask me if I give a shit," Andrew Andrewich proposed.

I didn't. He nodded with satisfaction and told me to climb into the van. There was a table set up, at which sat none other than Ivan Ivanovich. The back of the van was filled with equipment of unknown purpose.

There sat a man, wearing a white shirt and large headphones that covered his head and ears, with his back to us.

Andrew Andrewich and I sat next to each other opposite Ivan Ivanovich. Quietly and slowly, he told me that Samvel's gang was finished once and for all. He also said that Samvel had been detained with weapons in his hands while shooting at an on-duty police officer, wounding him in the shoulder.

"The bastard got himself a fifteen-year sentence," Ivan Ivanovich said.

Then, without changing his tone, he told me that the police had an arrest warrant for me. He asked if I liked that, and I said that I didn't like it at all. Then he asked if I would like to get away with it. My answer was a big *yup*!

"Okay," said Ivan Ivanovich, "in that case, we will agree, Sergey. We're looking for Tigran. You're looking for freedom. A very simple kind of transaction, isn't it? Go and find Tigran for us."

"Go and find him," Andrew Andrewich echoed. "The sooner, the better. Do you have a mobile phone, Sergey?"

He showed an imaginary phone with his thumb and little finger. In response, I showed him my first Nokia brick phone, with its tiny black-and-white screen and a battery that lasted days rather than hours. Andrew Andrewich dictated his contact number to me twice and told me that I could go. I was given two days to search for Tigran—a supertight deadline. I was completely at a loss, not knowing how to go on or what to do. Telling somebody might help, and my wife was the logical choice, but I didn't want to scare her. And there was another thing: What could Luba do, even if I did tell her? Shield me with her fragile body? But wasn't it I who should have shielded her?

The first place I went to the next morning was the Miner Club. The likelihood of finding Tigran there was less than zero, but I couldn't help but show up at the venue. It would look too suspicious if I suddenly disappeared. Tigran didn't answer my calls, so it seemed absolutely natural for me to look for him after the Berdyansk defeat. I needed to get ahead of Oksana and find Tigran before she'd had time to tell him about my conversation with the SBU officers.

Chapter 20

I usually entered the Miner via a small bar that served as a gathering place for Tigran's guys. Having crossed the threshold, I could not believe my eyes. The bar was trashed and looked like it had been through an earthquake. Mirrors, bottles, glasses, and lamps were smashed into bits that snapped and crackled underneath my boots as I made my way between overturned tables and stools.

Leaving the bar, I found myself in a small kitchen, where the same chaos reigned. Some clothes, mostly napkins and small towels, were all over the floor or hung out of drawers. Pots and pans lay everywhere, and the room stank with stale-food and garbage smells. The collapsed hood system mixed with overturned stoves and ovens formed a surreal barricade, which took me several minutes to overcome.

The next door, with its broken frame, was hanging from the upper hinge, and there were spots of blood on the white paintwork. I stopped. A large brown spot behind the door, sticky in appearance, blocked my way into the café. I didn't really want to step on it. And I hated the thought of going *over* it. The dried puddle looked ugly and smelly, like someone's puked curry on the tilted floor with ketchup then poured on top of it. I looked higher up at the door, spattered with blood, and barely restrained myself from vomiting.

Rattling the stainless steel kitchen stuff, I started to make my way back into the destroyed bar. There I found the two waitresses, Olya and Ira, who had just risen from the basement store, where they had taken their things.

"I don't think we will ever return to work here," Olya said sadly.

She was a very beautiful girl with expressive eyes and a disconcerting surname, which, if literally translated into English, would sound almost like "Toad." She and Ira had begun their careers as Tigran's lovers, but they later turned into girlfriends of his young guards. They told me that last night, two dozen bandits burst into the Miner and began to destroy everything here with bats. Tigran was not there (as always, in moments of danger), and his guards silently watched the massacre. Only the youngest of them, a handsome boy named Dima, dared to say something against the raiders. They took him into the kitchen, laid him face down on the floor, and shot him in the back of the head with a gun. Dima's body was taken by his mother, as no one had found the courage to call an ambulance or the police.

"The scum promised that they would return and kill whoever did this," Olya said. "They could, I think. They behaved like owners of the city. And they constantly asked where they would find Tigran."

While Olya was talking, Ira was crying and muttering that she and Dima had been getting ready to marry but now the wedding was off. I kept nodding and tried to imagine what the mother of the murdered lad was feeling now. He was eighteen. Why did he die? In the name of whom? And why were his brains scattered on the tiled floor of a venue that did not even belong to him?

Having finished her story, Olya asked me what they should do next. The girls looked at me hopefully, expecting me to know the answer. They feared for their lives, as they'd witnessed the murder. I calmed them down as best I could, saying that the murderers would have killed them the night before if they'd wanted. It was all I could do for the couple of pretty waitresses of the defunct nightclub. The Martirosyan brothers had lost their power and possessions in Donetsk. Nothing belonged to them here anymore, as it was at the beginning of their expansion. Samvel made his successful takeoff out of nowhere, and he fell into nowhere.

Tigran, for all his merits, was not capable of taking the place of his older brother. I suspected that he would not live to see his trial, perhaps even to his arrest.

Did he understand this himself?

Instead of searching for him all over Donetsk, I went straight to the house of Rita—"the mother of his son," as he'd once described her. His red Ferrari didn't fit in her small yard, so Tigran had left it a hundred yards down the street. It was too conspicuous a car for someone who wanted to stay incognito.

The gate in front of Rita's house was locked with a latch on the inside, so I had to hook my arm over the fence to undo it. I didn't knock on the door, knowing that Rita wouldn't open it for me. I just sat in the yard on a shaky box for an hour or two until she came out on her own, getting ready to go to the store or somewhere else. I jumped onto the porch before she could close the door and held it with my foot. Rita looked at me with fear and hatred and asked what I wanted. She had eyes like a cat whose kitten was about to be taken away.

I spoke to her loudly so that Tigran, who was hiding in the house, could hear me. His jacket and shoes were visible through the crack of the slightly open door.

I asked Rita to tell Tigran that not only the police were looking for him but also the SBU and some bandits. I said that he had exactly two hours to leave Donetsk. I also said that his shelter was not safe. Rita listened to me in silence. The fear and hatred did not disappear from her eyes, but their intensity decreased.

"Two hours, no more," I repeated insistently and left the yard.

At fifteen minutes to noon, I called Andrew Andrewich and told him Rita's address. He expressed his satisfaction with my efficiency and said that from now on, I could sleep peacefully. But for a long time, I could not sleep peacefully, expecting that the ghosts of the past would one day overtake me and drag me back to the 1990s, from which I'd somehow miraculously escaped into the year 2000—and then further, further, and further, until I found myself in 2022, when I started writing *Deadly Bonds*.

I've written a whole bunch of other books before this, but this one was and *is* special. Here, for the first time, I call Samvel by his real name and write the truth about him, about myself, and about our relationship. Actually, his moody figure has already emerged in my debut paperback, *For Thirty Pieces of Silver*, where he is introduced to the audience as Khan. As for me, I hid behind a pseudonym, so in 2001, readers had no idea how close to reality my story was.

Having escaped the Mafia's web, I never engaged in any business again for the rest of my life. Literature became my only source of income. I used to write several books a year, and every second one described the gangster underworld. For novels of this kind, I have long used the pen name Sergey Donskoy. Their back covers had the standard blurb: "The author was born in 1955 in the Donbass. After graduating from the economics department of a trade institute, he worked in commercial structures for a long time, then left this activity and devoted himself entirely to literature. His works vividly describe the life of representatives of the criminal world."

Samvel was the ideal prototype of the villain, whom I reproduced many times on the pages of my books—all under different names. My personal experience aside, it was a pleasure to describe it because he had a magnetic personality and lots of charisma. And at the same time, he was strong and fearless, like the leader of a wolf pack; for him, this was the only way to bend dozens of other predators to his will.

It was a shock for me when I saw Samvel broken, frightened, and suffering from pain. It was even more of a shock to see him ingratiating himself to his enemies. I don't remember exactly when it happened, but it happened. In the course of my ongoing research, I came across a YouTube video that turned my idea of Samvel and the Mafia upside down (The Back Door 2020). The footage was filmed in 2020 at the Lukyanovka pretrial detention center, where Samvel was serving a term while awaiting trial. Three men caught him in the prison corridor and began to beat him, muttering threats and curses. Instead of defending himself, Samvel sat down on the floor and, covering his head with his hands, asked over and over, "For what, brother? For what?" His voice broke into whiny notes.

He offered not the slightest resistance. He was dragged into some dirty nook, where he was beaten with hands, feet, and wooden clubs. Squealing in pain, he kept asking, "For what, for what? Ah! Ah! For what?"

"You are selling our brothers, scum," they told him, continuing to wield their hands and feet. Oh, how hard they beat him! One of the guys literally kneaded Samvel's sides and stomach with his fists until he switched to inarticulate whining. I had a hard time watching the video to the end. When Samvel promised that he would no longer write denunciations against his cellmates, he was left to lie where he lay. He was finished in a moral sense. He was not a prison boss. He'd turned into a small-time informer, who was publicly humiliated by the filmed video. It was a miserable end to the almighty bandit who'd once terrorized all of Eastern Ukraine.

Then there were other photographs and videos depicting the "alternate" Samvel, unknown to me before (Detective Info, 2023). He half-heartedly faked heart attacks, made rather comic suicide attempts by

Chapter 20

ramming his head into a plexiglass wall, and threw ugly tantrums in the courtroom, trying to present himself as an innocent victim.

All these were disgusting manifestations of the real Samvel, which I could not see before. The most glaring fact supporting this was that he didn't spare his own son, Robic, sending him to kill a certain Sarkisyan and dooming him to vegetate in prison until the end of his days.

In 2021 Samvel himself was sentenced to life imprisonment, but in February 2023, a new court dropped some of the charges against him and replaced his prison sentence with house arrest. Reading the court ruling, I also learned that Samvel is the actual owner of a terminal in the seaport of Berdyansk worth $250,000 (his wife, Oksana, turned out to be the nominal owner; Roschina, 2023; ua_katarsis, 2023).

As a result, this image of Samvel turned out to be complete and as truthful as possible. I peered at this image for a long time, trying to determine my attitude toward it and to get one main feeling that Samvel evoked in me after many years.

In the end I caught this feeling.

Pity.

I no longer hate this man. I don't feel afraid of him anymore. There is no respect and no sympathy. All I can find for the fearsome Mafia leader Samvel Martirosyan is pity. He maimed and took many lives, but he also destroyed his own life. Today he sits in his house with a transmitting bracelet on his ankle, like a wolf whose foot is caught in a trap. Tomorrow, in any case, he will again go to prison, where he will be beaten and quite likely killed (to the joy and relief of many people). He's not destined to die like Don Corleone, in his garden, playing with his grandson, whispering, "Life is so beautiful."

His death will be terrible and cruel, as he himself always was. And he will die completely alone, without hearing words of compassion and sympathy.

What a pathetic end for a man who could have achieved so much in this life!

Having put a period here or, rather, an exclamation point, I seek to understand my attitude toward myself because, after all, I—not Samvel—am the main character of this book.

The Last Chance

And guess what? I think it would be better if you do it yourself. It is for this purpose that I wrote these eighty-seven thousand words. I have made the signed confession, and it remains for you to pass judgment.

Guilty? Not guilty?

Hoping for your indulgence,
Sergey Maidukov

Bibliography

The Back Door. 2020. "What Happens in the Lukyanovka Pre-trial Detention Center with Those Who Cooperate with the SBU." YouTube Video, May 23, 2020. https://www.youtube.com/watch?v=9b6p4-WKYs8.

Detective Info. 2023. "The Story of the Rise and Fall of Samvel from Donetsk." YouTube Video, May 15, 2023. https://www.youtube.com/watch?v=9b6p4-WKYs8.

Kikvidze, Georgy. 2004. "Leader of OCG, Samvel." *Criminal Ukraine*, April 26, 2004. https://cripo.com.ua/gangsters/p-1942/.

Perovitch, Vitaly. 2006. "In the Regions with a Clear Conscience." ORD. Published February 22, 2006. https://ord-ua.com/2006/02/22/v-regionyi-s-chistoj-sovestyu/.

Semenetz, Georgy. 2019. "Bandit Samvel Martirosyan Is Alive." Argument. Published September 20, 2019. https://argumentua.com/stati/bandit-samvel-martirosyan-zhiv-spasibo-akhmetovu-i-prodazhnym-pravokhranitelyam.

Studio PE Info. 2019. "A Well-Known Criminal Authority Was Detained in Poltava." YouTube Video, September 20, 2019. https://www.youtube.com/watch?v=i4g2YztmPk4.

Roschina, Victoria. 2023. "The Kiev Court Began to Hear the Case of Samvel Donetsky, Who Is Called One of the Most Influential Gang Leaders of the 90s." Hromadske. Published November 3, 2023. https://hromadske.ua/ru/posts/kievskij-sud-nachal-slushat-delo-samvela-doneckogo-kotorogo-nazyvayut-odnim-iz-samyh-vliyatelnyh-liderov-band-90-h.

ua_katarsis. 2023. "Samvel Donetsky was Released Under House Arrest." LiveJournal. Published June 11, 2023. https://ua-katarsis.livejournal.com/1546398.html.

Zhukova, Ksenia. 2019. "The End of the Gang of the Most Terrible Mafia in Ukraine." Kompromat 1. Published September 23, 2019. https://kompromat1.guru/articles/129867-konetc_bandy_samogo_strashnogo_mafiozi_v_ukraine.

Index

agency agreement, 24
Agency for State Reserves: Martirosyan, T., refusing to pay, 139; sugar purchase from, 137–38
AK-47 Kalashnikov assault rifle, 51
Akhmetov, Rinat, 223, 237
Alchevsk Metallurgical Plant, 44, 46, 51, 55
Alexander (Rezany): army drafting, 181; Eugene and friends brawl with, 177–78; as Maidukov, Sergey, driver, 136
Amanda (pet dog), 152–54
American, image of rich, 34–35
American investment company, 37
Andrewich, Andrew, 218–19; bandits killing each other comment of, 52; face-to-face meeting with, 66–67; Globalinvest vulnerable due to, 73; Maidukov, Sergey, calling, 86; Maidukov, Sergey, cooperation and, 238–39; Maidukov, Sergey, leave mobsters advice of, 233; Maidukov, Sergey, meeting with, 47–48, 232–33; Maidukov, Sergey, never to call, 70; Maidukov, Sergey, warning from, 238; Martirosyan, T., location told to, 242
Angelika (accountant), 36; brother's death of, 70; Maidukov, Sergey, accepting invitation from, 77; Maidukov, Sergey, betrayed by, 78–79, 84; Maidukov, Sergey, critical situation discussion with, 71; Maidukov, Sergey, interviewed by, 31–32; Maidukov, Sergey, stick together with, 76–77; Momot comment by, 32; Momot defended by, 42; payroll duties of, 41; secret room hiding of, 72–73
Antonov (Iceworld owner), 209–10
anxiety, of Maidukov, Sergey, 230
Armenians, 127–28
army, violence and cruelty in, 16
arrest: Maidukov, Sergey, with *militsiya*, 83; of Martirosyan, S.,

191–92; possibility of, 72–73; sentence of house, 244
assassination attempt, of Martirosyan, S., 12, 187, 205–6
automobile repair shop, 120

Bag of Bones (King), 214
bank loan business plan, 160–62
beating: defenseless person getting, 115; George giving car driver, 172; Igor getting policemen, 149–50; Konstantin getting savage, 192; Maidukov, Sergey, getting mobster, 133–34; Martirosyan, S., detention center, 243
the Beatles (band), 4, 15, 47, 192
Benchley, Peter, 15
Berdyansk (port city), 231–32, 235–36
Berdyansk Seaport Administration, 236–37
blonde secretary, 114–15
Bogdanov, Arthur: fear of losing life, 130–31; Maidukov, Sergey, gun pointed at by, 130–31; Martirosyan, S., causing departure of, 131
Boris the Banker: bank loan unavailable from, 162; Martirosyan, S., and, 163; Martirosyan, S., wanting bank loan from, 160–61; mobsters visit office of, 161
boxcars, of steel rebar, 45–46

Bragin, Akhat (Alik the Greek), 39–40
Brezhnev, Leonid, 15
bribe money, Oksana providing, 184
building costs, for nightclub, 229
bulletproof vest, of Martirosyan, S., 100, 182
bullet souvenir, 51
business deals: Martirosyan, S., naive approach to, 118; unscrupulous partners in, 29
businessmen: create problem then solution for, 125; Donetsk with Akhmetov as rich, 223; Grousko as small, 178–79; Maidukov, Sergey, only available, 223; mobsters seeing cash cows of, 171; Momot playing role of, 41; SBU defending, 47–48; in Ukraine, 27. *See also specific businessman*
businesswoman, 215

caffeine and nicotine, 60
capitalism, 24
car dealership, 24, 69
car ownership, 105–6
Carpetbaggers (Robbins), 15
cellmates, 94–95
Chance Café: closing of, 191; luxury car pulling up to, 171–72; Maidukov, Sergey, with mobsters at, 170–71; Martirosyan

brothers arrival at, 169–70; mobsters gathering at, 169–70
charismatic leader: Martirosyan, S., as, 243; Martirosyan, T., as, 112
Charter Arms Undercover .38 Special, 178
children: family arguments and, 143; life of luxury for, 56; Maidukov, L., on prospects of, 21; Maidukov, Sergey, and threatening of his, 26–27, 29; Maidukov, Sergey, kids raising, 3, 16; Martirosyan, S., and safety of, 182–83; Martirosyan, S., court case and, 199–200; Martirosyan brother's fathers abuse of, 106; mobsters showing up at door and, 103; what's best for, 87–88
clothing market: Maidukov, L., selling goods at, 211–12; Martirosyan, S., approaching at, 212–13
Cobain, Kurt, 189
commodity exchange, 20
Communist Party of the Soviet Union (CPSU), 15, 24
company name change, 137
competition, between Martirosyan brothers, 226
construction site, 113, 136
copper wire, 19
court hearing: iron cage at, 202; judge entering, 203; judge wounded at, 207; judicial clerk in, 202; machine gun shots interrupting, 205; Martirosyan, S., entering, 203–4; Martirosyan, S., in-charge behavior of, 204; Martirosyan, T., pre-hearing greeting at, 201; for Martirosyan, S., 199
Cowboy (bodyguard), 159, 213–14
CPSU. *See* Communist Party of the Soviet Union
creativity, of Maidukov, Sergey, 15
crime fiction, writer of, 13
criminal activity, 56–57, 98. *See also* mobsters
criminal groups: Martirosyan, S., gang ceased to exist as, 192, 237–38; Martirosyan, T., organizing, 11; *militsiya* as organization like, 83; superiority proven by, 172–73; syndicates and, 11; in Ukraine, 5

dangerous, Martirosyan, S., as, 6
death threats, against Martirosyan, S., 11
debt: of Grousko to Maidukov, Sergey, 179; of Maidukov, Sergey, to Martirosyan, S., 145; of Martirosyan, T., 59–60, 63; of Petya, 163; Valery's liberation from, 119, 122
defenseless people, 115

Department of Combating Economic Crimes, 73, 83, 86, 89
detention center, Martirosyan, S., beating at, 243
Dima (young boy), 240
divide and conquer, by tyrants, 117
dog, death of pet, 152–54
dogs, ordered killed, 159–60
Donetsk (city): Akhmetov as rich businessman from, 223; Bragin as mafia mobsters in, 39–40; as crime capital, 38; horrible things happening in, 56–57; Lada cars in, 181; Maidukov, Sergey, growing up in, 123–24; Maidukov, Sergey, job difficulties in, 142–43; Martirosyan, S., buying store in, 183; Samson as mobster in, 50–51; as Soviet dictator name, 56
Donetsk Police Department, 192
Donetsky, Samvel. *See* Martirosyan, Samvel
driving accident, 120
drunk men, Robic and, 173–74

earnings. *See* income
employment, difficulties finding, 212
"The End of the Most Terrible Mafia King in Ukraine" (headline), 4–5
Eugene (Sergey's friend): as dead drunk mean, 177; Maidukov, Sergey, brawl with, 177–78; Maidukov, Sergey, meeting with, 176–77; minor bruises of, 178; no loan from, 23–24
Europe (rock band), 172

fabric and accessories, 58
family arguments, of Maidukov, Sergey, 143
family problems, of Martirosyan brothers, 128–29
father's abuse, of Martirosyan brothers, 106
faux arctic fox coat, 226
films, 17
The Final Countdown (album), 172
financing: from Momot, 44–45; for schemes, 43
first degree murder charge, 204–5
fishing vessel, 118–22
football club players, 100–101
For Thirty Pieces of Silver (Maidukov, Sergey), 242
fourteen year sentence, for Martirosyan, S., 206
freedom: Maidukov, Sergey, experiencing work, 135; Maidukov, Sergey, lost, 125; Maidukov, Sergey, rejoicing, 151–52

gang rape, 215
gangsters. *See* mobsters
gang wars, in USSR, 236
George (mobster), 172
gift, for lying, 109–10

girlfriends, of Martirosyan, T., 229
girls, for job interviews, 228–29
Globalinvest company: American investment company phrase and, 37; Andrewich and Ivanovich creating vulnerability for, 73; Maidukov, Sergey, as president of, 33; Maidukov, Sergey, future connected to, 57; Maidukov, Sergey, hired by, 31–32; Maidukov, Sergey, running, 69; new products needed by, 55; no longer existing, 75; police special forces breaking into, 71–74; racketeers invading, 39–40; relocation of, 33; responsibility as head of, 84; salary increase sought from, 36–37; SBU as *krysha* for, 47–48; SBU as protection for, 64; SBU no longer protecting, 70–71; searches and interrogations of, 74; special forces trashing office of, 74; steel rebar deal for, 45–46, 50; tax exemptions for, 37–38; useless people on staff of, 41
the Goblin (mobster), 155
goods. *See* products/goods
Gossnabsbyt (company name): liquidation of, 151; Maidukov, Sergey, creating name of, 137; mine headframe income for, 148
granny summer, 7

Grousko (businessman): Maidukov, Sergey, fired by, 26; Maidukov, Sergey, getting debt compensation from, 179; Maidukov, Sergey, threatened by thugs of, 27; rolled metal shipments and, 24–25; scheme financing by, 43; as small businessman, 178–79
gullibility, 78–79, 111

high pitched voice, 8, 104
holding cell, 89; Martirosyan, T., meeting at, 91–92; as monkey house, 90–91
home: Maidukov, Sergey, arriving at Martirosyan, S., 104; Maidukov, Sergey, kept at Martirosyan, S., 233; Maidukov, Sergey, staying at parent's, 179; Martirosyan, S., new, 186; Martirosyan, S., new Berdyansk, 232; Martirosyan, T., location of, 109; Martirosyan family courtyard of, 129
hostel, living conditions at, 176
house arrest sentence, 244
hydrochloric acid, 213–14

Iceworld exhibition center, 207–10
Iceworld regional manager job, 207
Igor (businessman): income increased by, 170; Martirosyan, S., arrest and, 192; Martirosyan,

T., stealing café success from, 148–49; at Martirosyan, S., court hearing, 203; policemen beating and interrogating, 149–50; Scientific Research Institute location of, 169; as witness, 202

"I'm Only Sleeping" (song), 192

incarceration: jail cell for, 93–94; Martirosyan, S., early release from, 213

income: fake ads selling air for, 20; Gossnabsbyt's mine headframe, 148; Igor increasing, 170; loss of, 18; Martirosyan, S., demanding, 166; retail store with declining, 187–88; scrap metal for, 19; workmates searching for, 18

indentured servant, 5

Institute of Soviet Trade, 16, 199

insurance company, 24; Maidukov, Sergey, fired from, 196; mobsters showing up at, 195–96; as psychotherapy, 193–94; in Ukraine, 193

intelligentsia, 16

Internet, Martirosyan, S., information on, 10

investment offer, 57–58, 60

iron cage, 202

Ivanovich, Ivan, 218–19; face-to-face meeting with, 66–67; Globalinvest vulnerable due to, 73; Maidukov, Sergey, cooperation and, 238–39; Maidukov, Sergey, meeting with, 47–48

jail cell, 93–94

Jakob the Samson. *See* Samson, Jacob

Jaws (Benchley), 15

John Paul II (pope), 192

judge, court hearing injury of, 207

judicial system, in Ukraine, 200

junk equipment, 59

KGB officers, 47

Kherson (city), 120–21

Kikvidze, Georgy, 10

King, Stephen, 214

Konstantin: Maidukov, Sergey, argument and, 141–42; Martirosyan, T., constant companion of, 112, 171; Martirosyan, T., scam with, 188; savagely beaten, 192; as witness, 202

Kranz, Janusz, 183–84

Krasnaya Shapochka cafe, 132, 157

krysha (roof), 47–48, 64

labor exchanges, 34

Lada cars, 181

law enforcement, 6–7, 218–19

lawlessness, 22, 76

Led Zeppelin, 152

Lennon, John, 178

life of luxury, 56
liquidation, of Gossnabsbyt, 151
Little Red Riding Hood. *See* Krasnaya Shapochka cafe
lower classes, 16
luxury cars, 171–72

machine gun shots, 205
mafia boss: day in life of, 8; Martirosyan, S., with death sentence from, 186–87; premeditated murder by, 6; SBU cooperation and, 218–19; in Ukraine, 13
magnetic personality, 243
Maidukov (Sergey's mother): business of, 155; pet dog's death of, 152–54
Maidukov, George (father), 128, 154–55
Maidukov, Luba (Sergey's wife), 3–4, 143; can't feed children with prospects from, 21; children at risk fear of, 29; clothing market goods sold by, 211–12; faux arctic fox coat for, 226; Maidukov, Sergey, changes not pleasing to, 124–25; Maidukov, Sergey, emotional separation with, 124–25; Maidukov, Sergey, explaining problems to, 87–88; Maidukov, Sergey, fights with, 175–76; Maidukov, Sergey, reconciliation with, 179–80; Maidukov, Sergey, reproached by, 29–30, 75; Maidukov, Svitlana, conversation with, 88; Martirosyan, S., birthday party invitation to, 157; Martirosyan, S., meeting told to, 102–3; Martirosyan, S., memories explained to, 12–13; Martirosyan, S., words like champagne to, 158; mobster introduced to, 157–58; police special forces searching flat of, 75; salary increase suggestion of, 36
Maidukov, Sergey: Alexander new driver for, 136; American company negotiations by, 35; Andrewich and cooperation of, 238–39; Andrewich calling, 86; Andrewich's advice to leave mobsters for, 233; Andrewich's meeting with, 47–48, 232–33; Andrewich's warning not to call, 70; Andrewich's warning to, 238; Angelika betraying, 78–79, 84; Angelika's critical situation discussion with, 71; Angelika's invitation offered to, 77; Angelika sticking together with, 76–77; anxiety of, 230; blonde secretary for, 114–15; Bogdanov pointing gun at, 130–31; cellmates of, 94–95; children raising kids of, 3, 16; children threatened of, 26–27, 29; Communist Party taking

255

care of, 24; creativity of, 15; as crime fiction writer, 13; Department of Combating Economic Crimes arrival of, 89; Donetsk childhood of, 123–24; Donetsk's job difficulties for, 142–43; don't lend money from, 60; double salary request by, 36–37; drinking by, 30; employment difficult to find for, 212; Eugene meeting with, 176–77; Eugene not lending money to, 23–24; Eugene's brawl with, 177–78; family arguments of, 143; family not involved in problems of, 189; first business job of, 25; *For Thirty Pieces of Silver* by, 242; freedom at work experienced by, 135; freedom lost of, 125; freedom rejoiced by, 151–52; freight train load of wood and, 21–22; Globalinvest company future for, 57; Globalinvest company hiring, 31–32; as Globalinvest company president, 33; Globalinvest run by, 69; Gossnabsbyt name created by, 137; Grousko firing, 26; Grousko paying off some debt to, 179; Grousko's thugs threatening, 27; in holding cell, 90; hydrochloric acid warning to, 213–14; Iceworld firing, 209–10; Iceworld regional manager job for, 207; as indentured servant, 5; insurance company firing, 196; Ivanovich meeting with, 47–48; job search by, 30–31; Kranz's widow meeting with, 184; as last available businessmen, 223; Maidukov, L., emotional separation with, 124–25; Maidukov, L., fights with, 175–76; Maidukov, L., not happy with changes of, 124–25; Maidukov, L., problems explained by, 87–88; Maidukov, L., reconciliation with, 179–80; Maidukov, L., reproaches to, 29–30, 75; Maidukov, Sergiy, pushed down by, 175; Maidukov, Svitlana, conversation with, 14; Martirosyan, S., always choosing, 214–15; Martirosyan, S., birthday party invitation to, 157; Martirosyan, S., debt owed from, 145; Martirosyan, S., demanding income from, 166; Martirosyan, S., first meeting, 99–100; Martirosyan, S., home arrival by, 104; Martirosyan, S., interaction with, 100–102; Martirosyan, S., keeping at house, 233; Martirosyan, S., man-to-man talk with, 107–8; Martirosyan, S., meeting warnings to, 98; Martirosyan, S., meeting with, 116, 145, 181–82, 216–18; Martirosyan,

S., memories by, 9; Martirosyan, S., million dollar demand to, 164–65; Martirosyan, S., name first heard by, 63; Martirosyan, S., nark accusation to, 101–2; Martirosyan, S., not trusting, 4–5; Martirosyan, S., part of family of, 182–83; Martirosyan, S., picture seen by, 4; Martirosyan, S., pitied by, 244; Martirosyan, S., questioning SBU cooperation by, 217; Martirosyan, S., sending men to pickup, 103, 214; Martirosyan, S., summoning, 115–16; Martirosyan, S., with defense witness as, 195; Martirosyan, T., accidental meeting with, 91–92; Martirosyan, T., argument with, 141–42; Martirosyan, T., buddies with, 195; Martirosyan, T., dinner with, 227–28; Martirosyan, T., friendship reassurance to, 142; Martirosyan, T., interaction with, 102; Martirosyan, T., location given by, 242; Martirosyan, T., looked after by, 224; Martirosyan, T., not sharing sugar profits with, 140; Martirosyan, T., protection of, 132; Martirosyan, T., reappearance to, 194; Martirosyan, T., repayment of favor to, 95–96; Martirosyan, T., reward promises to, 59–60; Martirosyan, T., warnings to, 98, 189; Martirosyan, T., with front man as, 112; Martirosyan, T., work meetings with, 110; Martirosyan brothers left by, 142; Martirosyan brothers new nightmare family of, 114; Martirosyan brothers thoughts of leaving by, 114; Martirosyan brothers work freedom for, 135; as merchandise broker, 20; *militsiya* arresting, 83; *militsiya* investigating, 85; *militsiya* lie accusations to, 85–86; *militsiya* offering bribe to, 85; mobster contact reduced for, 181; mobster gang beating up, 133–34; mobster life influencing behavior of, 175; mobsters as enemies surrounding, 216; mobsters at Chance Café with, 170–71; mobsters seeing, as outsider, 158; mobsters visiting mother of, 155; Momot handing visa card to, 49; Momot working with, 37; mother's pet dog death and, 152–54; new office space task of, 113; no experience as lawbreaker, 76; no payment from wood for, 22–23; not feeling safe, 52; Oksana testing, 185; Oksana working with, 182; panic attack feelings of, 202–3; parent's house stay for, 179; peace of mind lost for, 124; phone call threatening, 196–97; with pneumonia, 206; policemen beating and interrogating, 149–50; regional manager job obtained by, 193; research institute job lost by, 18–19; respectable treatment demanded for, 116–17; retail store investigation by, 188; rolled metal deal not paying, 26; rolled metal supply sought by, 43–44; as sales manager, 32; Salim becoming enemy of, 117; Samson's exchange with, 51; Sasha stayed with by, 176; SBU cooperation agreement with, 238–39; SBU questioning, 220–21; Scientific Research Institute kicking out, 150–51; secret room hiding of, 72–73; Sergey Donskoy nickname for, 242; set his own salary, 186; as softhearted but a fighter, 123–24; steel rebar deal by, 45–46, 50; testifying against Martirosyan, S., 200–202; as uncaring selfish man, 176; visa card's little value discovered by, 88; as wanted outlaw, 75; worthless feeling of, 29

Maidukov, Sergiy (son), 9, 18; gift for, 49; growing up, 187; at Institute of Soviet Trade, 199;

Maidukov, Sergey, pushing down, 175

Maidukov, Svitlana (daughter): bright blue hair of, 199; gift for, 49; growing up, 187; if you fall get up again from, 134; Maidukov, L., conversation with, 88; Maidukov, Sergey, conversation with, 14; school party of, 132–34

Makiivka (city), 58–59

Marat (mobster), 161–62

Martirosyan, George (father), 128

Martirosyan, Momma, 128

Martirosyan, Samvel: acts of violence by, 11; appearance of, 5–6; arrest and incarceration of, 191–92; article about, 6–7, 10–12; assassination attempt of, 12, 205–6; bank loan business plan of, 160–61; Berdyansk new home for, 232; Berdyansk Seaport Administration raided by, 236–37; Berdyansk seaport control sought by, 231–32; birthday party invitations from, 157; Bogdanov departure caused by, 131; Boris the Banker and, 163; bulletproof vest put on, 100, 182; business deals naive approach of, 118; car ownership discussion with, 105–6; Chance Café gathering spot for, 169; as charismatic leader, 243; children and court

INDEX

case of, 199–200; children's safety and, 182–83; as classic mobster, 126; clothing market approach of, 212–13; constantly on edge, 187; construction workers not paid by, 136; court hearing entered by, 203–4; court hearing for, 199; court hearing in-charge behavior of, 204; creating problem then solution by, 125; criminal charges acquittal of, 98; as dangerous, 6; days numbered of, 233; death threats against, 11; detention center beating of, 243; dinner at parents of, 127–28; dogs ordered killed by, 159–60; Donetsk store bought by, 183; early release for, 213; father's abuse and, 106; first degree murder charge against, 204–5; football club players protecting, 100–101; fourteen year sentence for, 206; gang ceased to exist of, 192, 237–38; gang members disunited of, 201; high pitched raspy voice of, 8, 104; house arrest sentence of, 244; Igor at court hearing of, 203; Igor to collect money for release of, 192; Internet information on, 10; mafia leader's death sentence for, 186–87; Maidukov, L., explained memories of, 12–13; Maidukov, L., told of meeting with, 102–3; Maidukov, Sergey, always chosen by, 214–15; Maidukov, Sergey, arriving at home of, 104; Maidukov, Sergey, as defense witness for, 195; Maidukov, Sergey, business income demanded by, 166; Maidukov, Sergey, can't be trusted by, 4–5; Maidukov, Sergey, deciding to testify against, 200–202; Maidukov, Sergey, feeling pity for, 244; Maidukov, Sergey, first time hearing of, 63; Maidukov, Sergey, forced to stay with, 233; Maidukov, Sergey, in debt to, 145; Maidukov, Sergey, interaction with, 100–102; Maidukov, Sergey, man-to-man talk with, 107–8; Maidukov, Sergey, meeting, 99–100; Maidukov, Sergey, meeting with, 116, 145, 181–82, 216–18; Maidukov, Sergey, memories of, 9; Maidukov, Sergey, million dollars demand of, 164–65; Maidukov, Sergey, nark accusation from, 101–2; Maidukov, Sergey, part of family of, 182–83; Maidukov, Sergey, picked up by men of, 103, 214; Maidukov, Sergey, respect demanded by, 116–17; Maidukov, Sergey, SBU cooperation questioned by, 217; Maidukov, Sergey, seeing picture of, 4; Maidukov, Sergey, summoned by, 115–16; Maidukov, Sergey, warnings against meeting, 98; Marat as close associate of, 162; Martirosyan, T., embezzling from, 229; Martirosyan, T., interaction with, 101; Martirosyan, T., on prison release of, 64; *militsiya* attempting criminal responsibility for, 186–87; Miner building shopping complex acquired by, 224; mobster overhead costs of, 125–26; mobsters scared off by name of, 208–9; moods of, 5, 126, 159, 170, 186, 230; National Police of Ukraine finally detaining, 7–8; new house of, 186; Oksana bringing tea for, 106–7; Oksana protected by, 184–85; outbursts of rage by, 229; Petya meeting with, 163–64; Petya's bankruptcy story told to, 164; Petya's ear drums damaged by, 165; as pitiless and vindictive, 7; police and special forces detaining, 237; at pretrial detention center, 192; preventive detention of, 10; prey in field of vision for, 122; as prototype villain, 243; punishment avoided by, 6–7, 11–12; Robic doomed to prison by, 244; Sasha stealing police radios from, 143–44; SBU meeting sought by, 218; SBU meeting violating mafia law, 218–19; SBU to contact, 221; smoking advice from, 106; society high status dream of, 223–24; store receipts anticipated by, 189; sugar purchase and, 139; as Ukraine citizen, 10; Valery owing money to, 118; words like champagne from, 158

Martirosyan, Tigran: Agency for State Reserves payment refused by, 139; Andrewich told location of, 242; assassination attempt claim by, 63; baseball bat to skull by, 174; as charismatic leader, 112; clothing store goods as gifts from, 226; cold and menacing demeanor of, 62; crime syndicate organized by, 11; debt of, 59–60, 63; disappearance of, 206–7; dressing style of, 97; fabric and accessories sought by, 58; fake receipt from, 61; girlfriends of, 229; girls interviewing with, 228–29; holding cell meeting with, 91–92; home location of, 109; Igor's café success stolen by, 148–49; Konstantin new partner for, 112, 171; Konstantin's scam with, 188; lying gift of, 109–10; Maidukov, Sergey, argument with, 141–42; Maidukov, Sergey, as front man for, 112; Maidukov, Sergey, buddies with, 195; Maidukov, Sergey, dinner with, 227–28; Maidukov, Sergey, don't lend money to, 60; Maidukov, Sergey, favor repayment to, 95–96; Maidukov, Sergey, friendship reassurance from, 142; Maidukov, Sergey, interaction with, 102; Maidukov, Sergey, promises of reward from, 59–60; Maidukov, Sergey, protected by, 132; Maidukov, Sergey, reappearance of, 194; Maidukov, Sergey, sugar profits not shared by, 140; Maidukov, Sergey, to look after, 224; Maidukov, Sergey, warned by, 98, 189; Maidukov, Sergey, work meetings with, 110; Makiivka drive with, 58–59; Martirosyan, S., embezzled by, 229; Martirosyan, S., interaction with, 101; Martirosyan, S., prison release from, 64; Miner building as bottomless pit for, 228; Miner building renovation plans of, 225–26; Miner building search for, 239–40; Momot drawn to affairs of, 58; Momot ordering attack on, 65–66; Momot's outrage with, 61; Momot's warning from, 64–65, 93; nightclub plans of, 225–26; office space of, 137; payment promises by, 111; pre-hearing greeting by, 201; products to sell acquired by, 113; research institute and business of, 97–98; Robic flagging down, 173; Scientific Research Institute lease agreement with, 146; sewing shop investment offer from, 57–58; son of, 227; spine problems of, 225; TVs not paid for by, 133

Martirosyan brothers: Armenians as family for, 127–28; bad circumstances for, 194; bank loan business opportunity for, 160–61; cars appear in courtyard of, 130–31; Chance Café arrival of, 169–70; company name change for, 137; competition between, 226; defenseless person beaten by, 115; employees sought for, 135; family home courtyard of, 129; family problems discussed of, 128–29; father abusing, 106; Maidukov, Sergey, leaving, 142; Maidukov, Sergey, new nightmare family as, 114; Maidukov, Sergey, thinking of leaving, 114; Maidukov, Sergey, work freedom for, 135; Scientific Research Institute kicking out,

150–51; seldom kept their word, 113; strangest job ever with, 109; survival from prey for, 148

medieval chaos, 22

memories, 147

metallurgical plants, 55

militsiya: as criminal organization, 83; Maidukov, Sergey, bribe offer from, 85; Maidukov, Sergey, investigated by, 85; Maidukov, Sergey, lies accusation by, 85–86; Maidukov, Sergey, under arrest by, 83; Martirosyan, S., criminal responsibility and, 186–87; you are criminal from, 98

Miner building shopping complex: bar area trashed at, 240–41; Martirosyan, S., acquiring, 224; Martirosyan, T., bottomless pit of, 228; Martirosyan, T., renovation plans for, 225–26; Martirosyan, T., searched for at, 239–40; renovations completed of, 230–31; women's clothing store at, 226

mine's headframe, 147–48

mobsters: Andrewich advice to leave, 233; Andrewich comment on mobsters killing, 52; Berdyansk winery tour with, 235–36; Boris the Banker office visited by, 161; Bragin as mafia, 39–40; businessmen as cash cows to, 171; Chance Café gathering of, 169–70; at Chance Café with Maidukov, Sergey, 170–71; children experiencing, 103; criminal activity of, 126; Globalinvest company invaded by, 39–40; the Goblin as, 155; Iceworld invaded by, 208; insurance company with, 195–96; Kranz's widow robbed by, 183; locked in trap with, 107–8; Maidukov, L, introduced to, 157–58; Maidukov, Sergey, almost beaten up by, 133–34; Maidukov, Sergey, as outsider to, 158; Maidukov, Sergey, behavior influenced by, 175; Maidukov, Sergey, contact reduced with, 181; Maidukov, Sergey, mother visited by, 155; Maidukov, Sergey, surrounded by enemies as, 216; Martirosyan, S., as classic, 126; Martirosyan, S., disunited members of, 201; Martirosyan, S., name scaring off, 208–9; Martirosyan, S., overhead costs for, 125–26; meetings in deserted locations by, 181–82; Momot on phone with, 40; money sought by, 39; nightclub trashed by, 240–41; personal courage of, 173; Petya as cash cow for, 163; racketeer invasion of, 39–40, 42; Samson as, 50–51; Sasha's interactions limited with, 136–37; SBU defenders against, 47–48; Scientific Research Institute parking by, 115; security by, 100; tedious life of, 171. *See also* mafia boss

Momot, Sergey Viktorovich: American company negotiations and, 35; Angelika defending, 42; businessman role played by, 41; as demanding, 32; disappearance of, 69; financing money from, 44–45; guards protecting, 38; investment offer accepted by, 57–58; investment return hope of, 60; Maidukov, Sergey, handed visa card from, 49; Maidukov, Sergey, working with, 37; Martirosyan, T., affairs interest of, 58; Martirosyan, T., attack ordered by, 65–66; Martirosyan, T., outrage from, 61; Martirosyan, T., warning about, 64–65, 93; mobster talking on phone with, 40; nasty character of, 35–36; personal business of, 58; profit increase expected of, 42–43; racketeer invasion questions by, 42; rich American image projected by, 34–35; rolled metal supply requested by, 43–44; Samson's exchange with, 51; SBU face-to-face meeting with, 66–67; SBU fining, 67; SBU money wasted by, 66; SBU officers as masters over, 48

money, mobsters seeking, 39

monkey house, 90–91

moods, of Martirosyan, S., 5, 126, 159, 170, 186, 230

Most Terrible Mafia in Ukraine (biography), 10

Nadezhda (businesswoman), 21–23

National Police of Ukraine, 7–8

nicotine and caffeine, 60

nightclub: building costs for, 229; Martirosyan, T., plans for, 225–26; Miner building's trashed, 240–41; profit made by, 230–31

nonferrous metals, 19

office space: Maidukov, S., task of new, 113; of Martirosyan, T., 137; mobsters visit Boris the Banker, 161; at Scientific Research Institute, 136, 140–41, 145–46; Scientific Research Institute layout of, 100; special forces trashing, 74

Oksana (Samvel's friend), 238; at Berdyansk Seaport Administration, 236–37; bribe money provided to, 184; as clothing market, 212–13;

Maidukov, Sergey, tested by, 185; Maidukov, Sergey, working with, 182; Martirosyan, S., brought tea by, 106–7; Martirosyan, S., protecting, 184–85; resentment created in, 185; retail store job without, 191; set her own salary, 186; as witness, 202

Olya (citizen), 240–41

open-air café, 133

opera house building, 50

panic attack, 202–3

parent's house, Maidukov, Sergey, staying at, 179

payment promises, by Martirosyan, T., 111

peace of mind lost, 124

penitentiary system, 90

Perestroika, 17, 104, 126

Perovitch, Vitaly, 10

personal courage, 173

Pescarus ship: as fishing vessel, 118–22; poor condition of, 121; scrap metal calculations for, 121–22

Petrovitch, Michael: agreement signed with, 46; appropriate approach to, 45; death of, 50; physical violence threats against, 45; from USSR, 44

Petya (businessman): bankruptcy story of, 164; debt of, 163; ear drums damaged of, 165; Martirosyan, S., meeting with, 163–64; wholesale cheese from, 163

physical strength, 172–73

physical violence threats, 45

pneumonia, of Maidukov, Sergey, 206

policemen: law enforcement and, 6–7, 218–19; Maidukov, L., flat searched by, 75; Maidukov, Sergey, beaten and interrogated by, 149–50; Martirosyan, S., detained by, 237; Scientific Research Institute director calling, 150; special forces, 71–74. *See also krysha; militsiya*

police station, 151

premeditated murder, 6

pretrial detention center, 192

preventive detention, 10

prey, in field of vision, 122

products/goods: Globalinvest company needing new, 55; Maidukov, L., selling, 211–12; Martirosyan, T., acquiring, 113; Martirosyan, T., giving as gifts, 226

profit increase, 42–43

psychotherapy, 193–94

punishment, Martirosyan, S., avoiding, 6–7, 11–12

purchasing power, 17

purchasing process, 111

rage, of Martirosyan, S., 229

rape, 215
Rea, Chris, 103, 124
regional manager, 193
research institute, losing job at, 18–19
resentment, Oksana feeling, 185
respectable treatment, 116–17
retail store: Maidukov, Sergey, investigation of, 188; Martirosyan, S., buying into, 183; Martirosyan, S., waiting for receipts from, 189; Oksana not showing up at, 191; revenue declining of, 187–88; scam stealing money from, 188
revenue. *See* income
rich American image, 34–35
Rinat (Bragin's nephew), 40
Rita (Tigran's girlfriend), 227–28, 241–42
"The Road to Hell" (song), 103, 124
Robbins, Harold, 15
Robic (Tigran's nephew): drunk men offending, 173–74; local men avoiding, 175; Martirosyan, S., dooming, 244; Martirosyan, T., flagged down by, 173
rolled metal: Grousko and shipments of, 24–25; Maidukov, Sergey, not paid for, 26; Maidukov, Sergey, seeking supply of, 43–44; shipments to Turkey, 25

Russia, Ukraine occupied by, 3, 14

sailing yachts, 119
sales manager, Maidukov, Sergey, as, 32
Salim (gang member), 143–44, 164, 215; cruelty of, 7; driving accident of, 120; Eugene brawl assistance from, 178; killings by, 117; Maidukov, Sergey, becoming enemy of, 117; phone threat and, 196–97; as poor driver, 119
Samson, Jacob, 50–52, 130–32
Sasha (Sergey's nephew): Maidukov, Sergey, staying with, 176; Martirosyan, S., police radios stolen by, 143–44; mobster interactions limited for, 136–37
SBU. *See* Security Service of Ukraine
schemes, 22, 43, 112, 188
school days, 161–62
school party, of Maidukov, Svitlana, 132–34
scientific intelligentsia, 16–17
Scientific Research Institute: construction work at, 110–11; Igor's cafe located at, 169; Martirosyan, T., lease agreement with, 146; Martirosyan, T., with business at, 97–98; Martirosyan brothers being kicked out of, 150–51; mobster cars parking at, 115; office

Index

construction at, 136, 140–41, 145–46; office layout in, 100; police called by director of, 150; purchasing process for, 111; remote location of, 135

scrap metal: calculations, 121–22; income from, 19; mine's headframe for, 147–48

Seagull company, 231

Sea of Azov, 231

secret agents, 47

Security Service of Ukraine (SBU), 46; as businessmen defenders, 47–48; Globalinvest company protected by, 64; Globalinvest no longer protected by, 70–71; Maidukov, Sergey, and questions about, 217; Maidukov, Sergey, cooperation agreement with, 238–39; Maidukov, Sergey, questioned by, 220–21; Martirosyan, S., to be contacted by, 221; Martirosyan, S., violating mafia law meeting, 218–19; Martirosyan, S., wanting meeting with, 218; Momot fined by, 67; Momot's face-to-face meeting with, 66–67; Momot subordinate to officers of, 48; Momot wasting money belonging to, 66; people avoiding building of, 219

self-preservation instinct, 101

Semenetz, Georgy, 10

Sergey Donskoy nickname, 242

sewing shop: empty, 61–62; junk equipment in, 59; Martirosyan, T., offering investment in, 57–58

Siberian penal colony, 21

Silver (gang member), 143–44, 195, 215, 237

smoking advice, 106

socialist economy, 24

socialist paradise, 16

social ladder, 17

society, in USSR, 16

society high status, 223–24

softhearted, but a fighter, 123–24

Soviet reserve stocks, 138

spine problems, 225

steel industry, 50, 55

steel rebar, 45–46, 50

sugar purchase: from Agency for State Reserves, 137–38; Martirosyan, S., not knowing about complete, 139

tax exemptions, 37–38

The Time Machine (Wells), 16

trapped, locked in with mobsters, 107–8

truth, liberation through, 14

Turkey, 25

tyrants, divide and conquer by, 117

Ukraine: businessmen in, 27; car ownership in, 105; criminal groups in, 5; difficult times in,

34; Donetsk as crime capital of, 38; honesty of businessmen in, 27; insurance company in, 193; judicial system in, 200; mafia boss in, 13; Martirosyan, S., becoming citizen of, 10; medieval chaos in, 22; *militsiya* as police in, 83; national police in, 7–8; Russian occupation of, 3, 14; search for earnings in, 18; upheaval in, 17; white cow among black cows, 44

uncaring selfish man, 176

United States, 37

unscrupulous partners, 29

USSR: collapse of, 138, 209; Donetsk as dictator's name from, 56; gang wars in, 236; life as paradise in, 15; *militsiya* as police in, 83; organization of society in, 16; penitentiary system conditions in, 90; Petrovitch from, 44

Valery (businessman), 117; debt liberation by, 119, 122; fishing vessel of, 118–19; Martirosyan, S., owed money by, 118; *Pescarus* ship of, 121; sailing yachts designed and built by, 119

Velichko (insurance agent), 196

video saloons, illegal, 17–18

villain, Martirosyan, S., as prototype, 243

violence: army with cruelty and, 16; Martirosyan, S., acts of, 11; threats of physical, 45

visa card, 49, 88

voice, high pitched, 8, 104

Wells, H. G., 16

white cow among black cows expression, 44

women's clothing store, 226

wood, freight train load of, 21–23

workmates, 18–19

writer, of crime fiction, 13

Youth Sports Palace, 207

Zhurba (businessman), 21–23

About the Author

Sergey Maidukov is a Ukrainian writer who has sold tens of thousands of copies of his published books in the countries of the former USSR, such as Ukraine, Russia, Belarus, and the Baltics. Widely recognized in Western Europe for his intimate knowledge of the criminal world, he worked for twenty-two years as a commissioned writer for the largest publishing houses in Ukraine. His first book for the Rowman & Littlefield, *Life on the Run*, received praise in the esteemed *Kirkus Reviews*, and Marcel H. Van Herpen, a security specialist in the post-Soviet states, endorsed it as well. Maidukov's political articles have been published in various US magazines, including *Newsweek*.